WRITING LOCAL HISTORY

Also available

*The Scottish family tree detective: tracing your ancestors
    in Scotland*   Rosemary Bigwood
*The family tree detective: tracing your ancestors
    in England and Wales*   Colin D. Rogers
*The Irish family tree detective: tracing your ancestors
    in Ireland*   Francis Dowling (forthcoming)

Writing local history

John Beckett

MANCHESTER UNIVERSITY PRESS
Manchester and New York
distributed exclusively in the USA by Palgrave

Published by Manchester University Press
Oxford Road, Manchester M13 9NR, UK
and Room 400, 175 Fifth Avenue, New York, NY 10010, USA
www.manchesteruniversitypress.co.uk

Distributed exclusively in the USA by
Palgrave, 175 Fifth Avenue, New York,
NY 10010, USA

Distributed exclusively in Canada by
UBC Press, University of British Columbia, 2029 West Mall,
Vancouver, BC, Canada V6T 1Z2

British Library Cataloguing-in-Publication Data
A catalogue record for this book is available from the British Library

Library of Congress Cataloging-in-Publication Data applied for

ISBN   978 0 7190 2950 9 hardback

ISBN   978 0 7190 7660 2 paperback

First published 2007

16 15 14 13 12 11 10 09 08 07   10 9 8 7 6 5 4 3 2 1

Typeset in Sabon 10.25/12
by Servis Filmsetting Ltd, N
Printed in Great Britain
by Bell & Bain Ltd, Glasgo

Contents

Abbreviations

CORAL	Conference of Regional and Local Historians
ECH	C.R.J. Currie and C.P. Lewis, (eds.), *English County Histories: A Guide* (1994)
JORALS	*Journal of Regional and Local Studies*
LH	*The Local Historian*
Richardson	R.C. Richardson, (ed.), *The Changing Face of English Local History* (2000)
VCH	Victoria History of the Counties of England, usually known as the Victoria County History, or VCH

Acknowledgements

This book has, in one sense, been under construction throughout my career. The University of Nottingham MA in Local and Regional History, which I co-founded in 1983, was not only one of the earliest of its kind, but also an opportunity for learning as well as teaching. I learnt from students, from guest lecturers, and from external examiners, and I hope that I can now bring some of that learning together in this book. I cannot begin to name or even recall in order to thank all of the people who have helped to mould my thinking about local history. Among academic historians I have benefited from discussions with Dr John Marshall, Dr Joan Thirsk, Professor Norman McCord, Professor Edward Royle, Professor Marilyn Palmer, Mr Philip Riden, Dr Trevor Foulds, Dr David Crook, Professor Brian Short, Dr Christopher Brooke and my fellow MA convenor, Dr David Marcombe. Above all, I am grateful to Professor David Hey, with whom I have had numerous discussions, many of them on coaches during conference field trips, about the nature of the subject, and who has kindly read this book in draft. I have learnt also from members of local societies whose interests have often been in fields far removed from my own, but whose willingness to give of their own (unpaid) time to run local societies, and to edit their transactions, reflects their concern that we should understand and learn from out localities. In this context I am particularly grateful to Adrian Henstock, the late Neville Hoskins, John Heath and Janice Avery. Finally, I have learnt more than they will ever realise from undergraduate and postgraduate students. Academic historians are often asked how teaching and research fit together: this book should provide at least one answer.

Preface

Local history is widely practised in England today, but what is it, how has it developed, and what do we understand by it? I began my life in local history like many young doctoral students, by tackling a national problem using a local case study. The locality was incidental to the problem, in my case the ownership and occupation of land between the Restoration in 1660 and the mid-eighteenth century. Even so, I could not but be aware that national issues tackled at a local or regional level produced a residuum, a body of knowledge about the area which was of interest locally whatever the 'national' issue. It was on this residuum that I cut my teaching teeth, lecturing to WEA groups in Windermere and remote areas of upland Westmorland where even finding the village hall on a foggy November night was a test of nerve, ingenuity and strong headlights. On these occasions I discovered just how interested people were in 'their' community, which was something which had entirely passed me by as I grew up, because history at school and even at university was about statesmen and their actions, and I had no empathy with these statesmen whatsoever. History only became real when I could study the papers of a Cumbrian landed family and at the same time visit the house in which they had lived, or walk on the quayside at Whitehaven which they had built. I realised that the house in which I had grown up, the ground on which I walked, the land on which my university was built, had a history which was interesting in itself, as well as being part of the wider history of the region and the nation.

In the early 1980s I started teaching local history to undergraduates and to postgraduate students at the University of Nottingham. I took up the baton at a time when local history was still almost exclusively the province of adult education departments, and I also taught on a Certificate in Local History and continued (and continue) to lecture to local societies across the East Midlands and, occasionally, beyond. I recognised that there were two historical communities: undergraduate students whose main interest was in nations, states, and a future career, and postgraduates, usually mature, whose interest was in local history and whose main concern was the subject itself. Faced with the enthusiasm of the postgraduate, I had both to think through the meaning of regional history,[1] and to practise local history to be sure I knew what I was talking about from first hand experience.[2] As a result I found, for example, that I understood the place where I grew up in a wholly new light.[3] Yet I remained aware of a residual hostile environment among professional historians, for whom 'local' meant parochial, antiquarian, and not 'proper' history.[4] That still remains somewhere in the background, and today the problem is compounded by the huge audience for local history, which means the term is used for anything which relates to the past and is perceived to be 'local', without much assessment of the 'history' involved. I do not think that this problem is insurmountable, and I have sought to combine my professional career with a commitment to local history in the community, both through lectures and through the practical, hands-on business of running a local society. I believe that at whatever level it is practised, local history can and should make a contribution not only to our understanding of national history, but also to our appreciation of our own communities. It is this duality which is one theme of this book: the other is to understand what the subject is, how it has been and is practised, and why it makes a significant contribution to our understanding of past societies.[4]

Notes

1   J.V. Beckett, *The East Midlands from AD1000* (1988).
2   J.V. Beckett, *A History of Laxton: England's Last Open-Field Village* (1989).
3   John Beckett (ed.), *A Centenary History of Nottingham* (1997); J.V. Beckett, 'The Church of England and the working class in nineteenth-century Nottingham: the building of St. Stephen's church, Hyson Green', *Transactions of the Thoroton Society*, 92 (1988), 59–73.
4   I initially developed the theme of this book in my inaugural lecture at the University of Nottingham, published as John Beckett, 'What future for the past in local history?', *East Midland Historian*, 4 (1994), 5–15.

I *Introduction*

It has long been a complaint, that local history is much wanted. This
will appear obvious, if we examine the places we know, with the histories that treat of them. Many an author has become a cripple, by
historically travelling through *all England*, who might have made a
tolerable figure, had he staid at home. The subject is too copious for
one performance, or even the life of one man. (William Hutton, *A
History of Birmingham* (2nd edn, 1783), xi–xii)

Local history is all around us. Our family, our house, our street, our
community, all have a 'history'. My workplace is a large house built
in 1800. Why was it built on this site in this year? From my window I
can see a road. It looks ordinary enough, but the modern tarmac hides
a much older road, which was turnpiked in 1789–90. I become a local
historian when I stop simply walking along the road and entering the
building, and I ask how the road and the building have come to be here
in the first place. Both house and road have a long history, but the
questions do not change just because we might live in a modern sub-
urban house. How was the land used before the house was built? Why
was this land turned into a housing estate? Who decided where the
streets should run, the size of houses and garden plots, the width of
pavements? And – the key historical question – what were the effects
of turning agricultural acres into houses, gardens and streets, of
allowing the town to expand at the expense of the countryside?
History is about peeling back the layers, whether it is the shaping and
formation of common law or parliamentary procedures, or the
process by which past landscapes were turned into present, or past
communities evolved into their present successors. The past begins in
the present, and for the local historian it begins where we are.

Local history encompasses a wide range of interests, concerns, and
outputs, serious and amusing, amateur and professional. Written
local history can range from a few pages of extracts about a particular place or community produced on a desktop PC, to a full-length
scholarly tome compiled by a professional historian and published by
a university press. But the written word is only a part of the story.
Modern media has altered the range and tone of local history, which
can now be presented on audio tapes, video tapes, and CD-Roms, and

through exhibitions and websites (which of course can be updated as work proceeds). It uses resources which were not available to earlier generations of historians, including photography and recorded oral testimony. It can be studied through university certificate, diploma or MA courses, and it can be listened to for information and, perhaps, amusement at one of the numerous local societies up and down the country. It shelters a range of interests, from community history to family history, railway, canal and turnpike histories, to folklore and custom, place-names and surnames, field names, footpaths and build-ings. And it comes packaged as heritage, advertised by the brown street signs up and down the country which summon us into museums, heritage centres and other places of local interest. Finally, it is about popular television series: local history at its most synthetic and, potentially, all too easily its most trivialised.

Today, local history is practised in one form or another by so many different individuals and groups, that offering any sort of definition will doubtless offend someone. But we need to start somewhere, and in this book it is taken to be the study of place, whether it is a house, a street, a village, a town, a county, or a region, or even a nation (in the context of the British Isles) and the people and communities who lived in them. Since it is history it is also about interpretation, not simply the collection of data, which is more accurately represented today, as in the past, as antiquarianism. It requires a range of basic skills if it is to be undertaken successfully, and that may be why the great majority of local historians research the relatively recent past. Apart from the scholars working on volumes of the Victoria County History, only the most intrepid explorers have the courage and the resources of knowledge to venture back far beyond the seventeenth century.[1]

The opportunities for studying and practising local history have never been greater. The county historians of the sixteenth and seven-teenth centuries were leisured gentlemen with the financial resources to allow them the time for study, and the social contacts to gain them access to documentary sources in country houses the length and breadth of their counties. Today there are no such social limits. Most of us have the time and resources to study the subject, the records are generally collected in accessible (and mostly publicly-funded) record offices and local studies libraries, there are courses by the score for anyone wanting to learn some of the basic techniques, and increas-ingly material is becoming available over the internet. Yet some things do not change; local history cannot be researched only in the warm confines of a study: the words of W.G. Hoskins, the founding father of modern local history, written in 1959, are as true today as they were then: 'no local historian ought to be afraid to get his feet wet'.[2] While the university historian studying states and nations may go no further than the relative comfort of the national archives of this or other countries around the globe, the local historian must come to terms with the importance of place, with understanding the landscape, the street pattern, the buildings – from medieval churches to modern estate housing – and the names. The ground rules are clear – to research, write or otherwise record and interpret the history of a community, we must understand what makes it work today, as a starting point for understanding its past.

As we shall see in this book, deciding on the community is sometimes the easy part of our work; the means of study are often more complex, because local history is invariably multi-disciplinary. John Tosh, assessing the aims, methods and directions in the study of modern history, called for an end to compartmentalisation, but in doing so noted that the search for 'total history' would inevitably reduce the geographical range of the practitioner: 'paradoxically, therefore, "total history" turns out in practice to mean *local history*'.[3] Of course, it was not always thus. Among professional historians, from the time that history degrees were introduced into universities in the 1880s, there was a strongly held view that local studies were relevant only insofar as they provided examples in support of a national agenda.

Local historians have often been intimidated by this professional view from among those practising what they choose to call 'proper', or national history, but since the Second World War this perspective has been challenged. As W.G. Hoskins pointed out in the 1950s, the in-depth study of a local community was likely to uncover an entirely new theme or issue. It is not the size or composition of the unit of study, whether the parish, the town, the county, the region, or even the nation, which is the issue, so much as the ends in view and the methods used. Local history, in other words, needed to justify itself by its results not its claims.[4] History is the result of rigorous analysis of the sources, thoughtful assessment of the methods, and clear presentation of properly assessed findings. Local and national history are both history, and both need to be treated and studied under the same rigorous conditions, whether by university academics for their doctoral theses, or interested amateurs examining their house, street or parish.

If there is a point at which English local history began,[5] it was probably with the medieval chroniclers, but it really blossomed with the post-Reformation preoccupation with a national – that is, protestant – identity. England is just one 'nation' on an island which encompasses three separate and distinctive national identities, and in which patterns of settlement evolution preceded the formation of the individual states. We should not assume that national 'cultures', which are in many cases a product of the nineteenth century, existed in earlier periods.[6] England may have evolved physically as a nation by the time of the Norman Conquest, but it remained part of an Empire which spanned both sides of the Channel and for 300 years it lacked a single language. This lack of harmony between the nations remained, despite the Act of Union with Wales in 1536, and the coming together of England and Scotland under a single monarch in 1603. Nor was it helped in the seventeenth century when a civil war on English soil during the 1640s could be viewed within the context of an Irish rebellion and a Scottish invasion. The union of England and Scotland in 1707 finally brought the concept of Britain into the public consciousness, but even today there is a tension between being Scottish, Welsh or English, and being British.[7]

Local history in England was driven in the sixteenth century by the search for a national, English identity. John Leland, William Harrison, Christopher Saxton, John Norden and, above all, William Camden, set out to gain an understanding of the past by studying documentary sources together with place names, inscriptions, coins and other artefacts. They wanted to justify 'Englishness', but for most researchers the county came to be recognised as a more practical level of research. William Lambarde set a new trend when he limited himself, for practical reasons, to a study of Kent (1576), and subsequently the county became the norm, so that by the eighteenth century only a handful of English counties lacked a major history. During the nineteenth century county histories became smaller in scale and more generalised, but the founding in 1899 of the Victoria County History is a reminder that local history still had, and indeed has, its base in the county. Not every would-be local historian had the time, resources and energy – or indeed, through time, the friends and contacts – to study a whole county, hence the growing importance of parish and town histories. Some of the latter were laudatory and rather servile accounts of the structures and personnel of past local government, but they are often still key sources for our understanding of the urban past. The early local historians drew no distinction between documents, artefacts, and landscapes. They were historians, archaeologists, and antiquarians, but what distinguished them was a tendency to collect rather than to interpret.

In the nineteenth century the rise of professional history, studied in the universities, brought a concentration on national and political history alien to the traditions of local history. The whole idea of studying localities was questioned, except insofar that 'local history' could contribute evidence towards the history of the nation. Other than this, local history was ignored by mainstream historians, dismissed as too concerned with the architectural study of churches and manor houses, the descent of manors, heraldry, and other similarly esoteric concerns. It was taught largely through the Workers' Educational Association and, from the 1920s, university adult education departments. Archaeology had become a separate discipline during the nineteenth century, and other branches of 'antiquarian' studies such as place names were also developing their own disciplinary approaches. Local history was associated with antiquarianism, a term which was beginning to acquire pejorative overtones, as the collection of data rather than the interpretation and dissemination of knowledge. The county societies, usually founded in the nineteenth century, flourished but were perceived to attract their members from among the gentry and clergy, rather than to represent local society more generally.

With the founding in 1948 of the Department of English Local History at the University of Leicester, local history began to gather academic credibility. The department was forced to defend its existence in a hostile intellectual climate by developing a methodology. Through the 1950s and beyond it questioned the meaning of 'local', and the relationship between different types of community. If these debates may have seemed rather arcane to the members of county societies, the debates inaugurated at Leicester enabled local history to flourish in universities under the wing of its adopted discipline, economic history. The rise of a separate discipline of social history from the 1960s was a further boost to the subject, but there was also fragmentation. Urban history turned into a separate discipline, and other related areas developed their own areas of interest, particularly industrial archaeology, the study of the family, and, of course, heritage. Economic history itself was ultimately undermined by local history, because the search for explanations of industrialisation through national income accounting fell foul of local and regional evidence, which demonstrated the weakness of any form of national approach to the subject of why England became the first industrial nation.

Local history also received a boost from the opening of county archive offices. A few were opened in the later nineteenth century, but the real breakthrough came after 1945, and provided access to a range of documents which had previously had to be located in numerous different places. Local archive repositories offered an alternative to relying for sources on the national archives – in England the Public Record Office, now known as The National Archives, in Scotland the Scottish Record Office and in Wales the National Library. The revolution in access transformed the study of the locality, as well as bringing about the development of whole new areas of interest.

Local historians traditionally studied the parish and the county, because they were manageable units, and because they reflected the governing structure in which most people lived. Today we identify with places, or with areas of interest such as the Lake District, the Derbyshire Peak District, the Lincolnshire Wolds, and so on. In other words our understanding of the 'local' in local history has changed. Today's local historian might be researching the history of a house, a street, or a family; equally, they might be looking at an area, a region, or a *pays*. None of these is necessarily defined in terms of parish or county boundaries. We still have county councils and parish councils, but the great majority of the population lives today in towns, under city and borough authorities. Parish boundaries still mean something in the countryside, and some communities have either retained or reinvented the traditional custom of beating the bounds at Rogationtide; but few townspeople even know where one parish begins and another ends.[8] Only the Victoria County History, with a format devised in Victorian England, continues to produce histories determined by the boundaries of parishes and townships, but it does so because, in the words of a former general editor, it 'has always been conceived as a national encyclopaedia rather than a series of books about individual counties . . . it uses an overall format which facilitates comparison but also aids uniformity'.[9]

Since 1945, and particularly since about 1960 local history has passed through what many of us would accept has been a 'revolution in the conception of local history'.[10] Simultaneously it has grown from an interest pursued by people of wealth and standing with time on their hands, into a national popular pastime. It is hard to disagree with Professor David Hey's conclusion that 'At no time in British history has the study of local history at all levels of achievement been so popular'.[11] It is about the evolution of place, community, and family. Its conclusions add to the jigsaw which represents the history of our nation, and yet at the same time it illuminates individual communities and shows us how they have developed through time. This book sets out how local history has come to be where it is today, and how through studying it we can better understand the nation, the region, and the locality.

Notes

1 This is, admittedly, an impressionistic view rather than the result of systematic study. Kate Tiller, *English Local History: An Introduction* (1992; 2nd edn, 2002) produced a useful starting point for broadly based courses in local history, but by devoting more than half the text to the period pre-1530 she examined areas where I find many students show an interest but fear to tread when it comes to preparing a dissertation, i.e. doing practical local history research. David Hey's approach in *Journeys in Family History* (2004), admittedly in this case relating to the specific case of family history, reflects my own preference for leading researchers backwards through time from the present, in other words peeling back the layers.

2 W.G. Hoskins, *Local History in England* ([1959] 3rd edn, 1984), 3.

3 John Tosh, *The Pursuit of History: Aims, Methods and New Directions in the Study of Modern History* (3rd edn, 2000), 89.

4 Kate Tiller, *English Local History: The State of the Art* (University of Cambridge, Board of Continuing Education, 1998) 3; Kevin Shurer, 'The future for local history: boom or recession?', in Richardson, 181. Hoskins's interpretation of local history in this way is discussed in chapter VI.

5 In this book I am concentrating on English local history, but every country has its local historians, and the principles outlined here are not limited to England. For a North American perspective see Carol Kammen, *On Doing Local History* (2nd edn, 2003).

6 H. Kearney, *The British Isles: a History of Four Nations* (1989).

7 K. Robbins, *Great Britain: Identities, Institutions and the Idea of Britishness* (1998); N. Evans (ed.), National identity in the British Isles (*Occasional Papers in Welsh Studies*, 3, 1989), 16; R. Colls, *Identity of England* (2002).

8 J.D. Marshall, *The Tyranny of the Discrete: A Discussion of the Problems of Local History in England* (1997), 85, and similar comments by Kevin Shurer, 'The future for local history: boom or recession?', in Richardson, 179–93.

9 Christopher Elrington, 'The Victoria County History', *LH*, 22/3 (1992), 128.

10 *ECH*, 103.

11 D. Hey, *The Oxford Companion to Local and Family History* (1996), 284.

II *The origins of local history*

Where, or when, did local history start? It is an obvious question with which to begin, and while we can be confident that it began with the study of antiquities, deciding on a suitable date is almost impossible. We can track back as far as the Venerable Bede in the eighth century, but perhaps a more realistic starting point is with the chronicles of Anglo-Saxon monks. William of Malmesbury, in his *Gesta Pontificum Anglorum* ('History of the Prelates of England') produced in 1125, used both topographical and antiquarian approaches in surveying the ecclesiastical history of England. Gerald of Wales's works included an early attempt to describe Ireland and the Irish: *Topographia Hibernica* (1187). He also wrote a travel diary of a preaching tour through Wales, produced in 1188 as *Itinerarium Cambriae*. Three years later, in 1191, his *Descriptio Cambriae* combined personal observation and the folklore of Wales in an account which ranged through geography, social life, popular customs, antiquities, and natural history. Other religious writers also concentrated on local subjects, among them Gervase of Canterbury (writing on Canterbury Cathedral) and Matthew Paris (writing on St Albans). Yet these were isolated studies in no particular tradition, and it was only during the fourteenth and fifteenth centuries that something more systematic began with the first descriptive works, known by the generic name of chorographies. Overlapping with, and eventually succeeding, the chorographies, were the county histories, and by the seventeenth century a tradition of writing local history had been established which still exists in an attenuated form today.

The chorographic tradition

Chorographies were studies of places. They brought together history with genealogies, antiquarian collections, and topographical description. One of the earliest was Ranulph Higden's *Polychronicon*, completed in 1327, translated into English in 1387, and partly published – the topographical section – by Caxton in 1480 as *The Discrypcion of Britayne*. William of Worcester (1415–c.1480) made notes during a number of journeys 1477–80 through Norfolk and the south-west, recording antiquarian details, distances between towns,

the size of cathedrals and monastic buildings, and compiling information for biographies and natural history. He wrote detailed descriptions of East Anglia, and of Bristol, and his daily journal remains a
valuable source material for modern historians, although it was published only in 1778, and he was little known in his own day.[1]

The chorographic tradition lasted into the eighteenth century.
Writers described landscapes and buildings, customs and laws, and
people and their language, and they used documentary sources as well
as artefacts such as coins. Yet in its earliest, medieval form, the chorographic method lacked any real sense of purpose or direction. This
changed with the Renaissance. Across much of Europe, the impact of
the Renaissance from the later fifteenth century was to encourage
humanist scholarship. In turn, this brought with it a desire to discover
more of the Classical world of Greece and Rome. Scholars began to
read the Classical historical texts, and to take a serious interest in the
physical remains of antiquity through topographical, archaeological
and antiquarian studies. In England, these concerns were waylaid by
the Reformation, which distracted attention from the Greek and
Roman historians. Tudor governments needed the sanction and
support of history, while the church was anxious to establish the legal
grounds for independence from Rome by uncovering the existence of
an early Christian Church in Britain which developed independently
of the Papacy. In addition, scholars grew concerned for the country's
heritage of medieval chronicles and other local records, when Henry
VIII and Thomas Cromwell began their systematic destruction of the
monasteries in the 1530s and 1540s.

Emerging from this mixture of motives was England's first major
topographical writer, John Leland (c.1503–52). In 1533 Leland was
commissioned by Henry VIII 'to peruse and diligently to serche al the
libraries of monasteries and collegies of this yowre noble reaulme', as
he put it in the *Itinerary*.[2] He toured the west country in 1533, and was
in York the following year. He visited monastic and collegiate libraries
for the purpose of bringing the work of ancient writers 'out of deadly
darkness to lively light'. He spent ten years travelling, making maps,
measuring distances, talking to local people, and examining books
and charters. In 1546 he told the King

> I have so travelled in your dominions both by the sea coasts and the
> middle parts, sparing neither labour nor costs, by the space of these
> 6 years past, that there is almost neither cape, nor bay, haven, creek,
> or pier, river or confluence of rivers, breacks, washes, lakes, meres,
> fenny waters, mountains, valleys, moors, hearths, forests, woods,

cities, burgs, castles, principal manor places, monasteries, and colleges, but I have seen them, and noted in so doing a whole world of things very memorable.

His work was never completed, and the numerous studies he envisaged were still unwritten when in 1547 he collapsed, probably suffering from some form of manic-depressive illness from which he did not recover.

Fortunately Leland's rough notes, made as he travelled the length and breadth of the country, became available to other scholars, who made full use of them in the sixteenth and seventeenth centuries. They were published in various editions in the eighteenth century, and fully at the beginning of the twentieth century. Leland set the pace. He showed why the topographer could not rely on previous chronicles, but needed to use personal observation and first-hand research. As a result of this attention to detail, his work was trusted as an accurate record of the destruction of monastic civilisation, the demolition of monastic buildings, and the dispersal and destruction of monastic libraries.[3]

Where Leland led, others soon followed, among them John Stow, William Harrison, and William Camden. Like Leland, they wanted to understand England – hence Harrison's great work was entitled *Description of England* when it was published in 1577. To do so, they sought to uncover the country's origins, and to strip away centuries of accumulated myth and legend that passed for history. These myths included the belief in a long line of English kings including Lear and Cymbeline, and the idea that Joseph of Arimathea brought Christianity to Britain shortly after Christ's life on earth. To dispel rumour, and to encourage truth, the sixteenth-century scholars worked with source materials, many of them documents saved when monastic foundations were dissolved. They are best described as antiquaries, a term widely used then and now to describe groups and individuals concerned with origins, whether these were the origins of nations, languages, religions, customs, institutions or offices. None was to play a more significant role in the development of antiquarian studies than William Camden (1551–1623).

William Camden

As a young man Camden taught at Westminster School. He spent the long vacations travelling the country in search of antiquities: he was in Norfolk and Suffolk in 1578 and Lancashire and Yorkshire in 1582.

In *Britannia*, the book published for the first time in 1586, and with which his name became synonymous, he argued that Britain had a Roman heritage which could stand comparison with her continental neighbours. As a good antiquarian, he refused to rely on the classical authors, and instead collected new evidence through travel and the use of documents, together with linguistic evidence such as place names, coins and inscriptions. 'I would', he wrote, 'restore antiquity to Britain, and Britain to . . . antiquity . . . I would renew ancientrie, enlighten obscuritie, cleare doubts, and recall home Verities by way of recovery.' He hoped 'to renew the memory of what was old, illustrate what was obscure, and settle what was doubtful'.[4] He succeeded beyond what can only have been his wildest dreams.

Britannia was published in 1586 in Latin, as a contribution, consciously made by Camden, to the wider world of European Renaissance scholarship. He was writing, not specifically for a local audience, but for his fellow antiquarians in Europe, because he wanted to establish Britain among the nations with roots in the classical world, while convincing the scholarly community more widely of his achievements in using topography, artefacts and documents, to recover the past from the time of the earliest settlers in the British Isles. Camden traced the distribution of tribes, identified monuments and barrows, and drew on the sources of Roman history which yielded information on the ancient British inhabitants. His conclusions did not always stand up to detailed scrutiny. The earliest inhabitants, he suggested, were Gomerians or Cimbri descendants of Noah, through his son Japhet. This rather speculative view was superseded during the seventeenth century, when Anglo-Saxon studies began to flourish, although the identity of the first inhabitants continued to arouse discussion.[5]

Camden moved on from the ancient Britons to the Romans. *Britannia* was originally planned with the intention of discovering the topography of Roman Britain, and Camden's travels were often associated with his search for evidence to establish the importance of Roman antiquities in Britain. He provided a first-hand account of Hadrian's Wall, and recorded and described numerous Roman coins.[6] His research also convinced him that to stop with classical civilisation would be a mistake, because England had many treasures dating from well after the Roman period. Camps, ditches, stone monuments, ruins, urn-fields, and mass graves, all pointed to a Saxon past virtually untouched by the chroniclers and ancient historians. Camden was fascinated, and he expanded his studies to look at the Saxons, the Danes and the Normans. To do so, he taught himself the rudiments of Anglo-Saxon. He also drew on the work of Leland, and on the research of two friends who were also pioneers in their own way: William Lambarde and Richard Carew. Like many later antiquarian studies, Camden was also well served by correspondents from different parts of the country, especially his colleagues in the Society of Antiquaries. *Britannia* covered history, geography, topography, anthropology and antiquarianism.

Camden's book was widely studied. It was reprinted time and again, as he developed his research and ideas. Successive editions gave more and more space to the Saxons and their religious and political life. So important did they begin to loom, that Richard Verstegan's book, *A Restitution of Decayed Intelligence in Antiquities*, published in 1605, even implied that the Saxons had been rather more significant than the Romans in the formation of the institutions, religious centres and, perhaps most significantly, the character of the English. This was the first book to be devoted entirely to Saxon matters.[7] The sixth edition of Camden in 1607 was substantially revised and enlarged, and was published as a large folio volume with maps by John Norden and Christopher Saxton. It had 860 pages, fifty-seven maps, and included illustrations of dozens of Romano-British inscriptions. In 1610 *Britannia* was translated into English, and after Camden's death it was republished with further material added in 1695, 1722 (when it reached two large folio volumes), 1753, 1772, 1789 (when it reached three large folios), and 1806 when it was four.[8] Of these, the two great revisions and enlargements were by Gibson in 1695 and Gough in 1789 (reprinted 1806), and the total publication represents a significant milestone in the history of British antiquarian thought from the Renaissance to the early nineteenth century. Additional material, collected by Camden but not used in *Britannia*, including the first study of the etymology of surnames, was collected in a later book, *Remaines of a Greater Worke Concerning Britaine* (1605).

Camden's inspiration came from a circle of friends with whom he frequently met in the first Society of Antiquaries. The Society flourished between 1586 and 1607 under the influence of Sir Henry Spelman, Sir Robert Cotton and Camden himself. They used to meet informally in Cotton's house to hear and discuss a scholarly paper on antiquarian matters, but in 1614 King James I took a 'mislike' to the Society, fearing it would encroach too far on matters of state, and the antiquaries considered it wise to end their meetings. By then *Britannia* had begun to provide the impetus for much of the antiquarian work undertaken in subsequent years.[9] Outside of London, Oxford became a centre for antiquarian and historical research, especially after the opening of Sir Thomas Bodley's library in 1602. Groups of like-minded scholars also gathered at the University of Cambridge, and at the Inns of Court. Antiquaries studied whatever material was available, including the written chronicles, ruins, relics, coins and other non-literary sources. Camden, more than any other individual, had inspired this interest in the past, partly through his scholarly method, but just as importantly because of its appeal to an English past.

In the sixteenth century the notion of 'Englishness' succeeded the earlier Celtic notion of 'Britishness'. This had been kept alive after the Norman conquest by scholars such as Geoffrey of Monmouth in the twelfth century, but it was increasingly difficult to maintain during the Middle Ages with the subjugation of Wales, and then by the English attempts to do the same to Scotland in the reign of Edward I. In the struggles which followed, the absence of harmony between the three nations sharing the one island was all too apparent, despite the so-called Act of Union with Wales in 1536.[10] The Reformation destroyed what was left of this idea. From 1533, when Henry VIII's Act in Restraint of Appeals [to Rome] declared that 'this realm of England is an Empire', the search was on for England.[11] In *Richard II*, Shakespeare evoked the idea of a 'sceptr'd isle . . . This fortress built by Nature for herself . . . This blessed plot, this earth, this realm, this England.'[12] Camden built on the work of Leland and Harrison in seeking to rediscover a self-consciously English national past. He provided an image of England as it developed through Saxon and medieval times and, with William Harrison, he was in part uncovering Englishness, the so-called 'discovery of England'.[13]

Christopher Saxton

The search for 'England' had other implications, particularly for sixteenth-century map making. The key role here was played by Christopher Saxton (c.1542–c.1610). Saxton used a combination of direct observation and surveying techniques, such as taking bearings from high vantage points, to identify coastlines, rivers and settlements. He then added in local features. Since the size of map was determined by the dimensions of the copper plate, counties were printed at different scales. Each plate was captioned with an appropriate scale bar and decorated with embellishments and a title. Between 1574 and 1578 Saxton published, with government backing, maps of all the counties of England and Wales. He issued them, together with a general map, as the first national atlas in 1579. Such was the interest in cartography that they were widely copied, despite restrictions granted by Queen Elizabeth I.[14]

Saxton achieved a new level of cartographic excellence, because his maps were superior to those of his predecessors in their depiction of land masses. They also helped to determine the visual image of England and its constituent parts for more than a century. He created the county atlas, a distinctive cartographic form for which there was no exact parallel elsewhere in Europe, and which was to become the characteristic of English map publication in the early modern period.[15] But they could also be seen as expressing national sentiment and, crucially, helping to meet the needs of central government.

The government's interest in Saxton's work arose from its own perspective, particularly the need to collect information to gain and maintain control in the provinces. Whether it was over religious practice, or the export of grain, or the encouragement of local industry, the government needed information. Saxton and his fellow cartographers tapped this demand to seek and often obtain semi-official sponsorship. Lord Burghley, Queen Elizabeth's long-serving minister and the dedicatee of Camden's *Britannia*, received proof sheets of Saxton's work.[16] Even Saxton's choice of the county may have been determined not just by the demands of the printer, but because it was the point at which central and local government interacted.

The significance of Saxton's achievement in setting out a particular visual image of England is hard to underestimate, particularly when from 1607 his maps were included in reprints of Camden's *Britannia*. Camden had regretted the lack of maps in the first edition of his work, and the inclusion of Saxton's greatly aided the presentation of his material. Not surprisingly, later map makers plagiarised his work. Among those who borrowed from Saxton was John Speed (1551/2–1629). Speed was an antiquary – a member of the early Society – and he knew and was influenced by Camden, Sir Robert Cotton and others. He adopted the same basic format as Saxton. His influence arose from the inclusion of original town plans, of which he drew the great majority himself. These depicted contemporary buildings and street plans, antiquarian remains, sites of battles and other information. Some of the buildings have subsequently disappeared. For example, his map of Nottingham, drawn in 1610, provides the only surviving depiction of the medieval church of St Nicholas, which was demolished in the seventeenth century and replaced by the current brick building. Speed's fifty-four county maps, completed between 1605 and 1610, were published in a large folio volume, *Theatre of the Empire of Great Britaine* (1611).[17] Not surprisingly there were plenty of other cartographers willing to follow where Saxton and Speed led, notably perhaps John Ogilby, whose ribbon route-maps were published in his *Britannia Depicta* (1675).[18]

County histories

The early antiquaries and cartographers saw their task in national terms, to justify Englishness. In doing so they set an agenda which has come down to us in the form of a distinctive *English* local history, but it was also an English history which depended, as Saxton showed, on its various parts to build up the whole picture. In researching 'England' Camden and his fellow antiquaries exposed great gaps in knowledge, which in turn inspired those who followed them to adopt a more manageable local approach. Antiquaries could research, and surveyors map individual counties more successfully and practically than they could the whole country, and the county was of symbolic importance for the gentlemen antiquaries who followed in Camden's wake. Many leisured gentlemen ruled and administered justice in their county as justices of the peace, and it is hardly surprising to find a new generation of antiquaries coming forward from among their number. It helped that the periodic heraldic visitations designed to establish the local legitimacy of gentry families took place on a county basis, as in Lincolnshire in 1562, 1592, 1634 and 1660. County histories gradually took the place of heraldic books of visitation, which fell into abeyance after the Restoration. A former sheriff of Kent commended William Lambarde's work on Kent 'to his countrymen, the gentlemen of the county of Kent', on the grounds that 'I know not (in respect of the place) unto whom I may more fully thus send it than unto you, that are either bred and well brought up here, or by the goodness of God and your own good provision are well settled here and here lawfully possess or are near unto sundry of those things that this book specially speaketh of'.[19]

County histories began, almost by accident, with William Lambarde, whose *A Perambulation of Kent* appeared in 1576.[20] Lambarde was the son of a London alderman. He trained as a lawyer and wrote a number of popular legal handbooks. In 1570 he married and moved to Kent, where he began collecting notes for a topographical dictionary which he turned into a systematic survey of the county. It was completed in draft in 1570 and read at that time by, among others, Lord Burghley. Lambarde continued collecting information, partly because he saw the *Perambulation* as a current handbook of the county. His aim was to describe Kent as he saw it, with some historical material including entries from Domesday Book, royal charters and Leland's work, but also with contemporary listings such as the local nobility and gentry recorded in the heraldic visitation of 1574.

The method adopted by Lambarde owed a good deal to the earlier chorographic tradition, because he examined each hundred (the ancient administrative unit) and parish in order. The reader was guided through the county, and current institutions were discussed as the journey proceeded. As Lambarde expressed it:

> It followeth therefore, that according to purpose and promise, I hande such particular places within this Diocese, as are mentioned in hysterie: in which treatie, I observe this order: first to begin at Tanet, and to peruse the East and South Shores, till I come to the limits between this Shyre and Sussex: then to ascend Northward, and to visit such places, as lie along the bounds of this Diocese and Rochester returning by the mouth of Medway to Tanet againe, which is the whole circuit of this Bishopricke: and lastly, to describe such places as lie in the body and midst of the same.

In this way Lambarde set an agenda for county histories, in which the study of antiquities was combined with topographical description, and current information.[21]

Lambarde conceived his study of Kent as a topographical dictionary, which would serve as a reference work for a series of county studies. These would eventually cover the whole country, but he soon came to recognise that this greater study was probably beyond him. Writing in the preface, he explained how experience had taught him that:

> it will be hard for any one man (and much more for myself) to accomplish all, I can but wish in like sort that some one in each shire would make the enterprise for his own country, to the end that by joining our pens and conferring our labours (as it were) . . . we may at the last by the union of many parts and papers compact a whole and perfect body and book of our English antiquities.[22]

Despite this apparent capitulation, Lambarde remained interested in the greater project of a national county-by-county study, at least until he received a manuscript copy of Camden's work in 1585. After that he accepted that such a project was beyond him, and when in 1596 a second edition of his *Perambulation* was published, he set out his revised vision:

> Nevertheless, being assured that the inwards of each place may best be known by such as reside therein, I cannot but still encourage

some one able man in each shire to undertake his own, whereby both many good particularities will come to discovery everywhere, and Master Camden himself may yet have greater choice wherewith to amplify and enlarge the whole.[23]

Lambarde may have become the first major county historian by accident rather than design, but he was soon followed. He inspired John Norden (c.1547–1625) who spent much of his later life as surveyor to the Duchy of Cornwall. In 1583 Norden conceived the idea of a 'Speculum Britanniae', a survey covering each county, complete with maps. His first work on the Speculum was in 1591. He used the opportunity of a surveying commission in Northamptonshire to compile a guidebook to the county, which included some historical and antiquarian background, a discussion of the economic and social life of the county, and a map, based largely on Saxton's work. The guide was not published until 1720, but his Speculum was under way and in 1593 he published *An Historical and Chorographicall Discription of Middlesex*. The text followed the prototype he had developed for Northamptonshire, but the map of Middlesex, and plans of Westminster and the City of London were his own. It was the first English county map to mark roads. As with so much early chorographical writing, Lord Burghley was involved, giving his permission for publication after seeing a manuscript copy.

With Middlesex completed, Norden was in business, and he worked with astonishing speed. In 1594 he produced descriptions and maps of Essex and Surrey, and in 1595 similar material for Hampshire, the Isle of Wight, Sussex, Jersey and Guernsey. The survey of Essex included a discussion of the county's hundreds, towns, parishes, hamlets, greater houses, parks and other features. His *Description of Hertfordshire* was published in 1598, with later editions in 1723 and 1903, despite the disparaging comment of one of his nineteenth-century successors that it was 'rather the survey of a geographer, than the description of an historian'.

Norden produced only one more part of the Speculum, the text and maps for Cornwall which he presented to James I in 1604. Like most of the Speculum, the description was not published in his lifetime, but his maps of Middlesex, Surrey, Essex, Sussex, Hampshire and Kent were printed in the 1607 edition of Camden's *Britannia*. Speed also used several of Norden's maps in his *Theatre of the Empire of Great Britaine* (1609). Norden followed some of Saxton's iconography, but he used a wider and more consistent set of conventional symbols with explanatory keys, as well as a marginal grid reference to relate maps and texts in complementary alphabetical gazetteers. Norden also included roads and triangular distance charts.[24]

Lambarde also influenced Sampson Erdeswicke's *Survey of Staffordshire*, begun in 1593 and still unfinished when the author died ten years later, Robert Reyce's *Breviary of Suffolk*, written at the end of the sixteenth century but published only in 1902, and Richard Carew's *Survey of Cornwall*. Carew belonged to one of the county's leading families, and from 1589 he was, like Camden and Lambarde, an active member of the Society of Antiquaries. His study of the county was published in 1602 after circulating for some years in manuscript, and was subsequently reprinted in 1723, 1769, 1811 and 1953. Carew examined the climate, geology, industry, education and recreations of Cornwall, he studied the county's history, and he described the hundreds on what was by now becoming the standard parish-by-parish basis.[25] Carew in turn inspired Thomas Westcote's *Devon*, which was concerned primarily with description and only incidentally with history. Like many similar studies it circulated in manuscript, and was not published until 1845.

Lambarde had started a new tradition in which landed gentlemen took the baton from him to research and write county histories. Thomas Denton, whose *Perambulation of Cumberland* was prepared in 1687–88, but finally printed only in 2003, was quite explicit in more or less cloning Lambarde's study for his own area.[26] But the method was also dictated by the manuscripts and the market. These histories were possible only because of the co-operation of the local gentry, either through permitting access to their muniment rooms for research purposes, or providing the information themselves. In such circumstances it is hardly surprising that county histories devoted many pages to manorial histories, the descent of property, the genealogies of gentry families, and the illustrations of their seats. County histories celebrated the power and wealth of the landed elite, while pandering to their fascination with family trees.

These histories also had a wider agenda, glorifying the local gentry, and providing a statement about the county as part of England for gentry elsewhere to admire. Thomas Habington started his work on Worcestershire to refute contemporary comments that there were 'few gentlemen of antiquity' in the county, and when he finished he was assured that 'the gentry of Worcestershyre will accept it as a great favour dewe unto theyre country'. William Burton saw his *Description of Leicestershire*, compiled 1597–1604, as serving to ensure that his native county 'should no longer lye obscured in darknesse'.[27] Of course some of this was cant: no one doubted the importance of marketing considerations as the antiquary appealed to the vanity of the gentry, and their family pride, in the expectation that they would purchase copies for their libraries.[28]

Dugdale and Thoroton

County history reached a new stage with the appearance in 1656 of Sir William Dugdale's *Antiquities of Warwickshire*. In many ways Dugdale followed earlier writers, using Leland's manuscript writings and, like Lambarde, following the chorographic tradition by dividing the county into its hundreds, and then proceeding along the routes of streams and rivers to describe each parish in turn. He also anticipated later interests by identifying deserted settlements, but he showed relatively little interest in the new approaches of his own day such as the detailed investigation of individual sites, or natural history. As a member of the College of Heralds, it is perhaps not surprising that his principal concerns were with genealogy and heraldry. The result was a county gentleman's history dedicated to 'the gentry of Warwickshire', and offered to them 'as the most proper persons to whom it can be presented; wherein you will see very much of your worthy ancestors, to whose memory I have erected it, as a monumental pillar'.[29]

What distinguished Dugdale's work was its scale and its range. It was far bigger than any of its predecessors, running to 800 folio pages, and it was meticulously researched. Dugdale was a master of the sources, and his notebooks displayed a methodical, selective approach. References were given throughout the text to the documents on which statements were based, and he left no known stone wittingly unturned. He read various classes of public records including plea rolls and patent rolls, together with papers in private hands, heralds' notes, monastic chronicles, and numerous printed books. He also followed where others had led by using the work of a circle of antiquarians and gentlemen with antiquarian interests in the Midlands.[30] He often relied on their knowledge of heraldry, antiquities and family trees, but families, and particularly Catholic families anxious to confirm their position among the gentry, were usually only too keen to help him.[31]

Conversely, their support and encouragement also enabled him to say a good deal about the individual families he assumed were potential purchasers of the book.[32] This necessary linkage to local gentry families did not prevent Dugdale from setting new standards of accuracy and method. His systematic and critical use of source materials went further than anything previously achieved.[33] He also established an innovative model by presenting the general history of the county since Anglo-Saxon times, followed by a parish-by-parish description with particular reference to manorial descent – one of the criticisms of Dugdale was that he mentioned only families who were lords of a manor or patrons of a church – and church monuments.

Dugdale's achievement was to 'perfect' the study of antiquities, and his work was widely admired even if his standards proved difficult to repeat. His most successful follower was Dr Robert Thoroton, whose *Antiquities of Nottinghamshire* was published in 1677. Thoroton, like Dugdale, was a country gentleman, and he followed the model established in the *Antiquities of Warwickshire* so closely that Dugdale has been described as Thoroton's 'mentor, guide and friend'.[34] Thoroton's interest in Nottinghamshire arose from a fascination with his own family history. He proudly traced his ancestry back to the Norman baronial family of Lovetot, and it was his experience as a genealogist which enabled him to compile pedigrees for a number of Nottinghamshire gentry families. He had researched at least nine prior to Dugdale's heraldic visitation of the county in 1663, the occasion on which Dugdale took the opportunity to encourage him, together with another local gentleman, Gervase Pigot of Thrumpton, to turn their research into a book. In the years that followed Thoroton was helped by Pigot, and by his father-in-law Gilbert Boun.

Thoroton used manuscripts lent to him by fellow gentry, and he visited many churches up and down the county, copying inscriptions and sketching coats-of-arms. However, he was reluctant to travel far from his home in Car Colston, and he hardly visited north Nottinghamshire. Despite his preference for working from home, Thoroton was able to base most of his research on original archival sources or, in their absence, transcripts and collections compiled by other antiquaries. Some of these were borrowed from fellow landowners, including the Rufford Abbey cartulary which came from Lord Halifax, and extracts from the Pipe Rolls compiled by the Yorkshire antiquary Roger Dodsworth.

Thoroton did not personally visit the national archives in London or the diocesan records in York, although he did employ a researcher to do some work at the latter. Dugdale's view was that these omissions affected the quality of the work: 'I do esteem the book well worth your buying', Dugdale told a friend, 'though had he gone to the fountain of records it might have been better done'. Thoroton also included little or nothing on any antiquities of archaeological significance, which is surprising given that Car Colston lies adjacent to the Roman

Fosse Way, and there was the site of a small Roman fort and town within a mile of his house. Despite such caveats the book remains a classic, not least for Thoroton's descriptions of the county in his own day, including his comments on Newark during the Civil War, the depopulation of the village of Thorpe-in-the-Glebe, and the building of fine town houses in Nottingham. His discussion of Nottingham was far more informative than Dugdale's rather sketchy account of Birmingham and its iron trade.[35]

No other volumes quite matched Dugdale and Thoroton in the seventeenth century, but by 1700 or thereabouts a great deal had been achieved, some of it particularly sensitive to locality, such as William Scawen's work in preserving knowledge of the Cornish language and tradition.[36] The more we learn of these antiquarian studies the more opportunity arises to judge their quality, but before becoming too critical the context in which these gentlemen-scholars were working should be remembered.[37] Dugdale and Thoroton emphasised the importance of antiquities. While they might occasionally comment on their own societies their major concern lay within a narrow range of topics, particularly the history of landed families, their heraldry and genealogy, their tombs, and the descent of their estates. This was the nature of county history at the time, and it reflected the market to which these scholars were appealing. Yet their achievement should not be underplayed. They were pioneers, and they laid the foundations of Anglo-Saxon and medieval scholarship, occasionally putting into print manuscript sources which local historians still use today.

Natural history

A parallel interest developing alongside county histories was in natural history, which traces its origins to William Turner's *New Herball* in 1551 and John Gerard's *Herball* of 1597. Sir Francis Bacon (1561–1626) argued that in human and natural history the value of any work depended on its use of measurement and induction. His empirical approach was based on the close observation and description of nature, and it led to the formation in 1660 of the Royal Society. Fellows of the new Society thought in similar ways to antiquaries, emphasising the importance of accurate measurement, specific data, and careful recording of material. These emphases had consequences for antiquaries, particularly those who lacked Camden and Dugdale's attention to detail, and who, as a result, had sometimes been rather cavalier with their evidence. Increasingly it was obvious that all material remains needed to be carefully recorded, because of the contribution they might make to studies of the past.

By the end of the seventeenth century most antiquaries still began from the written record, which they regarded as the most reliable form of evidence. In part, of course, this was also a reflection of their necessary emphasis on genealogical and heraldic descents for commercial reasons. The growth of understanding of the significance of objects and sites marked the emergence of archaeology, and Bacon's approach liberated the early archaeologists from depending on literary sources. His lead was followed by John Aubrey (1626–97). Aubrey, now remembered mainly for *Brief Lives*, an account of his contemporaries and of famous people from the sixteenth century, was in many senses the founding father of archaeology, place name and folklore studies. A Fellow of the Royal Society, Aubrey confessed to be interested in antiquities from childhood, and in 1649 he 'discovered' the megalithic monument at Avebury. Subsequently he visited and studied both Avebury and Stonehenge, both of which he believed long predated what was then the orthodox attribution to the Danes or Romans. His findings were included in a manuscript entitled *Monumenta Britannica*, which was published in full only in 1980. It included notes and drawings of sites from various periods, many of which have either disappeared or been significantly altered since he surveyed them.

In 1660 Aubrey began collecting evidence for a study of the antiquities of Wiltshire, which he hoped would be a collaborative venture. He undertook to write the section on north Wiltshire, and to that end collected material for two manuscript volumes, which he called 'An Essay towards the Description of the North Division of Wiltshire'. Since it was designed as a natural history he included lists of trees and plants and their medicinal and practical uses, reflecting the scientific concerns of Bacon. It was expanded and printed in the nineteenth century as a partial history of the county. He also worked on Surrey, where Richard Rawlinson subsequently reorganised his material into *The Natural History and Antiquities of the County of Surrey* (5 volumes, 1718–19).[38]

Similar studies, some of them carried out under the auspices of the Royal Society, led towards 'scientific antiquarianism' as theories about the relationship between human history and natural science filtered down from the Royal Society to the localities. Of these the most notable was Robert Plot's *Natural History of Oxfordshire*, published in 1676, which firmly established local natural history. Plot, an Oxford don who in 1683 became the first keeper of the Ashmolean Museum, originally planned a county-based survey of England and Wales, which was to include maps. In his study of Oxfordshire he surveyed the county's natural features, and devoted only a single chapter to antiquities. He used the same methods in his *Natural History of Staffordshire*, published in 1686. Although concerned primarily with botany, geology and mineralogy, Plot also found space for a discussion of human history and antiquities, as well as opening up new discussion areas such as buildings and building materials, and trying to develop an awareness of the relationship between natural and human history.

Like many who had gone before, Plot found the task of writing a natural history of every county well beyond him. In the end, only his studies of Oxfordshire and Staffordshire appeared, although as late as 1694 he issued prospectuses for natural histories of London and Middlesex, and Middlesex and Kent. He also started collecting material, some of which he gave to Edmund Gibson for his new edition of Camden. Plot died in 1696 before he was able to complete either of the studies. In his Oxfordshire and Staffordshire volumes, however, he successfully combined civil and ecclesiastical history with natural history, and this enabled him to describe the counties in terms of both nature and human activity.

By the end of the seventeenth century local history had come a long way from the work of monks and occasional travellers, to the increasingly sophisticated output of gentlemen scholars from Dugdale to Plot. The search for England from the 1530s had some unexpected results. Initially, and most remarkably with Camden, antiquaries sought to describe England from the earliest, pre-Roman times. After Camden, although there were still aspirants wanting to emulate the great scholar by writing about the country rather than a single county, the scale of the task made such efforts increasingly difficult. Richard Blome's *Britannia*, which appeared for the first time in 1673, was criticised by Bishop William Nicolson for its over-reliance on Camden and Speed. Nicolson called him the 'boldest Plagiary in the whole pack'.[39] Rev. Thomas Cox produced a new survey entitled *Magna Britannia et Hibernia, antiqua et nova* in six volumes between 1720 and 1731, reprinted in 1738. Using Camden as his base source, Cox added material including a survey of each English county which combined general history with a topographical gazetteer. It is still regularly cited by historians, and yet no one could really emulate Camden, particularly with the enlargements of his work which appeared in 1789 and 1806.

By 1700, in reality if not in theory, the county had become the accepted area of study. It made obvious sense, given that most of the gentlemen-scholars were county gentry, with relatively easy access to both the sites and documents of their shire. In cartography, Saxton had shown how it was possible to map each county and build the whole into a national atlas. Something similar was possible through county histories, but this was of less importance than the findings of individual scholars and their helpers. A great deal was now known about the pre-Roman, Roman, and Anglo-Saxon periods, and considerable doubt had been thrown on once accepted truths such as the supposed primitive nature of pre-Roman Britons.

Almost every volume of county history added to the collective knowledge of the surviving material evidence of Roman Britain. The enlarged edition of *Britannia* in 1695 consolidated the advances in Roman studies, and paved the way for the publication in 1732 of John Horsley's magisterial work *Britannia Romana*. Even so, perhaps the most impressive result of seventeenth-century antiquarian study was the clarification of the Saxon past, where answers were offered to previously open questions. By 1700 Saxon England was yielding up its secrets, and the language of the Saxons was understood by scholars in Oxford and Cambridge. Both the secular and the religious history of the period had been pieced together. Studies were also focusing on the antiquity of the landscape itself and the ancient monuments which survived, the beginnings of what we now know as archaeology.[40] A great deal had been learned, but there was still much more to be discovered.

Notes

1 J.H. Harvey (ed.), *The Itineraries of William of Worcester* (1969); R.N. Worth, 'William of Worcester: Devon's earliest topographer', *Transactions of the Devonshire Association*, 18 (1886), cited in M. Brayshay (ed.), *Topographical Writers in South-West England* (1996), 5.

2 Lucy Tomlin Smith (ed.), *The Itinerary of John Leland* (5 vols, 1964 edn.), I, xxxvii.

3 Ibid; Lucy Tomlin Smith (ed.), *The Itinerary in Wales of John Leland in or About the Years 1536–39* (1906); J.R. Liddell, 'Leland's lists of manuscripts in Lincolnshire monasteries', *English Historical Review*, 54 (1939), 88–95; J. Simmons (ed.), *English County Historians* (1978), 5; Brayshay, *Topographical Writers*, 6.

4 Quoted in S. Piggott, *Ancient Britons and Antiquarian Imagination* (1989), 18.

5 R. Sweet, *Antiquaries: The Discovery of the Past in Eighteenth-Century Britain* (2004), 124–5.

6 Stuart Piggott, 'William Camden and the Britannia', in Richardson, 12–29.

7 Graham Parry, *The Trophies of Time: English Antiquarians of the Seventeenth Century* (1995), 3–4.

8 Bernard Nurse, 'The 1610 edition of Camden's *Britannia*', *The Antiquaries Journal*, 73 (1993), 158–60; William Camden, *Britannia: Or a Chorographicall Description of the Most Flourishing Kingdoms, England, Scotland, and Ireland, and the Islands Adjoyning, Out of the Depth of Antiquitie* (1637).

9 See Joan Evans, *A History of the Society of Antiquaries* (1956), May McKisack, *Medieval History in the Tudor Age* (1971), and for the importance of the Cotton Library, Kevin Sharpe, *Sir Robert Cotton, 1586–1631* (1979); Sweet, *Antiquaries*, 82–3.

10 K. Robbins, *Great Britain: Identities, Institutions and the Idea of Britishness* (1998), 23–6.

11 Jonathan Clark, 'Sovereignty: the British experience', *Times Literary Supplement*, 29 November 1991.

12 William Shakespeare, *Richard II*, Act II, Scene 1, lines 40–50.

13 N. Evans (ed.), National identity in the British Isles (*Occasional Papers in Welsh Studies*, 3, 1989), 1; Esther Moir, *The Discovery of Britain: The English Tourists, 1540–1840* (1964).

14 W. Ravenhill, *Christopher Saxton's 16th Century Maps: The Counties of England and Wales* (1992), 17; P. Hindle, *Maps for Historians* (1998), 6–7.

15 S. Tyacke and J. Huddy, *Christopher Saxton and Tudor Map-Making* (1980); P.D.A. Harvey, *Maps in Tudor England* (1993).

16 Penry Williams, 'The Crown and the counties', in C. Haigh (ed.), *The Reign of Elizabeth I* (1984), 125–46.

17 John Speed, *The Counties of Britain: A Tudor Atlas* (1988), which includes a reproduction of the original frontispiece of Speed's work. Saxton probably died before the *Theatre* was published.

18 The first edition, unsuitable for the traveller to carry, was followed by *Britannia Depicta or Ogilby Improved*, and was published as a popular pocket travel book in 1720 by Emanuel Bowen (reprinted 1970); *ECH*, 441.

19 Quoted in *ECH*, 15–16.

20 William Lambarde, *A Perambulation of Kent* ([1576]; new edn 1970).

21 Lambarde's work is best described in R.M. Warnicke, *William Lambarde* (1973). See also Victor Morgan, 'The cartographic image of "the country" in early modern England', *Transactions of the Royal Historical Society* 5th series, 29 (1979), 129–54.

22 Lambarde, *Perambulation*.

23 Ibid. Lambarde's interim researches before he abandoned the greater project were finally published as *Dictionarium Angliae Topographicum et Historicum* (1730). Lambarde's latest biographer pays far more attention to his successful legal career than to his work as an antiquary: J.D. Alsop, 'Lambarde, William (1536–1601)', *Oxford Dictionary of National Biography* (2004), art 15,921.

24 Hindle, *Maps*, 8–9; *ECH*, 14–15, 86, 186.

25 J. Chynoweth et al. (eds), *The Survey of Cornwall by Richard Carew* (Devon and Cornwall Record Society, 47, 2004); F.E. Halliday (ed.), *Richard Carew of Antony: The Survey of Cornwall* (1953); F.V. Emery, 'English regional studies from Aubrey to Defoe', *Geographical Journal*, 124 (1958), 315; Brayshay, *Topographical Writers*, 8; *ECH*, 87.

26 A.J.L. Winchester and Mary Wane (eds), *Thomas Denton: Perambulation of Cumberland 1687–1688* (Surtees Society, 2003), 15–18.

27 *ECH*, 15–16; Jan Broadway, William Dugdale and the significance of county history in early Stuart England (*Dugdale Society Occasional Paper*, 39, 1999), 8. The subject is further developed in Jan Broadway, '*No historie so meet*': *Gentry Culture and the Development of Local History in Elizabethan and Early Stuart England* (2006).

28 Sweet, *Antiquaries*, 37–9.

29 *ECH*, 16.

30 Ibid., 16–17, 398; Broadway, *William Dugdale*, 15–20.

31 Richard Cust, 'Catholicism, antiquarianism and gentry honour: the writings of Sir Thomas Shirley', *Midland History*, 23 (1998), 40–70.

32 Broadway, *William Dugdale*, 9.

33 S. Mendyk, 'Sir William Dugdale and the antiquities of Warwickshire (1656)', *West Midlands Studies*, 17 (1984), 1–6; S. Mendyk, '*Speculum Britanniae*': *Regional Study, Antiquarianism and Science in Britain to 1700* (1989), 102–3.

34 A. Henstock and K. Train, 'Robert Thoroton: Nottinghamshire Antiquary, 1623–78', *Transactions of the Thoroton Society*, 81 (1977), 13–32.

35 Ibid. *ECH*, 312–17; M.W. Barley and K.S.S. Train, 'Robert Thoroton', in J. Simmons (ed.), *English County Historians* (1978), 22–43.

36 Mark Stoyle, *West Briton: Cornish Identities and the Early Modern British State* (2002).

37 Simmons, *English County Historians*, 13–16.

38 J. Fowles and R. Legg (eds), *Monumenta Britannica* (1982 reprint); Anthony Powell, *John Aubrey and His Friends* (1948); M. Hunter, *John Aubrey and the Realm of Learning* (1975); *ECH*, 411–12.

39 S. Mendyk, 'Blome, Richard (c.1635–1705)', *Oxford Dictionary of National Biography* (2004), 2662.

40 Parry, *Trophies of Time*, 358–64.

III *Antiquaries at large: the eighteenth and nineteenth centuries*

What had been planted in the sixteenth century, and had sprouted in the seventeenth, came into full blossom during the eighteenth century, before fading gently away in the nineteenth. In the course of the eighteenth century antiquarian studies started to fragment, and three separate if overlapping movements can be identified. The first was the evolution of topographical studies into travel and tourist accounts, particularly in conjunction with the picturesque movement of the later eighteenth century. The second was the development within antiquarianism of natural historical and archaeological studies. Archaeology, although still within the family of antiquarian study, was emerging as a discipline in its own right, particularly with the founding in 1770 of the journal *Archaeologia*. Finally, the county history grew in terms of both output and size. What Dugdale and Thoroton had achieved in a single folio volume now multiplied into two, four and as many as twelve to a county. Although quantity was not necessarily paralleled by quality, it would be churlish to deny that a huge step forward was taken by a great number of dedicated scholars in the eighteenth century, but this blossoming was not to last. By the early nineteenth century topographical writing had given place to travel writing, archaeology was established as a separate discipline, and county histories were changing in form and style. The heyday of these great studies was over by the 1830s, as they were gradually replaced by the trade directory and occasionally revived in shorter, single volume, more synoptic studies of individual counties – until the last flourish of this style of writing, the founding in 1899 of the Victoria County History.

Topographical studies

Topographical writing had developed in response to Camden's work.[1] Seventeenth-century studies included Edward Leigh's *England Described* (1659), Edward Chamberlayne's *Angliae Notitia* (1669), and Guy Miege's *The New State of England* (1691). Chamberlayne's work contained topographical descriptions of much of the country. It was frequently reprinted, reaching a thirty-eighth edition by 1755. This description of Oxfordshire taken from the eighteenth edition of 1694 gives an idea of the style of writing:

> Is in the diocese of Oxford, 130 miles in circumference, contains about 534,000 acres and 19,007 houses. The air is sweet and healthful. The soil is fertile in corn, and rich in pastures. Its chief commodities, corn, malt, cattle, fruit, wood. It has 280 parishes and 15 towns. The chief is the city of Oxford, 47 miles from London, one of the two noblest Universities in the world. Woodstock is noted for its Park, walled in, and the first in England: T[h]ame for its Free School. Henl[e]y for its malt, Witney for its Free School and Library: the rich and fine town of Banbury for cheese; Burford for saddles: Its principal seats are Woodstock, a Palace Royal; Cornbury, the Earl of Clarendon's; Bletchington, the Earl of Anglesey's; Caversham, the Earl of Craven's; Dichley and Lees Rest, the Earl of Lichfield's; Rycott and Chesterton, the Earl of Abington's; Broughton, North Newton, and Shetford, Lord Viscount Saye and Seal's; Sherborn Castle, Lord Abergavenny's; Water Eaton, Lord Lovelace's; Leadwell, Lord Carrington's; Wroxton Abbey, Lord Guildford.[2]

It was only a small step to tour writing, which added a personal touch to this rather stark description, and allowed the writer freedom to discuss both contemporary and antiquarian interests. References to antiquities appeared on many of the pages of Celia Fiennes's late seventeenth-century *Journeys* (although these were published for the first time only in the late nineteenth century).[3] John Macky, in his *Journey Through England* (1722), also revealed a fascination with Roman antiquities.[4]

Daniel Defoe noted in the first edition of what was probably the best known of these early guides, his *Tour Through the Whole Island of Great Britain*, published in 1726, that he would take no notice of antiquities because he was mostly interested in the current state of the nation.[5] Page after page of the *Tour* teems with information about the economy, urban growth, trade and other matters of contemporary interest, but Defoe could not resist reference to the past, and freely plagiarised Camden's *Britannia* whenever it suited him. Writing of Stonehenge, he enjoyed himself by poking gentle fun at the differences of opinion expressed by different antiquaries:

> Tis needless, that I should enter here into any part of the dispute about which our learned antiquaries have so puzzled themselves,

that several books, and one of them, in folio, has been published about it; some alleging it to be a heathen, or pagan temple, and altar, or place of sacrifice, as Mr Jones; others, a monument, or trophy of victory; others a monument for the dead, as Mr Aubury, and the like. Again, some will have it to be British, some Danish, some Saxon, some Roman, and some before them all, Phenician.[6]

Defoe was easily tempted into such diversions, and after a long discussion of Lincoln's post-Conquest history, much of it derived from Camden, he reprimanded himself in print: 'all this relates to times past, and is an excursion, which I shall atone for by making no more'. Returning rapidly to the present he condemned contemporary Lincoln as 'an old, dying, decayed, dirty city'.[7] Later editors of Defoe added additional antiquarian information as more information became readily available.[8]

Defoe was happy to suggest that his discussion of antiquities was no more than an 'excursion', but there was evidently a market for tour literature which reflected on antiquarian and historical issues as the traveller progressed. Charles Cotton's *Wonders of the Peak*, published first in 1725, was written in blank verse, and described St Mary's Well, Buxton, Poole's Hole, Tideswell, Mam Tor, Chatsworth, and several other features of the Peak District. In the 1770s William Bray's tour of the Midlands and Yorkshire included a place-by-place discussion of towns, country houses and other features, written as part of a journey through the area.[9] Bray (1736–1832), a solicitor from Surrey, is best known for his contribution to the *History and Antiquities of Surrey*. He became a Fellow of the Society of Antiquaries in 1771, and treasurer in 1803, finding the energy to combine his legal practice and other professional duties with a range of antiquarian interests.[10]

A further development of tour writing took place with the Romantic movement, which inspired a new genre of this type of tour in the more 'picturesque' counties, by drawing the attention of visitors towards ruins. The descriptive works of William Gilpin helped to open Georgian eyes to the beauties of the countryside, particularly the Lake District, which he described in terms both of its antiquities and its current economy and society.[11] Castles and abbeys could be drawn to the attention of would-be visitors and, still dwelling on the notion of Englishness, presented as symbolic reflections of the triumph of reformed religion over Catholicism. The ruin became an object of fashionable taste.[12]

In 1798 John Britton commenced a series of publications of this type, of which the most important were *Beauties of England and*

Wales: Architectural Antiquities, and *Cathedral Antiquities*. This was originally designed as a topographical study of Wiltshire entitled *Beauties of Wiltshire*, but it led to his more ambitious scheme, *Beauties of England and Wales*, which he undertook in collaboration with Edward Brayley, and which was aimed at a general market. Whereas most antiquarian publications had print runs of 200–1000, the *Beauties* sold in thousands. Britton insisted that the series should be based on original sources and illustrated by accurate engravings of antiquities, as opposed to the traditional combination of country seats and picturesque woodland scenes. Volumes grew progressively more detailed, as he and Brayley broadened their reading and built up their expertise. Their study of Cumberland took the form of a current description of the local economy, with supportive historical and antiquarian material.[13] Britton and Brayley researched their volumes on long field trips to collect information. What they planned as three volumes ended up as twenty-five, although some later studies contained contributions from other authors.[14] Britton took stock of the growth which had taken place in the discussion of architectural antiquities in England in 1825, in the concluding volume of the series, *The Architectural Antiquities of Great Britain*.[15]

Even more commendable were the herculean efforts of the brothers Daniel and Samuel Lysons who, between 1806 and 1822, were busy researching what they intended would be a uniform history of each county. Daniel (1762–1834), a clergyman, and Samuel (1763–1819), a lawyer, were both antiquaries. Daniel worked on Middlesex and Surrey, while Samuel combined field archaeology with a position from 1803 as keeper of the records in the Tower of London. Both were Fellows of the Society of Antiquaries and the Royal Society, and Samuel was also an accomplished artist. Both had published independently when they started working together on *Magna Britannia, being a concise topographical account of the several counties of Great Britain*. Their intention was to fill the gap they perceived between Camden's work, and the large-scale county histories, and their scheme was even more ambitious than Britton and Brayley's work.

The Lysons intended to produce accounts of each county in turn to form a complete whole. They travelled through each county to study churches, but they paid less attention to secular buildings except for brief notes on a handful of gentry seats. They also depended on a standard questionnaire for manorial information, which inevitably made their work patchy, even though the Post Office allowed replies by clergymen to be sent post-free. Nine volumes (numbered I–VI because some were in parts) were published 1806–22, covering

Bedfordshire to Devonshire. Samuel Lysons died in 1819 and Daniel felt unable to continue with the work, at least partly because he needed Samuel's archaeological skills. Their research, particularly on Berkshire and Cambridgeshire, helped to fill important gaps; indeed, for Cambridgeshire the Lysons' study was the only systematic account of the whole county. Their parochial histories provided useful summaries reused in trade directories and similar publications through the nineteenth and into the twentieth centuries. [16]

Similar topographical studies also came on the market, usually aimed at wealthier tourists. Every county had its local writers. For Nottinghamshire, G.A. Cooke's *Topographical and Statistical Description of Nottinghamshire* appeared about 1810, and included general and topographical description including towns and country houses, a discussion of the county's agriculture, and a complete itinerary of the county designed as 'a copious travelling guide'.[17] The Nottinghamshire section of F.C. Laird's *Beauties of England and Wales* was published in 1812. Rev. J. Curtis's *Topographical History of Nottinghamshire*, published 1843–44, quoted extensively from Thoroton's county history, reflecting the tradition of borrowing rather than researching from new, but took the form of a place-by-place gazetteer through the county and also included evidence on Nottingham's water supply prepared by the borough engineer Thomas Hawksley for a government enquiry in the 1840s.[18]

Archaeology

A second level of antiquarian fragmentation was associated in the eighteenth century with the study and excavation of sites, that is the development of the discipline we today know as archaeology. This was given something of a boost with the re-forming of the Society of Antiquaries in London, 1707–17, on lines similar to that of its Elizabethan predecessor in which Camden had played such an important role. Humfrey Wanley, John Talman and John Bagford sat down at the Bear, a tavern in the Strand, at 6 p.m. on 5 December 1707 to discuss how to revive the Society. It was not long before they attracted other like-minded antiquaries to swell their numbers, and by 1717 (when the minutes begin) the Society was meeting regularly in the Mitre Tavern on Fleet Street. It had twenty-three members, and the secretary was Dr William Stukeley.[19]

Stukeley (1687–1765), born at Holbeach, Lincolnshire, was a physician and clergyman, a friend of Sir Isaac Newton, a Fellow of the Royal Society, and a founding member of the Society of Antiquaries.

He wrote works on gout, the spleen and the anatomy of the elephant and, in 1750, *The Philosophy of Earthquakes, Natural and Religious*, in which he attributed earth tremors in London to electrical explosions in the atmosphere. He was in at the beginning of what was to be in eighteenth-century Britain a significant growth of interest in archaeology. Antiquaries had always been concerned with every aspect of the past, and Stukeley established his reputation by attempting to date some of Britain's best known prehistoric antiquities, notably Stonehenge and Avebury. He first visited these monuments around 1719, his interest aroused by reading a borrowed copy of John Aubrey's manuscript, and a concern that landowners regarded them only as potential stone quarries for building materials.

At Avebury, Stukeley found that a number of the features described by Aubrey had already disappeared, and the demands of agriculture were taking precedence over archaeological enquiry. Stukeley's painstaking survey of the sites revealed the sophistication and complexity of the design. His account of Stonehenge was published in 1740 as *Stonehenge: a Temple Restor'd to the British Druids. Abury: A Temple of the British Druids* appeared in 1743. Both volumes arose from fieldwork on the two sites, 1718–24, during which Stukeley took notes, made sketches, and carefully measured everything he saw. His views were not always accepted; indeed, by the early 1750s they were being received with barely concealed ridicule at the Society of Antiquaries, largely because of his interest in druidical science. As a result of Stukeley's work it was no longer possible for anyone seriously to challenge his theory that Stonehenge and other stone circles were of Celtic construction.[20]

The study of antiquities benefited from improvements in the means of communicating findings. From 1731 the *Gentleman's Magazine* regularly included contributions sent in by correspondents from around the country on the topography and antiquities of places they had studied. Local antiquaries formed their own societies, such as the Gentleman's Society of Spalding – which Stukeley joined when he moved in 1710 to Boston to practise as a physician – and its sister societies in Peterborough (1730), Stamford, and a number of other Lincolnshire towns. Smaller societies often depended on the dynamism of a single individual, and most survived only a generation or two. The Spalding Gentleman's Society, founded in 1710 and still active, initially depended on the enthusiasm and energy of local lawyer Maurice Johnson, whose own interests included numismatics, heraldry and sepulchral monuments, fossils, natural history and gardening, as well as legal history.[21] Societies like this enabled antiquaries to keep in touch with each other and to share their experiences of investigating and recording physical remains, particularly Roman remains. Perhaps not surprisingly, many members were more enthusiastic about fieldwork and recording than synthesis, but at their best they set new standards of accuracy, and raised the level of understanding of subjects ranging from the ancient Britons to medieval architecture.

Apart from correspondence and local society meetings antiquaries were increasingly able to keep abreast of each others' research with the founding by the Society of Antiquaries in 1770 of *Archaeologia*. The inspiration behind *Archaeologia* was Richard Gough, like Stukeley a fellow of both the Society of Antiquaries and the Royal Society. Gough was a regular correspondent of the *Gentleman's Magazine*, and director of the Society of Antiquaries 1771–97. In 1768 he published *Anecdotes of British Topography*, a gazetteer of published and unpublished work in local history and topography covering the British Isles, with particular emphasis on the Saxon era. Many other publications followed, including his new edition of *Camden* in 1789. In his role as Director, Gough persuaded the Antiquaries to establish a periodical miscellany. *Archaeologia* appeared for the first time in 1770, with a remit to record and illustrate British antiquities. Although Gough was one of the major contributors in the early years of *Archaeologia*, the journal enabled would-be scholars with limited resources to find their way into print.[22] The complete set of *Archaeologia* sits on the library shelves of the Society of Antiquaries at Burlington House, Piccadilly, to this day, a remarkable monument to the archaeological heritage of the past two centuries.

The importance for learning by communication is apparent from the career of a man in the second division of antiquarian studies, who was nevertheless a regular contributor to *Archaeologia*, Major Hayman Rooke (1723–1806). Rooke is best known today as the man who gave his military title to one of the great oaks of Sherwood Forest, still associated with the clandestine activities of the mythical outlaw Robin Hood. After a modest military career, Rooke spent the final thirty years of his life contributing to antiquarian and archaeological research on Derbyshire and Nottinghamshire, communicating his finds through numerous articles in *Archaeologia*, and compiling sketches, note books and other ephemera, still available and used for study today. He was elected a Fellow of the Society of Antiquaries in 1775.[23]

Antiquaries were essentially collectors of information rather than interpreters.[24] Gough was careful to distinguish between the historian, whose task was 'the arrangement and proper use of facts', and the antiquary, whose job was 'to record present transactions or gather the more ancient ones from the general wreck'.[25] Although he showed little interest in natural history, Gough was one of many antiquaries who moved easily between the Royal Society and the Society of Antiquaries, enjoying fellowships in both organisations. Dual membership was denoted by the initials FRSAS, and election to one society generally followed rapidly on election to the other. These overlapping interests ensured that the methodology and language of natural history and scientific enquiry coloured that of antiquarian and archaeological studies, but just what was achieved by the eighteenth-century antiquaries?

Any judgement has to take into account the way in which the study of antiquities is often associated with the emergence of archaeology as a separate study based on rigorous fieldwork. Praise is usually reserved for the work of a handful of field archaeologists from John Aubrey and Edward Lhwyd in the late seventeenth century, to Stukeley's work at Stonehenge and Avebury. After that, so the argument goes, came a decline in standards of accuracy and observation as antiquaries all too often collected indiscriminately. This negative view has remained in the literature until recent times. Stuart Piggott, for example, noted what he saw as a general collapse in intellectual standards within historical and antiquarian research from the 1730s: 'the necessity of an empirical approach was forgotten, the British foundation-myths were rewritten, philological speculation took on even more fantastic forms, and antiquarian studies became, understandably enough, discredited by serious scholars in other fields'.[26]

Of course, part of the problem Piggott identified was that men like Hayman Rooke engaged in antiquarian research as a hobby, a pleasant pastime, so that although they took their researches seriously they expected to enjoy them rather than to worry about more abstruse and academic issues. Rooke, as a recent biographer has concluded, 'was a collector and an aesthete with "archaeological" thoughts. He discovered and he speculated.'[27] The problem was that men like Rooke simultaneously employed new scientific methodologies, treated ancients' accounts judiciously, and appealed to natural religion for explanation and justification. This annoyed those in the scholarly community who had little time for what they considered to be excessive speculation. Stukeley's tendency to combine science with fantasy was similarly frustrating.[28] The situation improved only with the careful work of men such as James Douglas, William Cunnington and Sir Richard Colt Hoare at the end of the century. Once again, emphasis was placed on the importance of depending on facts rather than theory. Even so, there is plenty of evidence to suggest that the accusations levelled against many antiquaries of allowing standards of recording to fall away are wide of the mark: in Rosemary Sweet's words, 'a greater precision can be identified, whether in recording inscriptions, describing excavations or drawing the physical remains'.[29]

Rosemary Sweet also suggests that the antiquaries of the eighteenth century should be judged by their own standards. They were not especially concerned with Greece or Rome; rather, they were interested in the discovery and recording of the national pasts of England, Scotland, Wales and Ireland. As a result, the traditional fascination with Roman antiquities was supplemented during the eighteenth century by enquiry into the period following the departure of the Romans, which could be seen as the point at which national differences within Britain became more clearly differentiated. Saxon antiquities were a specifically English concern, and the study of them could be seen as a way of working towards a sense of English nationhood. By the early nineteenth century the admiration of antiquaries for all things Roman was not as dominant as a century earlier. This was despite a considerable increase in knowledge. When Thomas Reynolds compiled his *Iber britanniarum* in 1799, he calculated that it included at least 100 sites of Roman antiquities which had not been mentioned by Gough in his 1789 revised edition of *Camden*.[30] Hayman Rooke was one of those who contributed to this body of knowledge through the interest he took in Roman antiquities on either side of the Nottinghamshire–Derbyshire border.[31]

County histories

The third main development of the eighteenth century following topographical writing and antiquarian-cum-archaeological research, lay with the county history, which was both flourishing and changing. Between the publication of William Burton's *Leicestershire* in 1622, and the middle of the eighteenth century, twenty-five county histories were produced. Another twenty-two came out between 1750 and 1800,[32] and by the beginning of the nineteenth century only seven counties lacked a historian. Not only were there more books, they were bigger books: where Dugdale and Thoroton had written of Warwickshire and Nottinghamshire in a single volume, John Nichols's *The History and Antiquities of the County of Leicester* was conceived as four volumes, but Nichols wrote at such length that the four volumes were further subdivided and a total of eight large folio volumes appeared between 1795 and 1815, effectively – if confusingly – two per volume. Lined up on a library shelf they look particularly imposing.

County history was also stirring local passions. Philip Morant, whose twelve-volume history of Essex appeared between 1763 and 1768, endured a tirade of abuse from Gough, who accused him of being pompous, sedentary and lazy in his research, too easily quoting others rather than researching the sources himself. Morant responded by criticising Gough's own work, *Anecdotes of British Topography*, published in 1769. The bad feeling lasted beyond the grave. Gough reopened the issue as late as 1809, when Morant had been dead for nearly forty years. Modern scholars hold Morant's work in higher esteem than did Gough.[33]

In other counties, rivalry developed into alternative 'histories'. Rev. John Morton, rector of Oxendon and a Fellow of the Royal Society, dedicated his life to researching and finally writing his *Natural History of Northamptonshire with some Accounts of the Antiquities*. It appeared in 1712, when he had, or so he claimed, visited all but three or four of the county's villages, traced all the Roman roads, and inspected all the ancient earthworks of which he was aware.[34] Hardly had the book had time to circulate in the county than John Bridges started work on a further history in 1719. He spent some of his accumulated wealth, acquired as a lawyer and government sinecurist, hiring research assistants who drew maps and transcribed documents, many of which had not been used by Morton. In all he amassed more than fifty volumes of notes and transcriptions on a wide variety of topics, particularly – perhaps not surprisingly in the context of the time – on the descent of manors. He had done nothing with this vast collection when he died in 1724.

Bridges' material passed to his brother William, who in turn passed it to a man called Gibbons, a stationer and law bookseller at the Middle Gate Temple. In turn, Gibbons circulated a prospectus with the intention of raising money to fund writing and publishing of the proposed book. Dr Samuel Jebb of Stratford in Kent was engaged as author. He had custody of the notes for about four years, during which time five or six parts were published, before Gibbons was declared bankrupt. Jebb had as yet received no remuneration for his work.

A group of gentry in Northamptonshire met to discuss what should be done next. They agreed to pay Jebb for his work, but to hand over further production to Rev. Peter Whalley, formerly a fellow of St John's College, Oxford. Whalley took up the task, enlarging and correcting Jebb's work, but progress slowed down when he was appointed headmaster of a school, and by the time he was ready to go into print several members of the committee had died, and funds were insufficient to see the project to completion. For some years nothing further was achieved until the committee regrouped, and further funds were raised. Eventually, in 1791, John Bridges's *The History and Antiquities of Northamptonshire* appeared, seventy-two years after work had first commenced, and sixty-seven years after Bridges's death.[35]

Not surprisingly Bridges' book was already out of date in several important respects, and George Baker began work on a further county history covering similar ground to Bridges, but adding evidence from documents previously unavailable. Volume 1, which included the material he completed between 1822 and 1830, was published by subscription. By 1837 Baker was in financial difficulty. At a public meeting in October that year the Marquess of Northampton called for a new subscription list and a new committee.[36] Forty names were added to the list, and Baker was able to continue with his work. The last sections of his *The History and Antiquities of the County of Northampton*, were completed between 1836 and 1841, and appear as volume 2 in the surviving editions. Fortunately Baker's work complemented rather than superseded Bridges's, but from more or less the mid-seventeenth until the mid-nineteenth century work continued in researching or writing a major county history of Northamptonshire.[37]

Northamptonshire encapsulated many of the problems of researching and writing county history in the eighteenth century, particularly the confusion which could arise when more than one scholar was at work. Something similar happened in County Durham. Christopher Watson compiled four 'Books of Durham History' in 1573–74. Of these the first contained an account of the lives of the bishops, the second was a history of the county from the creation to the arrival of St Augustine, the third contained laudatory verses addressed to the author, and the fourth had another list of bishops and some miscellaneous ecclesiastical material. About the same time William Claxton also began collecting material for a history of the county. He lived at Wynyard and knew both Stow and Camden, but his collections were never turned into a completed history. During the seventeenth century Roger Dodsworth and James Mickleton, a Durham barrister, made further collections, but did not complete their work, and an early eighteenth-century scheme for a history of the county ran onto the rocks because no one had all the skills needed to undertake the work. Two Durham lawyers completed a book in 1729, but this was largely an attack on the bishop. It was only in 1785 that an acceptable history of the county was published.[38]

While some counties were struggling to produce a good county history, Warwickshire and Nottinghamshire were suffering from a surfeit of Dugdale and Thoroton. Dugdale's achievement overwhelmed any would-be followers. 'You have drawn the bridge after you – scarcely leaving any gleanings for the most exact of future undertakers', wrote William Somner in a letter to Dugdale.[39] In 1730 Rev. William Thomas, sometime rector of Exhall, started the process of rebuilding the bridge when he produced a second edition of Dugdale's *Antiquities* in two volumes 'revised, augmented and continued down to this present time'.[40] In Nottinghamshire later historians tended to be wary of criticising Thoroton. The centenary of the publication of his *Antiquities* in 1777 saw various attempts to promote a reprint. These were not successful, but in the 1790s it was republished with extensive revisions by John Throsby, a Leicester antiquary and parish clerk. Throsby reprinted Thoroton's text verbatim, but added his own comments based on a tour of Nottinghamshire following in Thoroton's footsteps. Because he followed Thoroton, Throsby's work is biased towards the southern end of the county, but he had the added reason for this bias because he lived in Leicester. When he travelled north he complained that roads around South Leverton were 'intollerably bad for the journeying of poor curates in the performance of their religious duties'. He did not use original archives, and he lacked the welcome to some of the country houses that Thoroton had enjoyed; but his edition of Thoroton's work remains an important work of reference, and was reprinted in 1972.[41]

Even the seven counties that lacked a history by the early nineteenth century had not been entirely neglected. In Derbyshire, various efforts were made during the sixteenth and seventeenth centuries to start a history. Samuel Sanders wrote a substantial piece of work between about 1663 and 1668, which subsequently became the basis of William Woolley's history of the county prepared in 1712, but published only in 1981. A proposal by Thomas Blore (1764–1818) for a county history failed because it met with 'a lack of proper encouragement'.[42] James Pilkington produced *A View of the Present State of Derbyshire* in 1789, but this was not a traditional county history because he had nothing to do with subjects such as armorial bearings, genealogy, history and antiquities. Pilkington noted that although his readers might expect him to cover such topics in the style of Thoroton and other county historians, it would be 'too laborious and expensive an

undertaking', and 'an unnecessary application' of his 'time and attention'.[43] The book appeared in two volumes, and much of volume two
consisted of descriptions of gentry family seats.

In Lincolnshire during the 1630s Gervase Holles (1606–75) began
collecting materials, records, charters and church monuments for a
history of the county. Several volumes of his (unprinted) collections are
now in the British Library. However, a proper county history was
started only when the Boston printer William Marrat (1772–1852)
issued the first parts of his *History of Lincolnshire, Topographical,
Historical and Descriptive* (1814–16). It was never finished, and no one
else managed to produce anything more substantial than incomplete
histories of parts of the county.[44] In Northumberland, Rev. John
Hodgson started work in 1817, but he soon ran into difficulties. He
published the first volume of his projected multi-volume study in 1820.
It was described as volume V. Another five volumes appeared before his
death in 1845, but further progress had to await the formation in 1890
of a county committee, which finally brought out a full study of the
county by 1940.[45] In Somerset, the county history by John Strachey, who
died in 1743, was never published, and is now an accessioned manuscript volume in the Somerset Record Office. John Collinson's *History
and Antiquities of Somerset* appeared in three volumes 1791–92.[46]

What did all this effort mean in terms of quality? Not surprisingly,
it varied considerably. Among the best, partly because it was one of
the first to try to synthesise the accounts of separate parishes and
manors which were the chief characteristic of county histories, was
John Hutchins's two-volume *History and Antiquities of the County
of Dorset*, published in 1774. Hutchins was born and lived most of his
life in Dorset, and he travelled the county to read documents, as well
as visiting archives in Oxford and London. His history was and still is
an indispensable tool for local historians, and it included a seventy-
page introduction covering archaeology and the ecclesiastical and
natural history of the county, as well as a discussion of markets and
roads.[47] Others who followed his example included Edward Hasted on
Kent, John Nichols on Leicestershire, and Sir Richard Colt Hoare on
South Wiltshire. Joseph Nicolson and Richard Burn, in their *History
of Cumberland and Westmorland*, published in 1777, did much the
same as Hutchins with a 130-page introductory section looking at the
ancient and modern state of the border counties. Like so many of
their type, however, they bequeathed a legacy which refuses to go
away, with many of the most common mistakes in the history of these
two historic counties being traceable to their work, which is not so
much a reflection on them as on those who followed.

Like Hutchins, some of the best county historians combined a number of skills. The impact of scientific thought, which had influenced the antiquaries, was also important in a number of county studies, particularly William Borlase's two books on Cornwall: *Antiquities* (1754) and *Natural History* (1758). Borlase (1696–1772) was born in St Just in Penwith, and after studying at Oxford became vicar of Ludgvan, Penzance. His *Natural History of* Cornwall published in 1758 was his most valuable work of topographical description. By writing extensively about geology and mineralogy, Borlase revealed interests firmly rooted in the tradition of natural historical studies developed in the later seventeenth century. He was able to handle both human and natural history, and he wrote on a grand scale covering geology and natural resources, climate, river systems, coasts, flora and fauna, as well as the economy and Cornish culture and language.[48] But for every example of quality, there was always one in which enthusiasm was not matched by ability. W.G. Hoskins has written of the historical chapters in Polwhele's *Devon*, published in three volumes 1793–1806, that they represent 'a miserable level of performance . . . and the work as a whole is third rate'. Other commentators have been rather less critical.[49]

County histories initially became popular because they were more manageable than national studies of the type undertaken by Camden, but as they grew in scale and size individual authors came to rely increasingly for support on collaborators in the manner of a Dugdale or a Thoroton. An example of how this worked was John Nichols's study of Leicestershire. Nichols' main role in the *History and Antiquities of the County of Leicester* was in bringing together a team of more than 100 helpers – among them Richard Gough – and turning their chapters into the *History*, which took nearly twenty years to complete (1795–1815). Despite the size of his research team, Nichols also made use of earlier studies. For the detailed gazetteer he consulted more than twenty corrected versions of the first edition of William Burton's earlier study of the county. Many of the annotations were by local landowners.[50]

The use of assistance was widespread and the recycling of information from earlier studies was less common over time. George Ormerod (1785–1873) married in 1808 the daughter of a Cheshire-born doctor who introduced him to papers collected by Thomas Foote Gower in 1771 with the intention of writing a county history. By 1813 Ormerod had begun work on a county history, and he divided his time for several years between London and Cheshire collecting material for his study. It was issued in nine parts 1816–19. He supplemented his own research from material sent to him by numerous correspondents among the county gentry. In some cases Ormerod asked them to copy out documents on his behalf.[51] Francis Blomefield's *An Essay Towards a Topographical History of the County of Norfolk*, published 1739–75 (although he died 1752), and in a second edition (1805–10), drew extensively on the manuscript collections of both contemporaries and predecessors. Much of the evidence was collected on tours during 1733–35, that left him seriously ill. He then solicited evidence through a detailed printed questionnaire sent to several hundred Norfolk incumbents early in 1735. Walter Rye, writing Blomefield's biography for the *Dictionary of National Biography*, thought he went too far: 'there is vastly more of Le Neve's work than Blomefield'. He added that Blomefield 'fell an easy victim to all the monstrous pedigree fabrications of the heralds', and his essay was 'full of errors'. Modern opinion is very much more positive.[52]

John Collinson, the named author of Somerset's first major county history published in 1792, relied heavily for the sections on topography and natural history on Edmund Rack. He also made extensive use of the collections of Thomas Palmer and Thomas Carew, as well as papers at Longleat and in the British Museum.[53] The final volume of Sir Richard Colt Hoare's *The Modern History of South Wiltshire* was completed by his friends following his death in 1838, in memory of the way they had been 'accustomed to assemble annually at Stourhead to assist him in preparing his history of Modern Wiltshire and partake of the graceful hospitalities of that splendid mansion'.[54]

As if researching and writing a county history was not sufficiently burdensome, authors often had to finance, or to raise the capital for their publications. The books were usually published in folio format, and funded either from the author's own resources, or by subscription. Publishing for a profit was a non-starter, since this was the mark of a tradesman rather than a gentleman, and consequently men of private means such as Richard Gough, who owned property in Middlesex, preferred to publish at their own expense. John Nicols, also a man of means, was able to bear the heavy financial loss incurred by his Leicestershire history. A few authors found a wealthy sponsor. This was William Cunnington's good fortune. *The Ancient History of Wiltshire* (1810–21) was financed by Sir Richard Colt Hoare.[55]

Those who lacked such resources usually solicited subscriptions, partly to find out whether there were sufficient potential purchasers to warrant publication. For obvious reasons, authors needed to be convinced of their market among the local gentry. As John Hutchins put it in reference to his work on Dorset, 'there is some satisfaction in a gentleman's knowing the particular history of his own family, and being able to point out through what hands his several lands and tenements have passed'.[56] Quite so, but such knowledge did not necessarily persuade gentry to part with their money, and more commercial methods sometimes had to be employed. In many volumes the illustrations were mainly engravings of country houses, and they were paid for by the owners. Edward Hasted thanked 'those noblemen and gentlemen who have so generously and liberally been at the expense of embellishing this work with engravings of their seats' in his *History of Kent*, and he told correspondents that the plates 'are done in a more elegant and expensive style where the donors have shown a more than ordinary liberality'.[57]

Authors found various ways of cutting costs and increasing sales. Francis Blomefield was so suspicious of printers who, he feared, would attempt to swindle him, that he set up his own press in a barn and employed a journeyman printer.[58] Some authors engaged in bargaining: 'I desire to be one of your subscribers', Francis Peck told Blomefield, 'conditionally that you take one of my Antiquities of Stamford in lieu of yours'.[59] But in the end, a lengthy subscription list was the best hope of breaking even. As George Ormerod found with his Cheshire history, as long as the subscriber list was long enough and the print run short enough, an author could expect to avoid being out of pocket.[60] Of course, having attracted the subscribers it was important to produce the book. George Baker was nearly bankrupted when his Northamptonshire subscribers dropped out because they considered his rate of production was too slow.[61]

The true scholar-antiquary had no time for such worldly considerations, and this could create serious difficulties. Edward Hasted was so obsessed with researching, writing, and then publishing a history of Kent that it almost ruined him. Hasted (1732–1812) was a remarkable man. In the 1750s he began work on *The History and Topographical Survey of the County of Kent*, and the first volume was finally published in 1778. He wrote of how he had spent twenty years in 'constant labour and assiduity' working in the Augmentation Office, the Chapter House at Westminster, the King's Remembrancer Office, the Tower of London, the Rolls-Chapel, the King's Surveyor's Office, and the Heralds' Office. He acknowledge the help others had provided, including making manuscript sources available, and he added a rather weary recognition of how he had neglected everything else in his passion for Kentish history: 'I can say truly I have spared neither labour, nor pains, nor any expense within the compass of my fortune, in the prosecution of this work'.[62]

Hasted's friends among the Kentish gentry allowed him access to their records, and he was elected to Fellowships of the Royal Society and the Antiquaries. His devotion to scholarship was such that corrections at the end of volume 4 of his study 'demonstrate an almost finicky concern'. Thus he made it clear in one of the corrections that when Matthew Parker, the Archbishop of Canterbury, died in 1575, his bowels were deposited in the Howard chapel in Lambeth church. As Joan Thirsk has noted, 'Hasted's work required thousands of facts to be discovered, transcribed, and checked, calling for monumental dedication and patience'. He did, however, lighten the load a little by incorporating within his text long passages written by others.[63] The great work was finally completed in 1799.

Unfortunately Hasted was so absorbed in his work that he entrusted his business affairs to an unscrupulous attorney, who gained possession of his estates. As Hasted noted in the first volume, he had 'too much neglected . . . the management of my own private affairs', and this had 'prevented my allotting more of my time, thoughts, and money in the prosecution of this work'.[64] Sadly, he was only the first of a long line of local historians to find that devotion to scholarship did not pay the bills, and he spent the years 1795–1802 in the King's Bench Prison when his financial affairs reached crisis point. Apparently undeterred by this inconvenience, he used his confinement to complete the final volume. He also revised the whole twelve-volume series for a second edition, although he had less control over this than the first edition and his editors altered the text in various ways. Hasted was by no means alone in finding the project more than his financial resources would allow, although he may have alienated some of his potential market because, as one reviewer put it, he had shown 'not much taste for the history of . . . mere landholders, or . . . mere squires: something more is necessary to obtain for them the record of a printed volume'.[65] Evidently engravings were not sufficient.

Hasted's case was unusual, but the financial commitment required of anyone who sought publication ensured that many county historians never saw their work in print. Some, like Hasted, suffered financial consequences, including Edward Lipscomb, whose four-volume history of Buckinghamshire was allegedly written, at least in part, while he was imprisoned for debt in the Fleet. Some may even have used the excuse of cost as a reason for not publishing at all, hence the large number of antiquaries' papers which either circulated in manuscript or were simply collections never really put into order. Others were grateful for the founding of *Archaeologia* in 1770, because it provided them with an outlet for publishing their work while relieving them of a potentially substantial financial burden.[66]

Multi-volume county histories ground to a halt towards the middle of the nineteenth century. Among the best of the later ones was Edward Baines's four-volume *History of the County Palatine and Duchy of Lancaster* (1836). Baines constructed his study of Lancashire to fulfil specific ideological and commercial purposes, and he made extensive use of the work of others, notably Edwin Butterworth, who acted as a rather poorly paid research assistant. The history was highly regarded and comprehensive, partly because he wrote of Lancashire as a whole, whereas previous 'Lancashire' studies had been confined to parts of the county. New editions, with significant revisions and updates, appeared in 1868 and 1888–93.[67] Other late, but well regarded examples of the genre included Robert Surtees' *History and Antiquities of the County Palatine of Durham*, published in folio in four parts 1816 and 1840. Surtees did his research thoroughly, so much so that his groom became bored with taking him round the county in a gig and having to stop at any 'auld beelding'. Surtees, it appeared, could never pass a place of historic interest without examining it in some detail.[68] Also well regarded, and another example of a history which virtually bankrupted the author, was Cussans's *History of Hertfordshire* (1870–81). Cussans, who claimed to have visited every parish and church in the county, lost £3,000 on the venture.[69]

By the time Cussans wrote, the old-style county history was going out of favour. The appearance of trade directories, with potted histories of each parish, had begun to undermine the old-style county histories. Directories had a commercial purpose, and appealed to middle-class audiences, with little time for pedigrees and manorial descents. The business material included in directories was supplemented by extensive sections on history and topography, in addition to useful information more generally about the county. Stephen Glover's *History, Gazetteer and Directory of the County of Derby* appeared in 1829, and White's *Directory of Nottinghamshire* for the first time in 1832. James Hatfield's *History Gazetteer and Directory of the County of Huntingdon* (1854), was just one of those which was worth buying for its detailed local history.[70]

County history was fragmenting, with new forms of writing coming into play. These included *Annals*, which were narrative histories of important events in a county's history compiled in chronological order. Thomas Bailey's *Annals of Nottinghamshire* was published in four volumes 1853–55, and Robert Gibbs produced a similar four-volume history of Buckinghamshire (1878–82). Gibbs published information on a selection of a miscellaneous events, arranged like a chronicle, from 1400 onwards. John Duncumb pioneered similar work in Herefordshire, and in Derbyshire the indefatigable Rev. John Charles Cox produced *Three Centuries of Derbyshire Annals as illustrated by the Records of Quarter Sessions* (1890) with a supplement in 1899.[71] The fragmentation that books like this highlighted was partly market driven: one of the reasons for the success of Baines's study of Lancashire was his ability to combine the family pedigrees of county society with an emphasis on economic, social and political developments. As such this enabled him to appeal both to the traditional market for antiquarian literature and a new, urban clientele. As Baines told his publishers, 'According to my plan, the work will . . . be sufficiently antiquarian and genealogical to give dignity to the subject amongst the principal families of the county, while it will be sufficiently popular to interest the manufacturing and commercial classes'.[72] Other authors lacked his breadth of knowledge.

Most counties can boast summary, and perhaps rather subjective histories from the late Victorian and Edwardian years, although these were often limited to parts of the county rather than offering complete coverage. All the south-western counties had a number of writers researching county history in these years,[73] while for Nottinghamshire Cornelius Brown's *History of Nottinghamshire* (1891) was a thinly disguised topographical history of places within the county. Other Nottinghamshire county historians of the period included J. Potter Briscoe, who produced antiquarian collections relating to the county, and William Stevenson, whose *Bygone Nottinghamshire* was published in 1893. Such volumes were on a much smaller scale than their predecessors. They were also of very varied quality. J.M. Falkner's *History of Oxfordshire* (1899) had a mixed reception, and J.A. Langford's *Warwickshire Past and Present* (1884) named two collaborators and various 'eminent assistants', but the book depended largely on secondary sources.[74]

Collaborative county histories

None of these later histories was in the same league as the great folio volumes selling at ten to forty guineas and intended for gentlemen's libraries, and for this there was good reason. The gentlemen were less willing to pay, the squire was rapidly being replaced by the parson as the historian, and the newcomers to antiquarian and historical studies, the middleclasses, were neither willing nor able to pay the sort of sums demanded for the great folio volumes – especially as they were not likely to find their family trees in the text. Perhaps the most serious problem, even so, was the scale of a county history. However hard they worked, successful authors relied on others to help them in one way or another, particularly through questionnaires to the parish clergy. At least in theory, it was only one step more to envisage the clergy writing the parish entries to be collated and edited by a county editor, and this idea was tried out in Lincolnshire.

Various attempts to promote a Lincolnshire county history came to nothing, but in 1872 the antiquarian Archdeacon Edward Trollope dedicated to Bishop Christopher Wordsworth of Lincoln his *Sleaford, and the Wapentakes of Flaxwell and Aswardhurn*. Trollope noted in the book that he had several times been approached to write a county history, but considered the work involved would be beyond him. Wordsworth clearly read this with interest, and he subsequently urged the Lincolnshire Diocesan Architectural Society to consider producing a county history with the clergy contributing individual entries. He suggested at his triennial visitation in 1873 that since 'the clergy in our county have usually much time at their disposal' they could use it to begin collecting and writing historical material relating to their parish. He was so enamoured of his proposal that he repeated it on a number of county occasions, and eventually in 1878 a committee was established under Trollope to examine the feasibility of the plan. The committee came up with a scheme for promoting uniformity in the arrangement of the materials for each parish, based on the work of Rev. John Charles Cox (1843–1919). A circular sent out to one Rural District referred in laudatory terms to the introduction to the first volume of Cox's 'Notes on the Churches of Derbyshire', published 1875–79, and Cox was asked to republish it for use in Lincolnshire. When he looked at the 'Notes' again, Cox decided that the material was really too narrowly focused on Derbyshire to serve the required purpose, and he decided instead to put something together on a more general scale 'that might prove a help to those who may be desirous of undertaking parochial history in any part of the kingdom, whether manorial, ecclesiastical or both'. The result was the first edition, published in 1879, of his *How to Write a Parish History*. The book was an immediate success, and Cox rewrote it for the third edition which appeared as early as 1886. A fifth edition came out in 1909.

By the end of 1879 details of the Lincolnshire scheme for promoting a county-wide research project using the skills of the local clergy had been issued to each parish parson – there are 605 parishes in

Lincolnshire – together with a copy of the first edition of Cox's book. Cox set out for them the range of issues he thought they should cover, from etymology and prehistoric remains to religious houses – he does not seem to have considered that it was particularly worthwhile studying periods later than the sixteenth century – but he directed their attention to sources in London, Oxford, and Cambridge, and to printed sources. There was not the slightest hint that they might start work with their own parish records.[75] Clearly some clergy were much better suited to local history than others, notably the Rev. William Oswald Massingberd, who had the skills to use all the available documentary sources critically, as well as to begin editing fundamental texts for the history of the county. Massingberd inherited his father's work on South Ormsby, which he published in 1891 after adding to it a great deal of historical research in the Public Record Office, the Prerogative Court of Canterbury, and local family papers. He went on from his book on Ormsby to compile a number of other detailed and scholarly works.[76] But Massingberd was unusual, and most of the clergy failed to pick up the baton thrown down by their bishop. No history was forthcoming.

A closer approximation to the idea of a collaborative history was in Northumberland where Henry Hodgson, a leading antiquary in the county, had proposed as long ago as 1819 a six-volume series beginning with a general volume including sections on agriculture, mining, geology, and natural history. It was to be followed by three volumes of 'parochial history', and two volumes of historical documents. The first volume to be published, in 1820, was the fifth in the series, and was one of the two designed to be volumes of records. The first volume of parish histories appeared in 1827, the second volume of records in 1828 and further volumes of parish history in 1832 and 1840. Hodgson died in 1845, and the Newcastle Society of Antiquaries undertook to complete the scheme. John Hodgson Hinde was appointed to compile an introductory volume, which appeared in 1858, but apart from a few piecemeal volumes on particular places nothing much more had been achieved by 1890, when the Newcastle antiquaries were reminded by Dr Thomas Hodgkin of their promise to bring the *History* to completion. A committee was formed, subscribers and donors were sought, and Edward Bateson was appointed editor. The intention was to provide the missing parish histories, and between 1893 and 1940 the committee successfully oversaw the production of fifteen volumes produced by six different editors.[77]

Lincolnshire may not have succeeded, but Northumberland did, and in an environment where collaboration was widely perceived to be the way forward, a scheme which would bring authors together to write county history on a parish-by-parish basis made sense. In addition, the late nineteenth century saw the rise of the modernist movement, which suggested that the ultimate history of individual places could be written. Into this environment came in 1899 the Victoria County History, a creation of enthusiasm and optimism summed up most vehemently in a 1904 document that claimed it would be 'the standard for all time, and also the nearest thing possible to supplying each Englishman with a history of his own individual ancestors and of his native land'.[78] Just when county history seemed to have reached the end of its particular road, came a brand new, nationally conceived project on a scale of which even Camden could not have dreamed.

We shall return to the VCH in chapter V. While it was in many respects the lineal descendant of the older county histories, it also represented a break with the past in terms of its research and writing, because of the way in which it encompassed town and parish histories. As research proceeded in the nineteenth century, and as the study of the past began to fragment with topographical, antiquarian, archaeological and historical study, as well as natural history, increasingly going their separate ways, the unit or area of discussion also changed. County historians of means and leisure could afford the time, and perhaps also they had the influence to persuade their friends and neighbours to help them out, as they proceeded with their work, but in doing so their books were becoming ever larger and more expensive. The bubble, if that is what it was, burst by the middle of the nineteenth century, hence the appearance of single-volume, far less detailed studies in the later Victorian period, but for the antiquarian-scholar who wanted to research and write the history of a community in detail, increasingly it made sense to concentrate on a study area smaller than the county. Parish and town histories were a major development in the eighteenth century, but they require separate treatment, and to these we turn in chapter IV.

Notes

1 H.C. Darby, 'Some early ideas on the agricultural regions of England', *Agricultural History Review*, 2 (1954), 30–47.

2 Edward Chamberlayne, *Angliae Notitia or The Present State of England* (18th edn, 1694), 25–6.

3 C. Morris (ed.), *The Journeys of Celia Fiennes* (1947). The *Journeys* were first published in an incomplete edition of 1888 with the title *Through England on a Side Saddle in the Time of William and Mary*.

4 John Macky, *A Journey Through England* (1722), 241, for his description of the Roman antiquities at Carlisle.

5 Daniel Defoe, *A Tour Through the Whole Island of Great Britain* (1726).

6 Defoe, *Tour* (1962 edn), 196–7.

7 Ibid., 93.

8 Such was the popularity of these tours, that Macky went into five editions by 1732, but seems not to have been reprinted since the eighteenth century. Macky was a government spy, and the book may have been written while he was in gaol for debt. Defoe's *Tour* had reached a ninth edition 'with additions and improvements' by 1779.

9 Charles Cotton, *The Wonders of the Peak* (2nd edn, 1744); William Bray, *Sketch of a Tour into Derbyshire and Yorkshire* (2nd edn, 1783).

10 Rosemary Sweet, *Antiquaries: The Discovery of the Past in Eighteenth-Century Britain* (2004), 45–6; ECH, 378–81.

11 William Gilpin, *Observations Relative Chiefly to Picturesque Beauty, Made in 1772, on Several Parts of England* (1786).

12 Sweet, *Antiquaries*, 316–17.

13 J. Britton and E.W. Brayley (eds), *Topographical, Historical and Descriptive Delineations of Cumberland* (1803).

14 Sweet, *Antiquaries*, 326–7. The importance of research contrasted with the more cavalier approach of Defoe, who did not visit all the places he described: J.H. Andrews, 'Defoe and the sources of his tour', *Geographical Review*, 126 (1968), 268–77; F.H. Bastian, 'Defoe's tour and the historian', *History Today*, 17 (1967), 845–51.

15 Sweet, *Antiquaries*, 266–7.

16 J. Simmons (ed.), *English County Historians* (1978), 15; ECH, 65–6.

17 G.A. Cooke, *Topographical and Statistical Description of the County of Nottingham* (c.1810).

18 F.C. Laird, *The Beauties of England and Wales* (1812); J. Curtis, *A Topographical History of Nottinghamshire* (1843–44).

19 Joan Evans, *A History of the Society of Antiquaries* (1956), chapters 3–4; Sweet, *Antiquaries*, 83–110.

20 David Boyd Haycock, *William Stukeley: Science, Religion and Archaeology in Eighteenth-Century England* (2002); Neil Mortimer (ed.), *Stukeley Illustrated: William Stukeley's Rediscovery of Britain's Ancient Sites* (2003); Theodor Harmsen, *Antiquarianism in the Augustan Age: Thomas Hearne, 1678–1735* (2000); Sweet, *Antiquaries*, 128–33.

21 M. Honeybone, 'The Spalding Gentlemen's Society: the communication of science in the East Midlands of England, 1710–1760' (Open University, Ph.D thesis, 2001); D.M. Owen (ed.), *The Minute Books of the Spalding Gentlemen's Society, 1712–55* (Lincoln Record Series, 73, 1981); Sweet, *Antiquaries*, 115–16.

22 Evans, *Society of Antiquaries*, 134–47.

23 Sarah Speight, 'An officer and an antiquary: Major Hayman Rooke and the beginnings of archaeology in eighteenth-century Nottinghamshire', in John Beckett (ed.), *Nottinghamshire Past* (2003), 116–36.

24 Historical Manuscripts Commission, *Papers of British Antiquaries and Historians* (Guides to Sources for British History, 12, 2003) lists the papers of 1,300 antiquaries, historians, genealogists, heralds, archaeologists and others between the mid-15th and late 20th centuries. Many are simply collections of papers which were never written up in any coherent form, including the 16 volumes of antiquarian material collected by William Stretton (1800–24), now in Nottinghamshire Archives Office, DD/TS/6/4/4 and still a useful source of information for local historians.

25 Quoted by Evans, *Society of Antiquaries*, 146.

26 S. Piggott, *Ruins in a Landscape: Essays in Antiquarianism* (1976), 21; Sweet, *Antiquaries*, 8–9.

27 Speight, 'Major Hayman Rooke', 135.

28 Sweet, *Antiquaries*, 1–30; Ronald Hutton, 'The religion of William Stukeley', *Antiquaries Journal*, 85 (2005), 381–94.

29 Sweet, *Antiquaries*, 176–82.

30 Ibid., 185–92.

31 Ibid., 190–1, 197, 229; Speight, 'Major Hayman Rooke'.

32 A.H. Eakle, 'Antiquaries and the writing of English local history, 1750–1800 (Genealogy, Heraldry, 18th Century Art, Folklore)' (University of Utah, Ph.D thesis, 1985).

33 W.R. Powell, 'Antiquaries in conflict: Philip Morant verses Richard Gough', *Essex Archaeology and History* 20 (1989), 143–6; *ECH*, 145–6. Many of the county histories referred to in subsequent paragraphs have been reprinted since the 1970s, an indication of their enduring usefulness.

34 J. Mordaunt, *The Natural History of Northamptonshire* (1712).

35 J. Bridges, *The History and Antiquities of Northamptonshire* (1791), i–vi.

36 G. Baker, *The History and Antiquities of the County of Northampton*, 2 vols (1836–41), 260.

37 L. Stone and J.C.F. Stone, *An Open Elite? England 1540–1880* (1984), 56–7; *ECH*, 291–7.

38 *ECH*, 132–6.

39 Ibid., 400–1.

40 Sir William Dugdale, *The Antiquities of Warwickshire* (2nd edn, in 2 volumes, revised, augmented and continued down to this present time by William Thomas D.D., sometime rector of Exhall in the same County, 1730).

41 John Throsby (ed.), *The Antiquities of Nottinghamshire by Robert Thoroton* (3 vols, 1790–96), 1 (1790), xix–xx; 3 (1796), 272; *ECH*, 316–17.

42 Philip Riden, 'John Hieron, William Woolley, Samuel Sanders and the history of Derbyshire', *Derbyshire Miscellany*, 7 (1974–76), 74–81; P. Riden and C. Glover (eds), *William Woolley's History of Derbyshire* (Derbyshire Record Society, 1981); *ECH*, 107–8, 138–9.

43 J. Pilkington, *A View of the Present State of Derbyshire with an Account of its Most Remarkable Antiquities* (1789), iii–iv.

44 *ECH*, 246–50.

45 Simmons, *English County Historians*, 3–4; *ECH*, 302–11.

46 M. Brayshay (ed.), *Topographical Writers in South-West England* (1996), 13.

47 *ECH*, 126–7.

48 Brayshay, *Topographical Writers*, 12.

49 W.G. Hoskins, *Local History in England* ([1959], 3rd edn, 1984), 23. Professor Joyce Youings, who has researched and written extensively on Devon, suggests that at its best the text 'is full of invaluable details concerning the descent of landed property, the local economy, and, here and there, crude population data'. Even so, she considered that Rev. Thomas Moore's *History of Devonshire* (1829–36) was better: *ECH*, 120. Polwhele's *History of Devonshire* was reprinted as recently as 1977, and his *History of Cornwall* in 1978.

50 *ECH*, 232.

51 Ibid., 77–80. I am grateful to Charles Foster for information on Ormerod's working methods.

52 Norfolk historians now consider Blomefield to have written 'one of the great county histories': *ECH*, 282–3. See also the rehabilitation in David Stocker, 'Francis Blomefield as a historian of Norfolk', *Norfolk Archaeology*, 44 (2003), 181–201. Also David Stocker, 'Blomefield, Francis (1705–52)', *Oxford Dictionary of National Biography* (2004), 2663.

53 *ECH*, 350.

54 Richard Colt Hoare, *The Modern History of South Wiltshire* (5 vols, 1822–44), dedication in vol. 5.

55 *ECH*, 417–18.

56 Sweet, *Antiquaries*, 39.

57 Edward Hasted, *The History and Topographical Survey of the County of Kent Containing the Antient and Present State of it Civil and Ecclesiastical; Collected from Public Records, and Other the Best Authorities, both Manuscript and Printed*, 1 (1778), viii; Alan Everitt, 'Edward Hasted', in Simmons, *English County Historians*, 189–219.

58 Stocker, 'Blomefield', 2663.

59 Sweet, *Antiquaries*, 67–8.

60 *ECH*, 79–80.

61 Stone and Stone, *Open Elite*, 56–7; *ECH*, 298–9.

62 Hasted, *Kent*, 1, iii–v.

63 Joan Thirsk, 'Hasted as historian', in Richardson, 69–82; Shirley Burgoyne, *A Scholar and a Gentleman: Edward Hasted, the Historian of Kent* (2001).

64 Hasted, Kent, 1, v.

65 Sweet, *Antiquaries*, 40, 68.

66 *ECH*, 55; Sweet, *Antiquaries*, 68.

67 M. Winstanley, 'Researching a county history: Edwin Butterworth, Edward Baines and the *History of Lancashire* (1836)', *Northern History*, 32 (1996), 152–72; *ECH*, 221–2.

68 *ECH*, 132–6.

69 Ibid., 136–7, 188; John Edwin Cussans, *History of Hertfordshire* 3 vols (1972 edn. of [1879–81] original).

70 Ibid., 204; J. E. Norton, *Guide to National and Provincial Directories, Excluding London, Before 1856* (1950); G. Shaw and A. Tipper, *British Directories: A Bibliography and Guide to Directories Published in England and Wales (1850–1950) and Scotland (1773–1950)* (1989).

71 *ECH*, 113.

72 Quoted in Winstanley, 'Researching', 154; *ECH*, 57.

73 Brayshay, *Topographical Writers*, 13–33.

74 *ECH*, 334, 407.

75 J.C. Cox, *How to Write the History of a Parish: An Outline Guide to Topographical Records, Manuscripts and Books* (5th edn, 1909).

76 Dorothy Owen, 'William Oswald Massingberd', in C. Sturman (ed.), *Some Historians of Lincolnshire* (1992), 44.

77 *ECH*, 305–8.

78 K. Tiller, 'The VCH: past, present and future', *The Historian*, 42 (1994), 18.

IV *The parish and the town*

If the county was the preferred unit of study, the parish increasingly came to be viewed as the practical limit of most scholars and, following loosely from this, it was only a short step towards discussion of the town as a separate place. Studies of towns inevitably began with London, particularly the great survey published by Stow at the end of the sixteenth century. No other towns were in the same league in terms of size and status, but it is no surprise to find histories being compiled of cathedral towns and some of the larger provincial towns including Norwich, which was both. The business of writing such histories really took off with the expansion of the new industrial towns, as a group of historian-commentators produced detailed histories of Manchester and Birmingham, Nottingham and Leicester, and smaller centres such as Hinckley. These studies were important not just as histories, but for the contemporary comment and description they included. Hardly surprisingly, the quality varied, and where corporations offered sponsorship there was an obvious tendency for authors to write in a more laudatory manner than they might otherwise have done. There were parallels also with county histories, with developments such as the production of Annals by the mid-nineteenth century, and also the writing of slighter and more generalised volumes by the late Victorian period. In this chapter we look at parish and town studies from the seventeenth century to the nineteenth.

Parish histories

By the seventeenth century the county had become the accepted focus of gentlemen scholars, but because each county was itself divided internally (into wapentakes or hundreds, parishes, manors and townships), the less-ambitious (or perhaps more realistic) antiquary could turn his attention to one of these smaller units. This made practical sense in terms of manageability, and marketing sense because smaller books were more saleable. W.G. Hoskins has suggested that William of Worcester founded the study of English topography and antiquities, Lambarde the county history, and White Kennett the parish history. In the latter case this was not strictly true. White Kennett's book was published in 1695, and a number of parish histories, not all of them published, are of earlier date. Wargrave, in Berkshire, was the subject of a study by a former vicar in 1690. It had more to do with the church's rights than historical enquiry, and the unpublished manuscript is now in the county archives office. Consequently, the Rev. White Kennett enjoys the accolade of being first in the field, with his *Parochial Antiquities Attempted in the History of Ambrosden, Burcester and Other Adjacent Parts*, published in 1695.

White Kennett concentrated almost exclusively on legal and ecclesiastical affairs, but this was because he had a particular purpose: 'Next to the immediate discharge of my holy office, I know not how in any course of studies I could better have served my patron, my people and my successors than by preserving the memoirs of this parish . . . which before lay remote from common notice and in few years had been buried in unsearchable oblivion'. This was laudable, but the study was also scholarly and constituted as such a pioneer piece of work which justified a new edition as late as 1818.[1] White Kennett was one of the earliest of a long line of country parsons who filled their spare hours by unravelling the parochial antiquities of their own small corner of the English countryside.[2] It was only when this became an expectation, as the case of Lincolnshire revealed in the late nineteenth century, that they were less enamoured of scholarly study.

Another study from roughly the same period as White Kennett, was Richard Gough's *Antiquityes and Memoyres of the Parish of Myddle*, written about 1700 although not published until 1834, and not in full until 1875. It was anecdotal rather than antiquarian or historical, although Gough – no relation of the later eighteenth-century antiquarian – was inspired by Camden, and he wrote a history of the church and the descent of the manor as well as discussing local administration, topography and place names. In 1701–2 he went on to write *Observations Concerning the Seates in Myddle and the Familyes to which they Belong*, in which he outlined the seating arrangements in the parish church to provide a context for studying parish families. Using the parish records, manorial records and the oral testimony of his neighbours, Gough produced the most detailed account that we have of a rural community in late-Stuart England. Some of the anecdotes reveal the real world of village life, and are a far cry from the dry manorial descents found in county histories. Thus Elizabeth Kyffin, wife of Francis Clarke, was:

> a sad, drunken woman. He went to fetch her from the ale-house in a very dark night, but she, being unwilling to come, pretended it was so dark that she could not see to go; he told her he would lead

her by the arm, and got her away almost half way home, and then she pretended she had lost one of her shoes; and when he had loosed her arm, and was groping for the shoe, she ran back to the alehouse and bolted him out, and would not come home that night.[3]

Similar early village studies included Gregory King's account of the Staffordshire village of Eccleshall in the 1690s, and John Lucas's *Topographical Description of the Parish of Warton*, Lancashire, compiled between 1710 and 1744. Lucas's study was something of a ramble through the parish, the manor, the church, the school, religion, funeral rites, the tithe barn, the maypole, hunting, and a few comments on neighbouring villages. It contained a good deal of interesting local detail, particularly on customs and local life, as well as the more traditional concentration on the parish church. It was published only in 1931.[4]

Despite Kennett's lead, few parish histories were written in the eighteenth century, although those that appeared often combined the contemporary interests in antiquities and natural history. Rev. Gilbert White published *The Natural History of Selborne* in 1789, with a second part entitled *Antiquities of Selborne* in which he traced the history of the area from Roman times. Most of the text concentrated on the parish church and its associated priory, and like so many similar studies White had little to say about local people. This interest in the church reflected growing antiquarian interest in the Middle Ages. Similar studies continued to be written through the nineteenth century, but often they concentrated almost entirely on the detail of manorial history, and neglected the history of the village itself. As with the county histories, the preoccupation was with the descent of manors and landed properties, and the pedigrees and heraldry of the local gentry. As W.G. Hoskins put it in a phrase he liked sufficiently to repeat in several publications: 'the dead hand of the seventeenth century squire still guided, until recently, the hand of the living antiquary'.[5]

Town histories of the sixteenth and seventeenth centuries

From the county and village history, it was only one short step to studying the town. Medieval authors attempted only chronicles and annals, usually compiled in Latin by monastic scribes, and there was no tradition of historical work on a par with the great town chronicles of fifteenth-century Germany. The earliest chronicles were for

London. They were written in English from about 1414, and by the 1430s were being brought up to date annually. London apart, most English towns were quite small before the late eighteenth century, but they did attract a number of chroniclers. Bristol had its mayor's kalendar, compiled by Robert Rickart, the town clerk, in Edward IV's reign, and other towns, including Reading, Lincoln and Kings Lynn, have chronicles dating from the fifteenth century. Medieval chronicles survive for more than twenty provincial towns, and most have been published. Towns were evidently aware of the uniqueness of their privileges, and the importance of historical events in shaping their fortunes. Additionally, the chronicle compilers were usually men of standing who had access to the records, and chronicles generally include notices of the major events in the urban calendar such as civic elections, commercial negotiations and agreements, council ordinances and, more rarely, significant national and international events.[6]

Chronicles were not the only way of recording town history. John Rous (1411–91) was said to have written a history of Warwick, which has since been lost, while William of Worcester included in his 'Itinerary' a detailed topographical survey of Bristol, including a street-by-street description of the town c.1480. A handful of more advanced town histories appeared during the sixteenth century, including John Twyne's study of Canterbury, compiled in Henry VIII's reign, although apparently never published.[7] The real breakthrough in urban history came at the end of the sixteenth century with the publication in 1598 of John Stow's A Survey of London.

John Stow (1524/5–1605) was a prolific collector and author and, with Camden, a prominent member of the Society of Antiquaries. His survey of London was based on the model established by Lambarde's Kent, and he made full use of Leland's manuscript notes. Stow wrote that he had 'attempted the discovery of London' in his topographical and antiquarian account of the capital. In good antiquarian fashion he drew attention to the remains of the great Roman town lying just beneath the Elizabethan city, and he included a discussion of features of London such as the walls, rivers, institutions and government. These sections preceded a topographical survey of the city, the suburbs, and Westminster, with boundaries, monuments, and a history of each area in the manner pioneered by Lambarde. Stow drew on a lifetime of study in medieval historical literature, public and civic records, and his own knowledge of the city. He left a good deal out, such as the London theatre, while providing copious details on subjects that interested him, including pageantry, and descriptions of many buildings. Overall, he provided a picture of London at the end of the sixteenth century which is significantly fuller than any other town can muster.[8] The survey went into three further editions between 1598 and 1640, and a folio edition in 1720. It remains an indispensable source of reference for anyone studying the capital.[9]

Stow may have taken the lead, but he was by no means alone at the end of the sixteenth century. Also finished in 1598, although not published in full until 1919, was John Hooker's *Description of the Cittie of Exceter*. With Stow's London, this represented the real beginning of urban history, and two manuscript histories of Great Yarmouth also date from around the end of the sixteenth century: Thomas Damet's *A Booke of the Foundacion and Antiquitye of the towne of Greate Yermouthe*, eventually published in 1847, and Henry Manship's manuscript completed in 1619. Both men had been town clerks, and heavily involved in the business of Great Yarmouth.[10] As with the county histories, these early studies often left much to be desired. Frequently, they were concerned with cathedral towns and chronicled in detail the bishops, the chapter and other aspects of ecclesiastical life without much indication that the towns had any other life at all. John Shrimpton's *Antiquities of St Albans* (1631) was not about a cathedral town, but he concentrated on the abbey and the three parish churches, particularly their monumental inscriptions.[11] The abbey was consecrated as a cathedral only in the 1870s.

Six town histories were published between 1640 and 1660. They included William Somner's *Antiquities of Canterbury*, and one of the contemporary studies that influenced Dugdale. Richard Butcher's *The Survey and Antiquitie of the Towne of Stamford* appeared in 1646. Butcher was the town clerk, as well as an innkeeper and victualler. William Grey's *Chorographia: A Survey of Newcastle upon Tyne* came out in 1649. Grey wrote an account of the fabric of Newcastle at a time when it was threatened by destruction in the Civil War.[12]

Further town histories appeared in the twenty years after the Restoration. They included Silas Taylor's and Samuel Dale's *History and Antiquities of Harwich and Dovercourt* (1676) which discussed topography, industries, maritime history, local government and public services in addition to the usual material on churches and the manor. Altogether twelve urban histories are known to have been published prior to 1700, while others circulated in manuscript. These included Abraham de la Pryme's history of Hull, which he was reluctant to publish 'till some are dead that are now living', largely because of his detailed (and therefore divisive) account of borough politics in the political turmoil of the 1680s.

Other unpublished studies included Abel Wantner's early eighteenth-century account of Gloucester, and Sir Thomas Widdrington's study of York, which he presented to the city in about 1660 in the hope that the council would help to finance its publication. His timing was unfortunate; he was told that in the aftermath of the Civil War such an account of the city's former prosperity was not welcome because 'it seems to add to our unhappiness that our predecessors were happy'. It was published only in 1897.[13] This was an unusual response, and later town historians found civic authorities willing dedicatees, and sometimes even sponsors.

Town histories of the eighteenth century

The growth of interest in town studies can really be dated to the eighteenth century when no fewer than 116 are known to have been printed. Most of the towns enjoying their first history in the early part of the century were seats of bishops, and their historians tackled ecclesiastical rather than municipal affairs. They included two histories of York published in the 1730s: Thomas Gent, *The Antient and Modern History of the Famous City of York* (1731) and Francis Drake, *Eboracum: or the History and Antiquities of the City of York* (1736). Drake, a local surgeon and a member of the Spalding Gentleman's Society, made use of the civic and minster records, but he was an antiquary who sought Roman origins in every remnant of antiquity he could identify. His book went through several editions, and was reprinted as recently as 1978. It provided the basis for later works including William Hargrove's history of York published in 1818. John Watson on Halifax, John Whitaker on Manchester, and John Brand on Newcastle, also gave considerable space to Roman antiquities.[14]

During the eighteenth century a succession of works appeared on London, and others were published on Norwich, Exeter, Maidstone, Beverley and Gloucester. At least two books were published on Manchester, and others on rising trade and manufacturing centres such as Liverpool, Birmingham, Halifax, Derby, Nottingham and Leicester, as well as spas like Bath and naval stations such as Harwich. Other studies included histories of Lowestoft (1790), Chichester (1804), Richmond in Yorkshire (1821) and Banbury (1841). Philip Morant's study of Colchester, published in 1789, was a particularly good example of the genre.[15]

Over time the quality and, indeed, the nature of these books changed. In the sixteenth century community consciousness was demonstrated by civic annals, and the chronicles were often defensive and parochial. By the eighteenth century urban society was changing. Towns were more popular places in which to live, partly because of the post-Restoration 'urban renaissance'.[16] The decline of civic annals, and the appearance of histories mirrored the growing ascendancy in town life of business and professional groups.

Town histories still paid homage to the traditional subjects such as churches and monastic houses, town endowments and monumental inscriptions, and they still included potted biographies of worthies. They discussed the charters and the structure of local government to identify what was unique about the town, and they included a chronology of the more noteworthy occurrences. Other features included lists of the holders of major offices, and brief biographies of civic dignitaries. Churches were frequently described in detail, often with transcriptions of monument inscriptions, lists of incumbents, and accounts of charities. They still had a tendency to roll out well known civic myths such as the Lady Godiva legend at Coventry, and the representation of Leicester as King Lear's capital, and they tended to gloss over social problems, although public utilities such as the water supply were often mentioned. Sometimes they included transcripts of documents, which can still be useful to historians if the original has disappeared.[17]

Many town studies doubled as visitor guide books rather than simply promoting civic patriotism and describing antiquities. New sections were included to appeal to a wider readership beyond the urban elite. As a result, attention was focused on the recent past, with details of trade and manufacturing, street widening and civic improvement, and extracts from improvement acts, all sitting alongside surveys of newly opened town halls and theatres, and reports of concerts, assemblies and other social occasions. Economic change was also described. Charles Deering, in his history of Nottingham published in 1751, set out to show 'the antiquity of Nottingham, its extremely inviting natural as well as acquired beauties; its importance in ancient times, and its flourishing state in our days'. The book combined accounts of neighbouring gentry seats with important material on the current state of Nottingham. Consequently Deering's work was, and is, chiefly of value for his description of the town as he saw it, particularly the chapters on demography, food supply, climate and local industries; indeed, his description of the hosiery industry provided one of the earliest accounts of a trade which was to play a critical role in Nottingham's industrial development, as well as providing a detailed description of the hand-operated stocking-frame.[18]

Deering wrote his history with no underlying coherence or structural unity. The intention was to convey information on a variety of subjects relating to Nottingham in a clear and accurate fashion, rather than to offer literary scholarship. As he wrote in the introduction, the book was intended to be 'a consistent account drawn from well attested facts, and drawn from a curious and judicious ocular inspection, after having duly compared things with things, like a reading glass which only clears up the letters but neither magnifies or diminishes them, serves the reader to see the truth in a proper light'.[19] Deering's ideal typified the antiquarian who saw his subject as a precise science, and the book has the hallmarks of many eighteenth-century urban histories with lists, annotations and footnotes, juxtaposed with undigested transcriptions and other matter. Sadly, Deering also shared the fate of some town historians in relation to the financial problems surrounding publication: he died in 1749 with his history as yet unpublished and left personal possessions valued at just £17 7s 5d, of which nearly half (£8) was the value placed by his appraisers on his Nottingham manuscript.[20]

Another example of the same method was John Nichols's study of Hinckley, published in 1782. Nichols wrote at length on the usual topics of the church, the public buildings, the fairs, and the civic buildings, but he also provided what remains a fascinating and informative description of the coming of the hosiery trade to the town. The first frame, which cost £60, was brought to Hinckley in 1640 by William Iliffe, and by the time of Nichols's book there were a thousand framework knitters in Hinckley, another 200 in the surrounding villages (usually operating frames owned by Hinckley hosiers), as well as 300 seamers, fifty-five woolcombers, thirty framesmiths and setters up, and 100 spinners, doublers and twisters, a total of 2,585 people from a population of 4,600.[21] This is still the earliest and most authoritative account of the introduction of framework knitting into Leicestershire.

Other town studies can be found in the pages of county histories: Robert Thoroton included a detailed discussion of Nottingham in his *Antiquities of Nottinghamshire*. Francis Blomefield devoted a whole volume of his history of Norfolk to a study of Norwich published in 1740. He also included a substantial history of Thetford in the first volume.[22] Richard Gough, the antiquary, was subsequently involved in seeing into print a second history of Thetford, by Thomas Martin, following the author's death in 1781. John Nichols devoted more than 600 folio-sized pages in his *History of Leicestershire* (1815) to Leicester, and a whole volume on Salisbury was contributed to

Hoare's *History of Modern Wiltshire* (1843).[23] The quality of these histories also improved. John Watson, in his *History and Antiquities of the Parish of Halifax in Yorkshire* (1775), suggested that the reputation of antiquarian publications such as his own had risen because the public was better satisfied of their utility when they were known to have been read in the highest courts of justice.[24]

Deering and Nichols provided descriptions of the East Midlands hosiery industry which remain authoritative sources. Similarly, William Enfield's study of Liverpool, published in 1774, looked not only to the past, but also to the immediate economic, commercial and cultural achievements of the present,[25] and William Hutton's *History of Birmingham* was similarly important. Hutton may well have been influenced by Deering's history since he was a journeyman stocking maker in Nottingham in the 1740s, and although he moved to Birmingham in 1750 he maintained family links with Nottingham. He set up as a paper merchant, but it was not until the 1770s that he began to collect material for a history of Birmingham, which he wrote in 1780. It was published in 1782 (although dated 1781). Hutton had first-hand experience of local industry and trade, and he set out to glorify Birmingham by presenting a portrait of what was by then a vigorously expanding commercial and industrial town. The book went into a second edition in 1783, when Hutton added additional material on gentry seats, and a third edition in 1795.[26]

Not all the town histories of this period reached or even aspired to the standards of Deering, Enfield and Hutton. Charles Caraccioli's *The Antiquities of Arundel* (1766) was 'ineptly compiled from secondary sources and dealt chiefly with the town's successive lords'; Alexander Hay's *History of Chichester* (1804) was also 'poor, badly arranged and insufficiently localised'. Rather better were the studies of Lewes and Brighthelmston by Paul Dunvan (1795), and Hastings by W.G. Moss (1824). Subsequently another Brighton author, J.A. Erredge, did not live to see his book into print in 1867, because he died at his desk while engaged in discussions with his publisher.[27]

Quite why was there was so much interest in town histories during the eighteenth century? It must have been connected with a change in the cultural position of English towns after 1660. Research flourished as local gentry began to acquire town houses and to form clubs and societies dedicated to antiquarian pursuits.[28] Civic annals declined in popularity as new-style histories mirrored the growing role in town life of the landed and professional classes. Corporations often contributed to the cost of illustrations in these histories. The result was a series of books which shed useful light on the mental and cultural world of the eighteenth-century town, and demonstrated a growing pride in the regeneration of towns as economic, political and cultural centres. Travel writing helped to bring urban history into the wider public consciousness, even if visitors were mostly concerned with the finer and more unusual features of towns rather than the mundane and less attractive. Visitors to Nottingham wrote in glowing terms of the spacious market place surrounded by the town houses of wealthy merchants and manufacturers,[29] and elsewhere pen-portraits drawn by visitors were the key to popularising the spa waters of Tunbridge Wells, Buxton, Leamington Spa, Cheltenham, Malvern and Knaresborough, and the seaside resorts of Brighton, Hastings, Whitby, Margate, Ramsgate, Poole, and Weymouth. It was in the resorts that the first recognisable guidebooks emerged, often produced by local printers or booksellers looking to exploit the visitor market. Bath's histories were written from the beginning with this audience in mind.[30]

What did this all amount to? Some years ago Peter Clark argued that by the end of the eighteenth century town histories had acquired a vital communal motif. They demonstrated growing pride in the regeneration of towns as economic, political and cultural centres.[31] More recently, Rosemary Sweet has argued persuasively that the enthusiasm for urban histories during the eighteenth century was not simply a result of a change in the mental and cultural world of post-Restoration towns, but also a change in the market. Urban histories were no longer written for the town elite, but were aimed at a broader section of society. As a result, they needed to be readable, and to contain a wider range of subject matter than the preoccupations of antiquarians. William Hutton, in writing about Birmingham, sought to create a strong sense of community, an image of Birmingham as a society of industrial, upright, and moral citizens, with a cultural and social life of their own.[32] The history of towns owed much to the desire to participate in and contribute to national improvement: in Sweet's words, 'to buy an urban history was a demonstration of local feeling; to undertake to write it demanded some sense of commitment to and pride in the town'.[33]

Rev. John Milner's *The History, Civil and Ecclesiastical, and Survey of the Antiquities of Winchester*, published in 1798 (with a second enlarged edition in 1809 and further editions to 1851) reflected some of these general considerations. Milner's history appealed to the expanding professional classes who both wrote and read the new urban histories. Although it was a commissioned history, in the sense that Milner was approached to write it by the Winchester printer and bookseller James Robbins, he took it on because he believed previous histories to be muddled and unconvincing where they were not downright wrong, and he thought local guidebooks were more or less worthless. He was not primarily interested in studying the town purely in its own right, but within the context of national history; in particular, as a Roman Catholic priest, he tended to view the greatness of Winchester in its pre-Reformation days. His book was a blend of antiquarian scholarship and Roman Catholic conviction, 'a politico-religious statement by a Roman Catholic priest which boldly correlates Winchester's past greatness in the Middle Ages with the ascendancy of the old religion'.[34]

Urban histories were not just about description: they often had a purpose. Just as Deering and others had no qualms about including within their histories descriptions of contemporary life, other authors saw themselves as having a political role in validating political claims and upholding legal judgements within the pages of a 'history'. Town histories reflected the concerns and preoccupations of the inhabitants. John Wood's history of Bath illustrated many of these issues. By asserting the antique origins of Bath he was able to establish the importance of the town in its own right, not simply as a resort for visitors, but he also set out to show how much Bath's rise to fashionable popularity owed to his own effort and vision, rather than to what he saw as the inconsequential role of the corporation. In this way town histories might be peddling a contemporary political message, hence Sweet's conclusion that 'urban histories cannot be resorted to as a reliable commentary on eighteenth-century municipal government, since so often they were written to argue a particular case'.[35]

Corporations had their own worries about town histories. Francis Drake was well connected in York, and he was welcomed into the library of the chapter of York Minster to read both books and manuscripts. Perhaps as a result, when in April 1731 he requested permission from the corporation to inspect the city records, he was immediately granted access. John Brand 'found a very copious source of unedited materials in the archives of the corporation of Newcastle upon Tyne' to which John Ball, the mayor, gave him 'liberal' access, and 'permission to make what extracts I thought proper'.[36] Corporations were not always so accommodating. Charles Deering had lived in Nottingham for some years before he began work on his *History*, and had enjoyed the active support and help of John Plumptre, a leading Nottingham townsman and a local MP. On the other hand he was not very popular in the town so, despite his connections, he was granted permission to consult the borough archives only under supervision.[37]

Some corporations actively attempted to block access. Browne Willis, a known Jacobite, writing in the aftermath of the 1715 rebellion, perhaps ought not to have been surprised to find Leicester Corporation 'possessed such a strange jealousy or envy as had hindered me from the proper means of doing it, and upon many accounts deter me from it'. Samuel Seyer was denied access to Bristol corporation's records in the early nineteenth century, partly because of rumours that in Newcastle, following the publication of John Brand's study of the town in 1789, various people found reason to withhold dues and other taxes previously paid without question. Conversely some historians found access granted simply because of who they were. The Bristol surgeon, William Barrett, author of *The History and Antiquities of Bristol* (1789) remarked that his profession had gained him admittance to many families from whom he procured important manuscript records.[38]

Of course, on occasion there were good reasons to toe the local political line, particularly if corporation sponsorship was promised or anticipated, since as with county histories, subscription lists were of variable success. Francis Drake could not bring himself to solicit directly for subscribers to his history of York, but a friend undertook the work for him, and did very well, gathering no fewer than 540 subscriptions for a book costing five guineas. The Archbishop of York was conspicuously absent from the list. A subscription list for Charles Deering's history of Nottingham attracted only ninety-one names. This was not sufficient for publication, and in his later years Deering continued to add to and revise the manuscript in the hope that further subscribers would come forward. The book remained unpublished when he died.[39] Clearly there were significant benefits for urban historians if corporations agreed to sponsor their work, but this was likely to affect the way they presented their research.

Town histories of the nineteenth century

Urban histories continued to appear in the nineteenth century and, predictably, they varied in range and quality. John Blackner published a new history of Nottingham in 1815, updating Deering, and at the same time celebrating the prosperity of the town's commercial and manufacturing groups.[40] William Dyde's *Tewkesbury* (1790) was updated and expanded by James Bennett in 1830 and again in 1849. Lewis Turnor's *Hertford* (1830) combined antiquarian thoroughness with institutional, political and social history. Studies of Huntingdon, Godmanchester and St Neots all appeared 1820–31.

Robert Carruthers's *History of Huntingdon* (1824) covered institutions, churches, historical events, and the usual material on eminent people, MPs and mayors. James Thompson's *History of Leicester from the Time of the Romans to the End of the Seventeenth Century* (1849) is regarded as the best of several histories of the town because it was based on extensive documentary research.[41] William Hutton's *History of Derby* (1791) self-confessedly borrowed heavily from Pilkington's history of Derbyshire published two years previously.[42] Stephen Glover's history of the town, which appeared as part of a Directory, included a discussion relating to the new arboretum.[43]

Many town histories were still pedestrian in style and content relying heavily on the familiar formula of dealing with the history of the corporation, charities, the parish church and ancient buildings, and usually illustrated with contemporary engravings. Among them were William Rastall Dickinson's histories of Southwell (1787) and Newark (1806). His work attempted to establish for the reader some kind of framework for distinguishing the characteristics of Roman, Saxon, Danish, Norman and Gothic architecture, the classic work of antiquaries by this date. His intention was to form a 'sort of architectural index, or nomenclature of columns, arches, and ornaments, by means of which the origin of every ancient building might, almost on a first view be dated'.[44]

Few of these histories were great works of literary scholarship, and studies such as W. Harrod's *Mansfield* (1801), J. Holland's *Worksop* (1826), and John Piercy's *Retford* (1828), reflected provincialism in a way that studies of larger towns affected by the urban renaissance did not. Piercy was master of the National School in Retford, parish clerk, and a regular contributor to the *Doncaster Gazette*. His preference in compiling and writing his history was for a straightforward narrative approach, but he was also concerned to do something before ancient documents were 'buried . . . in oblivion'.[45] He reproduced in full the Charter of James I, which he regarded as the key authority under which the borough operated, together with numerous other extracts from civic records, extracts from private records including wills, and copies of inscriptions in the churches and chapels. He could not resist including sections on two ancient families.[46]

Some town histories of the nineteenth century took much the same chronicle form as those produced for counties. Charles Henry Cooper, town clerk of Cambridge, compiled an *Annals of Cambridge* in five thick volumes taking a chronological order without interpretation. John Latimer (d. 1904) did much the same for Bristol, collecting a vast amount of information, largely from local newspapers.[47]

It is no surprise to find town histories being turned out in significant numbers by the late Victorian period, paralleling the briefer series of county histories. In Essex these included studies of Dagenham, Coggeshall, Brightingsea, Romford, Waltham Abbey and Upminster. Studies of smaller Gloucestershire towns in the late nineteenth century were 'generally undistinguished' except for P.H. Fisher's work on Stroud (1871). Better quality was achieved by George Fyler Townsend with his *Town and Borough of Leominster* published about 1863, perhaps because the chapter on the parish church and priory was written by the Oxford historian Professor E.A. Freeman.[48]

Later Victorian books on Nottinghamshire towns included studies of Worksop by Edwin Eddison in 1854 and Robert White in 1875, Newark by Cornelius Brown in 1879, and Mansfield by W. Horner Groves in 1894. Cornelius Brown later expanded his study into a monumental two volume work published 1904–7 and based on the borough archives and other original records.[49] Many of these later works were neither very comprehensive nor very intelligible, and the level of historical analysis varied considerably, but they clearly tapped a market for town histories, which was also recognised by Professor Freeman in his series on *Historic Towns* launched in 1877. Freeman was mainly interested, as a national historian, in local history, insofar as town histories could throw light on national political development. He did not read the original records for himself, or spend laborious days in muniment rooms deciphering the manuscripts. It was left to Maitland, the Cambridge historian, in his studies of borough history in the 1890s, to lay the real foundations for the study of urban history.[50]

By the end of the nineteenth century the world of local history was changing. Neither the later county histories, not their contemporaneous urban histories, were viewed in particularly positive terms, and the reason had something to do with changes in thinking about the study of history in the second half of the nineteenth century. While there were still large numbers of clergymen and gentlemen working away at the history of their communities, and while the setting up of the Victoria County History in 1899 appeared to be a new take on an old theme, the business of researching and writing in the locality was under fire from national, and often professional historians intent on establishing their own discipline as intellectually and academically superior. By this time the all-encompassing antiquary, who collected and recorded written documents and monumental inscriptions, studied place names and coins, and engaged in field walking, was an increasingly marginalised character. From the 1840s archaeology came increasingly to be a separate discipline, and by the late nineteenth century much the same was happening in history. There were – indeed there still are – people who can best be described, and would describe themselves as antiquaries, but far from occupying centre stage as they had in the eighteenth century, they were marginalised. It is to these developments in the world of local history that we turn in chapter V.

Notes

1 W.G. Hoskins, *Local History in England* (3rd edn, 1984), 27; *ECH*, 330.

2 *ECH*, 51, 330. Rev. Christopher Collinson, vicar of Laxton, Nottinghamshire, 1898–1916, spent many hours in the muniment room at Thoresby Hall working meticulously through papers in the Manvers MSS relating to Laxton. His working history of the village, which includes copies of documents now lost, is in Nottinghamshire Archives Office, PR 4082–6.

3 R. Gough, *Myddle* (ed.), D. Hey (1981), 109.

4 Margaret Spufford, 'Poverty portrayed: Gregory King and Eccleshall in Staffordshire in the 1690s', *Staffordshire Studies*, 7 (1995), 1–150; Hoskins, *LH*, 29; J.R. Ford (ed.), *John Lucas's History of Warton Parish, compiled 1710–1740* (1931).

5 Hoskins, *Local History*, 26.

6 Rosemary Sweet, *The Writing of Urban Histories in Eighteenth-Century England* (1997), 75–80; Peter Clark, 'Visions of the urban community: antiquarianism and the English city before 1800', in D. Fraser and A. Sutcliffe (eds), *The Pursuit of Urban History* (1983), 107.

7 Clark, 'Visions', 112.

8 M.J. Power, 'John Stow and his London', in Richardson, 30–51. Power presents a relatively negative view of Stow's achievements. John Strype produced in 1720 what he called a 'corrected, improved and very much enlarged' edition, and a 6th edition appeared in 1754. Today the edition edited by C.L. Kingsford in 1908, is regarded as the most authoritative modern edition.

9 Peter Ackroyd, *London: The Biography* (2000), 784 notes that 'accounts of sixteenth-century London are of course dominated by Stow's *A Survey of London*'.

10 Sweet, *Writing*, 86–8.

11 *ECH*, 189.

12 Sweet, *Writing*, 80–6; R. Sweet, 'The production of urban histories in eighteenth-century England', *Urban History*, 23 (1996), 174–6.

13 Clark, 'Visions', 106; Sweet, *Writing*, 89–90; Stephen Porter, *Exploring Urban History: Sources for Local Historians* (1990), 13; *ECH*, 147.

14 Sweet, *Writing*, 295–310; Rosemary Sweet, *Antiquaries: the Discovery of the Past in Eighteenth-Century Britain* (2004), 164, 173, 177–8; Francis

Drake, *Eboracum: Of the History and Antiquities of the City of York from its Original to the Present Times, Together With the History of the Cathedral Church and the Lives of the Archbishops of the See* (1736); John Whitaker, *The History of Manchester in Four Books*, 2 vols (2nd edn, 1773); John Brand, *The History and Antiquities of the Town and County of the Town of Newcastle upon Tyne* (2 vols, 1789).

15 Porter, *Exploring*, 13; ECH, 148, 452–3; Philip Morant, *The History and Antiquities of Colchester* (1789).

16 Peter Borsay, *The English Urban Renaissance: Culture and Society in the Provincial Town, 1660–1770* (1989).

17 Porter, *Exploring*, 14–15.

18 C. Deering, *Nottinghamia Vetus Et Nova: Or, an Historical Account of the Ancient and Present State of the Town of Nottingham* (1751), introduction.

19 Ibid. 24.

20 Nottinghamshire Archives Office, Probate inventory of Charles Deering. Note that the date on the inventory is given as 1748, Old Style, before the change of New Year's Day from 25 March to 1 January in 1752. The original manuscript of his history, in Deering's own hand, is in Bromley House Library, Angel Row, Nottingham. John Beckett and Catherine Smith, 'Dr Charles Deering: Nottingham's first historian', *Nottinghamshire Historian*, 63 (1999), 14–16; A.C. Wood, 'Doctor Charles Deering', *Transactions of the Thoroton Society*, 55 (1941), 24–39.

21 John Nichols, *The History and Antiquities of Hinckley in the County of Leicester* (1782).

22 D. Stoker, 'Francis Blomefield as a Historian of Norfolk', *Norfolk Archaeology*, 54 (2003), 181–201; Sweet, *Writing*, 92–8.

23 Richard Colt Hoare, *The Modern History of South Wiltshire* (5 vols, 1822–44). Subsequently an unnumbered volume was added on Salisbury by Robert Benson and Henry Hatcher in 1843.

24 Sweet, *Writing*, 38.

25 William Enfield, *An Essay Towards the History of Liverpool* (1773).

26 William Hutton, *A History of Birmingham* (1783 edn), 1–110, 123–40.

27 ECH, 387–9.

28 P. Clark, *British Clubs and Societies, 1580–1800: The Origins of an Associational World* (2000).

29 Robert Sanders, *Complete English Traveller* (1772), 492–3; C.P. Moritz, *Journeys of a German in England in 1782* (1965), 176.

30 Sweet, *Writing*, 22–30, 50–1, 73, 107, 113–16.

31 Clark, 'Visions', 124.

32 Sweet, 'Production of Urban Histories'; *Writing*, 184.

33 Sweet, *Writing*, 275.

34 R.C. Richardson, 'Writing urban history in the eighteenth century: Milner's Winchester', in Richardson, 83–93.

35 Sweet, *Writing*, 188–204.

36 C.B.L. Barr, 'Drake, Francis (1696–1771)'. *Oxford Dictionary of National Biography* (2004), 8023; Brand, *Newcastle*, iv.

37 *Records of the Borough of Nottingham*, VI (1914), 167, 169, 174.

38 Sweet, *Writing*, 47, 205, 235.

39 Barr, 'Drake'; Sweet, *Antiquaries*, 69; James Orange, *History and Antiquities of Nottingham* (2 vols, 1840), 953.

40 John Blackner, *The History of Nottingham* (1815); Sweet, *Antiquaries*, 341–2.

41 *ECH*, 160, 202–3, 235.

42 W. Hutton, *The History of Derby from the Remote Ages of Antiquity to the Year MDCCXCI . . .* (1791), viii–ix.

43 S. Glover, *Glover's Derby: The History and Directory of the Borough of Derby Intended as a Guide to Strangers Visiting the Town* (1843).

44 Sweet, *Antiquaries*, 265, quoting from William Dickinson, *Antiquities Historical, Architectural, Chorographical and Itinerary in Nottinghamshire and the Adjacent Counties* (1801), viii.

45 J.S. Piercy, *The History of Retford* (1828), v.

46 Ibid., 196–8, 227–31; B.J. Biggs, 'J.S. Piercy, Retford historian', *Transactions of the Thoroton Society*, 79 (1985), 60–71.

47 C.H. Cooper, *Annals of Cambridge* (3 vols, 1842); *ECH*, 66, 164.

48 *ECH*, 149, 160, 181.

49 http://www.nottshistory.org.uk, June 2006.

50 F.W. Maitland, *Domesday Book and Beyond, Township and Borough* (1897); Hoskins, *Local History*, 23–5.

V *Local history marginalised*

Until the nineteenth century no real distinctions existed within historical studies, hence the convenient term 'antiquary' to describe the various practitioners. There were no particular skills or methodologies, and the study of the past was in the hands of men with at most a classical training and a deep interest. The Society of Antiquaries may have been a meeting place, but it was not the keeper of standards; indeed, one of the more difficult accusations to counter, both for the Antiquaries and the Royal Society, was that they gave too much space to incredulous and fanciful material. In the course of the nineteenth century the amateurism that this reflected came into conflict with the professionalisation of archaeology and history and, in the process, the 'seamlessness' of past studies began to break down. As archaeology developed into a discipline, it continued to maintain close links with the antiquaries, largely through the county societies which sprang up across the country. The professionalisation of history had a different impact. It was bound up with the discovery of a national identity, which was believed to be best studied through the national archives on a national basis. Antiquarianism seemed alien to this position. Professional historians sought to distance themselves from what they saw as the amateur and the unscholarly. They promoted journals for disseminating their findings among their professional colleagues, and they sought to hide links they may have enjoyed with the societies. By the end of the nineteenth century local history was marginalised: even the Victoria County History, founded in 1899, was primarily concerned with studying the nation, admittedly through the locality, but from the national records. Ironically, all this was taking place just as the societies had brought more people into contact with archaeology and antiquarian study than at any time in the past. In this chapter we examine how local history ran into the buffers as it was increasingly marginalised in Victorian England.

Clubs and societies

Perhaps the most important development for the study of antiquities in the nineteenth century was the associational movement. Antiquaries had always sought to communicate, through organisations such as the

Society of Antiquaries, or by publishing in widely read journals such as *Archaeologia*. Since they were mostly gentlemen of private means they could afford to travel to a convenient meeting place. What changed in the nineteenth-century was both the clientele and the meeting location. The growth of towns from the later eighteenth century was matched by social change in which the middle-classes came to identify together in clubs and associations, and to engage in an associational world. The movement began with groups like the Spalding Gentleman's Society, and by the early nineteenth century clubs were being formed in a whole range of areas from freemasonry, through friendly societies, trade unions and co-operative societies, all the way to societies with an intellectual agenda including literary and philosophical societies, subscription libraries, archaeological and, belatedly, antiquarian societies. The 1851 census listed 1,057 literary and scientific societies and mechanics' institutes.[1]

Most middle-class societies were non-political, non-sectarian, and 'improving'. In Leeds, the middle-classes were able to act in a united fashion only in voluntary organisations. These groups helped to promote middle-class values because political and religious differences were suspended in the search for common cultural interests.[2] Much the same was true in Manchester, where the Manchester Institution was founded in 1823 with the idea that it would 'serve as a point of union for the enlightened and liberal part of this widely scattered and in some respects unconnected population . . . many people who might otherwise have continued strangers to each other, would thus be brought into harmonious cooperation.'[3]

The first provincial learned society to be devoted exclusively to the study of antiquities was the Newcastle Society, founded by a local bookseller, John Bell, in 1813. The north of England, with its rich heritage of Roman antiquities, had obvious attractions for the antiquary, and in Newcastle and its environs there was no shortage of materials to discuss at meetings. The Duke of Northumberland agreed to act as patron, which was expected to boost membership, but the society struggled, finding it difficult to attract members, in competition with the Newcastle Literary and Philosophical Society founded in 1793.[4] The breakthrough for local societies was usually in the study of archaeology, rather than in antiquities more generally, and on a county basis, even if they normally met in the county town. Among the early societies of this type were the St Albans and Hertfordshire Architectural and Archaeological Society (1845), the Sussex Archaeological Society (1846), the Buckinghamshire Archaeological Society (1847), the Norfolk and Norwich Archaeological Society

(1847), the Essex Archaeological Society (1852), which was formed in Colchester and brought together gentry, clergy and professional men, the North Oxfordshire Archaeological Society (1853), the Surrey Archaeological Society (1854), the London and Middlesex Archaeological Society (1855) and several others.[5]

The context in which the learned societies operated changed over time. In the early days they were informal, and meetings concentrated on the discussion of objects of 'curiosity'. This approach was gradually superseded as publication became more important than the simple exchange of ideas; indeed, failure to publish was regarded as a sign of a society's deficiencies. As a consequence, the societies gradually divided into two camps: printing clubs and 'social' clubs.

The printing clubs or societies were passive organisations, but they reflected the demand to publish as a sign that they took their studies seriously because, implicitly, their unstated mission was about conserving the country's heritage of public records. The interest in publishing began in London and spread to the provinces, where the earliest printing societies were the Surtees Society in Durham founded in 1834, quickly followed by the Camden Society in 1838, the Chetham Society, founded in Manchester to serve Lancashire and Cheshire in 1843, and the Sussex Archaeological Collections 'illustrating the history and antiquities of the county' in 1848. The Surtees Society, published a wide range of records relating to the county and north Yorkshire, and the Buckinghamshire Archaeological Society, founded in 1847, began in 1854 to publish the records of the county. The Norfolk and Norwich Archaeological Society (1847) published historical source material from its foundation, both in its transactions and in separate occasional volumes.[6]

Printing club members received a publication in return for an annual subscription. The Camden Society, named after the great antiquary himself, published edited historical texts with introductions. It continues today, as the text-publishing arm of the Royal Historical Society. The Chetham Society, founded for the publication of *Remains Historical and Literary Connected with the Palatine Counties of Lancaster and Cheshire*, was designed to develop the private printing of historical records in the two counties. Later printing societies included the Record Society of Lancashire and Cheshire in 1878.[7] Few counties failed to establish some form of printing club, and urban records were often transcribed for printing in the record series of county societies. Beverley and York records have both appeared in volumes of the Yorkshire Archaeological Society.[8]

The social clubs were forums in which members gathered for events and meetings. Many of them came through time to issue *Transactions*, and these in turn paralleled at a local level the material which appeared in *Archaeologia*. Some of these clubs were primarily interested in architecture, especially ecclesiastical architecture in the wake of the Gothic Revival. In Lincolnshire, the emergence of a new generation of scholarly incumbents and professional men in the 1840s and 1850s brought great enthusiasm for change. This owed something to the Oxford Movement, many of whose adherents were interested in parochial history and archaeology, and found expression in the Lincoln Diocesan Architectural Society, founded in the 1840s to cater for the widespread enthusiasm of the time for the restoration of the parish churches of the diocese. Members visited churches to see for themselves how they were being restored and improved, and the society began publishing in 1851. From c.1885 to c.1902 the Lincoln Architectural Society became the Lincoln and Nottingham Architectural Society, and published an annual journal concerned with church history. It finally disappeared as a separate publication only in 1964, when it became part of the Society for Lincolnshire History and Archaeology.[9]

More numerous and successful were the social clubs which were not linked specifically either to printing, or to a particular area of interest such as archaeology and architecture. These groups were encouraged by the Victorian concern with the loss of what was considered to be the 'traditional heritage'. As a result they saw themselves as antiquarian, club-type successors to the individuals who had dominated the eighteenth century, so that whatever their titles they usually took an interest in the whole range of antiquarian study. The Yorkshire Archaeological Society grew out of meetings held in Huddersfield from 1863 and issued its first journal in 1869, while the Cumberland and Westmorland Antiquarian and Archaeological Society dates from 1866, when it was founded – mainly by gentry and parsons – with the intention of publishing annual transactions and a record series. Other societies included the Historic Society of Lancashire and Cheshire (1848) and the Lancashire and Cheshire Antiquarian Society (1883).

The 1870s saw the formation of many such societies, including the Dorset Natural History and Archaeological Society (1875), the Bristol and Gloucestershire Archaeological Society (1876), and the Derbyshire Archaeological Society (1879). By 1886 there were fifty-five county and local societies from Penzance to Cumberland and from Chester to Louth. In England and Wales the number of new societies nearly doubled between the 1870s and 1900s.[10] Mostly they met in the county towns, but they brought together old land with a new middle-class audience. As Dr John Beddoe expressed it at the founding of the Bristol and Gloucestershire society in 1876, 'among the landed proprietors, among the local clergy and among the residents of such towns as Clifton and Cheltenham there must be many people who were fit to be members of such an association'.[11]

One other feature is worth mentioning. These societies were not, and were not intended to be, democratic institutions. Although they often depended on aristocratic patronage to get under way, the dukes, bishops and earls who graciously allowed their names to appear on the headed notepaper generally disappeared from view to be replaced by a core of working individuals, drafted from among the gentry, the clergy and the county town social elite. The Sussex Archaeological Society was accused of courting the aristocracy, and the Historic Society of Lancashire and Cheshire charged a subscription rate designed to determine the pedigree of its members.

Although we would identify these societies as social clubs, their aims were serious. The first general meeting of the Devonshire Association, held in August 1862 in Exeter, heard six papers. Although the weather put paid to the planned excursion, the sixty-nine members enjoyed a conversazione given by the Devon and Exeter Graphic Society. Predictably, the professed aims of the Society were 'to give a stronger impulse and a more systematic direction to scientific inquiry, and to promote the intercourse of those who cultivate science, literature or art in different parts of Devonshire, with one another, and with others'. In the early years papers were delivered at their peripatetic meetings on Devonshire geology, Darwinism, and science. The 1868 meeting at Honiton had an excursion to an excavation of three barrows. Ladies were admitted as members from 1873, and in 1876 the volume of transactions ran to 912 pages. Members began transcribing the Domesday Book entries for the county.[12]

The philosophy which drove these societies is nowhere clearer than with the founding on 21 March 1883 of the Lancashire and Cheshire Antiquarian Society at a meeting in the rooms of the Manchester Literary and Philosophical Society on George Street, Manchester. Proceedings followed the anticipated form. A committee was set up and an annual subscription agreed. Six weeks later, on 4 May 1883, a conversazione was held at Owens College (subsequently Manchester University) to mark the formation of the society. Some 400 people also heard a lecture by Dr John Evans entitled 'The Seven Ages of Man' covering the Palaeolithic to the Medieval, which was subsequently published as the first article in the newly commenced

Transactions. Early lectures were mainly on archaeological matters, but the society's aims included the examination, preservation and illustration of ancient monuments and records, the study of history, literature, arts, customs and traditions and, more generally, the antiquities of Lancashire and Cheshire. If the lectures concentrated on archaeology, the early volumes of transactions were more eclectic, with contributions on church bells, Anglo-Saxon crosses, and many other topics. The common denominator was the interest of contributors in collecting classifying and describing a range of objects which included Phoenician vases, flint tools, Roman coins and ecclesiastical architecture.[13]

The fascination with archaeology and scientific issues probably explains why the titles of most of the new societies omitted the word 'history'. Few of them were interested in the present or recent past, or the narrative form associated with historical writing, to which we shall come shortly. They can be most appropriately classified as antiquarians trying to conserve a distant past that they feared was in danger of disappearing, and which they thought should be recorded. It is no surprise that the first chairman of the Bristol and Gloucestershire Archaeological Society (founded in 1876) was Dr John Beddoe, a Fellow of the Royal Society and a distinguished anthropologist. The Society took itself extremely seriously: it intended to undertake proper scientific research, not to engage in 'junketings and picnics'. Beddoe told the inaugural meeting that the intention was to 'collect the scattered fragments of archaeology which existed in the county and give them some sort of cohesion'.[14] In subsequent years, like many other societies, this was indeed their chief goal.

The emphasis here was on serious research, and many antiquarians specialised in particular areas and saw themselves as serious scholars contributing to the development of human knowledge. They came from a variety of occupations and included architects, librarians, legal clerks, clerics and occasionally university academics, but their focus was usually on the 'local', rather than the national. Their interests were reflected in the activities of the societies, and the standard form which developed included winter lectures, summer excursions, and an annual conversazione with a guest speaker and a chance to view exhibits from members' collections. The societies also looked, from the outset, to fund research, usually archaeological fieldwork. Some members wrote in local newspapers on antiquarian and local historical matters. W. Doubleday's series of articles on Nottinghamshire villages is a typical example of this genre of local historical writing.

Often they went under titles such as 'local gleanings', 'notes and queries', or 'historical notes'.[15]

Nottinghamshire was relatively late acquiring a society, although the *Nottinghamshire and Derbyshire Notes and Queries* ran to six volumes between 1893 and 1898, suggesting a demand. This was met in 1897 with the founding of The Thoroton Society, named after Dr Robert Thoroton with, entirely predictably, the intention of holding meetings, running excursions, and publishing an annual volume of transactions. The driving force was W.P.W. Phillimore, whom we shall meet again in another context, and he pressed ahead despite being told that 'nothing of this kind was possible in Nottingham'. The rules proposed that the society's proceedings should include 'papers on antiquarian, genealogical or historical subjects relating to Nottingham and Nottinghamshire'. However, the early volumes paid more attention to society excursions than to academic study, and for the first twenty years or so a 'great deal of space was devoted to architectural descriptions of local churches'. It was not until the 1920s that articles on local history, topography and architecture came to predominate. These were, in the view of Professor A.C. Wood, the long-serving editor of *Transactions*, 'designed to enlarge the corpus of knowledge of Nottinghamshire history rather than to record the year-by-year doings of the Society'. Even so, descriptions of churches continued to fill a good deal of space.[16]

The societies varied in their aims and intentions. Some combined both printing and social clubs (i.e. issuing record series as well as journals and transactions). Thus the Yorkshire Archaeological Society started a journal in 1869 and a record series in 1885. Nottinghamshire's Thoroton Society also combined both the printing and social, but others (as in Derbyshire) concentrated only on historic and antiquarian matters; indeed, the Derbyshire Archaeological and Natural History Society was founded in 1878, but the county's record society dates only from 1977. By the end of the nineteenth century hardly any counties lacked one or more organisations devoted to studying the past of the locality, although Huntingdonshire did not have a separate society until 1900, and a serious county-wide society was formed in Bedfordshire only in 1914.[17]

The societies successfully brought together an audience which ranged across antiquarianism, archaeology, natural history, and other interests, which can be summed up as a concern with the loss of what was coming to be seen as the nation's 'traditional heritage', from folklorists recording the decline of customary forms of popular culture, to architectural societies promoting the Gothic Revival. The range

reflected the fact that members of the societies were seldom specialists. In almost all respects they were the successors to the eighteenth-
century antiquaries, interested in every aspect of the human past. Of
168 papers read to the Leicester Literary and Philosophical Society
between its inauguration in 1835 and 1848, twelve related to
Leicestershire's history, thirty-nine to literary and artistic subjects,
eighteen to contemporary society, and ninety-nine to scientific and
general historical subjects. In 1849 sectional committees were formed
for geology, zoology, botany archaeology and the fine arts.[18] Although
there were, perhaps inevitably, many dilettante dabblers, most antiquaries regarded themselves as serious scholars contributing to the
development of knowledge, but they lived and worked quite separately from the academic worlds of the universities.[19]

This distinction was important. The societies provided an outlet for
the historical and antiquarian talents of their members, but they did
not promote a consistent subject matter or a methodology, and they
continued to interweave archaeological, architectural and antiquarian
study at a time when these were being separated out by the professionals. The societies had combined sociability with intellectual discussion, but where did antiquarianism end and archaeology or history
begin?

Archaeology

Archaeology developed a more self-consciously scientific methodology in the course of the nineteenth century, partly reflecting developments in geology associated with the work of Charles Lyell and in
biology with Darwin. Scientific discovery got around the chronology
problems which had dogged earlier antiquaries, while Britain's imperial expansion gave archaeology a further impetus. For antiquaries,
archaeology was a supplement to the written record, but as Britain
came to rule large parts of the world which had no written sources the
significance of archaeology became more apparent. Inspired by the
work of General A.H. Pitt-Rivers (1827–1900), archaeology became
increasingly professionalised, with the organised dig becoming the
main form of investigation. Pitt-Rivers recognised that objects can be
placed in chronological sequence on the basis of slight changes in
design, and so nothing should be wasted. In turn this meant that his
field archaeology needed to be rigorous. He mapped and pho-
tographed sites with great precision, because he understood the
principles of stratigraphy, the sequence of layers and deposits that
make up an archaeological site. From these findings came the gradual

evolution of a system of ordering ancient artefacts and some concept of chronology as the past was divided into the Palaeolithic (old stone age), Mesolithic (middle stone age), Neolithic (new stone age), Bronze Age and Iron Age.

As these developments were in progress, archaeologists formed the British Archaeological Association in 1843. This was a professional body 'to promote the study of archaeology, art and architecture and the preservation of our national antiquities'. The BAA offered a focal point for work undertaken by professional scholars and the societies. In 1888 the Congress of Archaeological Societies was founded, and it met at Burlington House under the patronage of the Society of Antiquaries.[20]

Professional history

The changes taking place in archaeology were never such as to threaten the link with the societies, but the same could not be said about history. The study of antiquities was a product of the Renaissance. It began with a desire to recover the history and antiquities of ancient Rome, and – like archaeology – it expanded into other historical periods. Antiquaries used manuscripts, inscriptions and coins to retrieve and record this past. Renaissance humanists, by contrast, understood history as the study of events in classical antiquity. In their view it should be written within a narrative form. Events after the fall of Rome were recorded in Chronicles, but these were considered an inferior form of literature because they lacked the intellectual standing of classical history. Through time this rather arbitrary division was increasingly unclear as historians began to draw on the evidence of coins or inscriptions in writing the history of the ancient world. The literary materials on which historians conventionally depended were tested and found to be suspect, while the testimony of coins, inscriptions and statues came to be regarded as sound because it could not be forged. As a result, empiricism was seen as the basis of historical truth. In the eighteenth century this convergence of historical narrative and antiquarian discourse reached a notable milestone with the publication of Edward Gibbon's *The Decline and Fall of the Roman Empire* (1776–88).

The true historian continued to preserve a lofty distance from the antiquary, because history was perceived to be superior to the mere study of antiquities. While the antiquary was busy discovering the past, the historian was using that past as a vehicle to improve the present. The historian sought to understand the grand panorama, while the antiquary seemed obsessed with minutiae, which could have no significant bearing on the historical narrative. Expressed slightly differently, historians were concerned with narratives written about statesmen or nations, politics or war, while antiquaries were perceived to be interested only in specific localities such as a town, a parish or a county, or even just a collection of inscriptions. Since antiquaries were equated with localities, antiquarianism came to be regarded as parochial.[21] This sharp divide was widened and deepened by the different means they used to present their work: the antiquary often drew tables, transcribed documents or illustrated coins, but critics argued that this work lacked both analysis and the narrative form which was the backbone of history.

The way in which the divide grew is curious, given that many of the societies began life as printing clubs, and the earliest professional historians were linked to record publishing. The printing of official records started in 1783 with an edition of Domesday Book, and in the early nineteenth century a series of royal commissions began the work of publishing texts and calendars of the public records. The setting up of publishing clubs in the counties was a direct response to this national initiative, which led indirectly to the founding of the Public Record Office. The Public Records Office Act of 1838 was designed to create a national archive, professionally administered and properly curated. Until 1838 England's public records were scattered through fifty-six separate record repositories, each separately administered. The Public Record Office was established to bring together this vast collection of scattered documents, particularly with its move to Chancery Lane in 1862. But in addition to centralising the records the Public Record Office also served to stimulate historical research. Some of the earliest professional historians were the keepers and custodians of the public records.[22] Numerous transcripts of catalogues of the main classes of medieval administrative records were printed, multiplying the sources from which historians could work. By the 1850s the Public Record Office began its monumental series of Calendars of State Papers. Between 1857 and 1900 the Rolls Series published 250 volumes of records relating to the Middle Ages. In 1869 the Royal Commission on Historical Manuscripts was established with a remit to investigate manuscript sources in private hands. From 1870 it published reports on what were considered to be the most important collections. These reports often included transcriptions of documents. Finally, in 1888 the British Record Society was set up to publish indexes of historical records such as Chancery proceedings, inquisitions post mortem, wills and marriage licences.[23]

The most obvious allies of the Public Record Office keepers were the professional historians who benefited from the expansion of history as a separate university discipline, and for whom the subject was primarily about the nation, not the locality. The great narrative historians of the mid-century, among them Macaulay and Froude, addressed a wide general readership, and their interpretations of the national past helped to provide a sense of identity. This was the history of Englishness, which did not sit easily alongside the history of a place, whether it was a county, a town, or a parish. Over time this form of writing history was challenged and gradually displaced by more 'scientific', archive-based research, as the subject became professionalised. In 1871 Oxford established a School of History, and in 1873 Cambridge set up separate History Tripos. History came to be written on a smaller scale, and arguments had to be justified from the source materials. The key figures of these years were masters of their craft – as their footnotes demonstrated. In turn, these new research historians began to found their own associations and journals from which the 'amateur' was effectively excluded. The Royal Historical Society was founded in 1868 by a miscellaneous group of scholars, antiquarians and genealogists, but by the 1880s it had largely been taken over by a group of professional, academic historians. The new university academics were primarily interested in founding a journal which would cater for their strictly scientific historical interests, and which would be for scholars rather than general readers. This was to be the *English Historical Review*, founded in 1886.[24]

National history

The title of the *English Historical Review* says everything. The new professional scholars were writing national history, steeped in the documentation of the Public Record Office, and driven by a methodology learned from the earlier 'German School' of Ranke, Niebuhr and Mommsen, that concentrated on constitutional, legal and political history. Men like Trevelyan and Churchill, let alone J.L. and Barbara Hammond, considered themselves to be writing the history of England. This was not 'state' history, probably because professionalisation was neither as rapid nor as extensive as elsewhere in Europe, but it was about the history of countries rather than localities.[25] The *English Historical Review* was a carefully chosen, symbolic title, as was its equivalent north of the border, the *Scottish Historical Review*, founded in 1904. The prefatory note to the first edition of the *English*

Historical Review commented that 'states and politics will . . . be the chief part of its subject, because the acts of nations and of the individuals who have played a great part in the affairs of nations have usually been more important than the acts of private citizens'. The *Review* was to represent serious academic opinion among full-time scholars anxious to raise the prestige of their profession through publication of a journal which would be read primarily by fellow professionals. Articles were not confined to the history of England, but the title and editorial policy reflected a broad consensus as to the importance of nations and states for the study of history. Such thinking also chimed with late nineteenth-century ideas of Englishness.[26]

Whether intentional or not, these ideas helped to marginalise local history and its practitioners. To put it another way, the professionals claimed the scholarly high ground, a view neatly encapsulated in the words of Sir Henry Howarth, President of the Royal Archaeological Institute, in 1892. Howarth argued that 'the processes of writing history have become more difficult, more precise and more methodical, and . . . there is less and less room for the untrained, untaught, and unscholarly amateur'.[27] On another occasion Professor F.J.C. Hearnshaw told a meeting of the Historical Association that 'of course we all agree that local history must be used in a way entirely subsidiary . . . a lamp for the guidance and entertainment of the learner'.[28] G.M. Trevelyan saw it as the training ground for good historians who, once they were proficient, could then move on to higher studies.[29] With sentiments such as these prevailing the amateurs were viewed as operating only on the fringes of historical enterprise where, as Philippa Levine has written in her study of this movement 'their efforts posed no threat to the monopoly of expertise necessary to the standing of the new professions'. She continues:

> Local history, increasingly spurned by cosmopolitan academics, was reinforced as their [the antiquaries] particular concern; amateurism and antiquarianism were becoming synonymous. Curricular control further helped the new professionals to define with authority the components of the subject.[30]

Men like J.R. Green, William Stubbs and E.A. Freeman on occasion, disassociated themselves from or, in academic circles, did not admit to membership of local societies, and saw their work as superior. Green, for example, was always quick to emphasise the distinction between the antiquary and himself as a 'professional' historian. He reputedly dreaded being included among the ranks of the 'picturesque compilers'.[31]

Some professional historians retained links with the societies. Freeman was an active member of the Somerset Archaeological and Natural History Society, and he accepted that local studies contributed in some way to national history. As he observed on one occasion:

> There is hardly any better historic training for a man than to set him frankly in the streets of a quiet little town like Bury St Edmunds, and let him work out the history of the men who lived and died there . . . It is just in the pettiness of its details, in its commonplace incidents, in the want of marked features and striking events that the real lesson of the whole story lies.[32]

Freeman may have thought that walking the streets of Bury St Edmunds was the way to find out about the past, but the emphasis on 'the whole story' was more explicit when he became one of the first scholars to address the Lancashire and Cheshire Antiquarian Society in 1884:

> local researches were of very, very little profit unless they were brought to throw light on the general history of the country. A local antiquarian society . . . should work out the history of every district and spot, not merely the towns but the smallest villages; should work out every local detail, remembering as they went along that all they were working at locally was part of the history of England, and that the history of England was only part of a greater history – that of the whole of Europe.[33]

Local history, in other words, was valid only in so far as it added to the greater view of national history. Another contemporary, Sir John Seely, professor of history at Cambridge from 1863 until his death in 1895, is said to have remarked scathingly that 'the history of the Staffordshire potteries is not history'.[34] Even the great county historians were, in the words of Professor Jack Simmons, passed over by professional historians 'in silence, sometimes even in ignorance, or at best with a nod of condescension as amateurs, useful in recording the minute details of local life but certainly not to be considered historians in the full sense of the word'.[35]

By contrast, professional archaeological societies were never as exclusive, welcoming antiquarians both socially and intellectually. Most archaeologists belonged to their local county society as well as to national societies.[36] The real loser was the traditional antiquary, belonging to the county society and quietly working away at his or her chosen topic. In part, we can see why this happened. Antiquaries had failed to come to terms with the new history, and the description too easily acquired pejorative overtones, encouraged by the affectionate portrait of an enthusiast in Sir Walter Scott's *The Antiquary* (1816). But it was also about sources. The new professional historians worked with the public records, while the archaeology societies were frequently involved with establishing museums where local finds could be displayed and studied. The British Museum was set up in the eighteenth century to display exhibits from overseas and, later, the Empire. Individual collectors had their own 'cabinets of curiosities', which often found their way into civic sponsored museums where they could be studied and observed. The Warwickshire Natural History and Archaeological Society was founded in 1836 as a section of the Warwick and Leamington Phrenological Society, and although it failed to establish a county-wide presence, it established the county's first museum, in Warwick market hall. This became the official county museum in 1951. The Cambridgeshire Antiquarian Society, founded in 1840, collected coins, prehistoric weapons, pottery and other objects which were given in 1885 to the University Archaeological Museum, established with the society's assistance. The Buckinghamshire county museum opened in Aylesbury in 1907 to house collections brought together by the Buckinghamshire Archaeological Society, founded in 1847.[37]

Antiquaries had no such base; indeed, as we shall see in chapter VI they were actively encouraged to pursue their research in the Public Record Office rather than in the locality, an indication perhaps that even when it came to archives they had somehow to chase the professionals. Meantime they were seen not as genuine historians, but as collectors, too easily satisfied with a relatively low quality of published output. The Bristol and Gloucestershire Archaeological Society started producing annual *Transactions* from its founding in 1876, but with a range of discursive articles with titles such as 'Some Notes on the History of. . .'.[38] Editors found it difficult to move on from such material, and may indeed have positively welcomed it, although in 1946 Professor A.C. Wood expressed the view that 'the aim of the *Transactions* [of the Thoroton Society of Nottinghamshire] should surely be . . . to place on permanent record information which will swell the sum total of our knowledge of local history and so help students, both now and in the future'. His aim was to move the Thoroton Society away from its fascination with church bells and monuments towards 'other sides of life in the past', including agricultural and industrial developments as well as family histories. Wood was still an academic voice crying in the antiquarian wilderness, and in reality he frequently found the only way to achieve the end he had in view was to write the articles himself.[39]

Even the Victoria County History began life as a national organisation writing national history on a parish by parish basis, but primarily from the national records. It is no coincidence that the development of local history after the Second World War was in part possible because of the opening of local archive offices across the country, which suggested for the first time that documentation relevant to the study of history could be found locally, not just nationally.

Local history, however we choose to define it, was a feature of nineteenth-century middle-class culture, particularly provincial as opposed to metropolitan culture. It highlighted the relationship of region to nation in an age when civic pride and local identities were more marked than today. The great county histories may have had their day, but the county societies provided a more than adequate substitute. Yet the antiquary was marginalised as he struggled to keep up with the increased information available in specialist areas such as geology, philology, architectural history and, particularly, archaeology. Gradually these came to be viewed as separate areas of study in their own right, but what was left tended to be viewed rather patronisingly as pedantry, a futile accumulation of the detritus of the past.

This attitude became increasingly problematic as the study of history as a discipline became professionalised, and evolved into a distinct university subject. The professional community viewed the societies as dabbling in issues which were of little or no interest to real historians, who wrote about the nation, the rise of England, the state, and politicians. They researched and wrote in order to recover and preserve the nation's heritage, and they saw their subject as relevant for educating the governors and administrators of future generations. Today we would reverse this order, to argue much as the eighteenth-century antiquarians did, that the nation and its history are the sum of its parts. Yet, at the time, the trend was to brand antiquaries as amateur (i.e. unpaid) students of localities and, by implication, methodologically weak. By contrast, the professionals developed their methodologies and guarded their standards.

Since the most obvious 'historical' work of the antiquaries had been the county histories, succeeded in turn by annual transactions and proceedings, where material remains and manuscript sources were often treated alike, it is perhaps not surprising that professional historians wanted to distance themselves from this type of writing. It simply did not fit the new ethos. In time, the work of the antiquaries came to be viewed as what was left when the subject specialisms over which it had believed itself to hold a proverbial umbrella left it high and dry. By the 1880s, antiquaries were increasingly marginalised. Whatever Dr John Beddoe may have believed when he told the Bristol and Gloucestershire Archaeological Society in 1876 that they would be engaging in research not frolicking in 'junketings and picnics', antiquarians were considered insufficiently rigorous, generalists when professional historians and archaeologists were becoming specialists. In this context, the study of the past at the local level was to suffer in the first half of the twentieth century.

Notes

1 Peter Clark, *British Clubs and Societies, 1580–1800: The Origins of an Associational World* (2000), 473.
2 R.J. Morris, 'Clubs, societies and associations', in F.M.L. Thompson (ed.), *The Cambridge Social History of Britain, 1750–1950*, 3 (1990), 405–9.
3 J. Seed, 'From "middling sort" to middle-class in late eighteenth and early nineteenth-century England', in M.L. Bush (ed.), *Social Order and Social Classes in Europe since 1500* (1992), 132–4.
4 George Jobey, 'The Society of Antiquaries of Newcastle upon Tyne', *Archaeologia Aeliana*, 5th series, 18 (1990), 197–216.
5 *ECH*, 56, 148, 192, 251, 275–6, 285, 334, 390; Philippa Levine, *The Amateur and the Professional: Antiquarians, Historians and Archaeologists in Victorian England, 1838–86* (1986), 61; Stuart Piggott, 'The origins of the English county archaeological societies', in *Ruins in a Landscape. Essays in Antiquarianism* (1976), 171–95.
6 *ECH*, 56, 285–6; A. Hamilton Thompson, *The Surtees Society, 1834–1934* (Surtees Society, 90, 1939).
7 F.J. Levy, 'The founding of the Camden Society', *Victorian Studies*, 7 (1964), 295–305; A.G. Crosby, '*A society with no equal': The Chetham Society, 1843–1993* (1993); V.I. Tomlinson, 'The Lancashire and Cheshire Antiquarian Society, 1883–1983', *Transactions of the Lancashire and Cheshire Antiquarian Society*, 83 (1985), 1–39; A.J. Kidd, 'Between antiquary and academic: local history in the nineteenth century', in Richardson, 97–9, also published in *LH*, 26/1 (1996).
8 Stephen Porter, *Exploring Urban History* (1990), 16.
9 Terence R. Leach, 'Edward Trollope and the Lincoln Diocesan Architectural Society', in C. Sturman (ed.), *Some Historians of Lincolnshire* (1992), 13–26.
10 *ECH*, 101, 128, 160; E.L.C. Mullins, *A Guide to the Historical and Archaeological Publications of Societies in England and Wales, 1901–33* (1968)
11 Elizabeth Ralph, 'The Society 1876–1976', in Patrick McGrath and John Cannon (eds), *Essays in Bristol and Gloucestershire History* (1976), 3.

12 H.H. Walker, 'Centenary Lecture: the story of the Devonshire Association, 1862–1962', *Transactions of the Devonshire Association*, 94 (1962), 42–52.

13 J.W. Jackson, 'Genesis and progress of the Lancashire and Cheshire Antiquarian Society', *Transactions of the Lancashire and Cheshire Antiquarian Society*, 99 (1933), 104–12; A.J. Kidd, 'Between antiquary and academic', 94–109.

14 Ralph, 'The Society 1876–1976', 1–5.

15 Richardson, 101–2, 107.

16 A.C. Wood, 'Fifty years of the Transactions', *Transactions of the Thoroton Society*, 50 (1946), 1–12; John Beckett (ed.), *The Thoroton Society: a Commemoration of its First 100 Years* (1997).

17 *ECH*, 35, 205.

18 Richardson, 95; F.T. Mott and T. Carter (eds), *The Transactions of the Leicester Literary and Philosophical Society from June 1835 to June 1879* (1884).

19 Richardson, 94–109.

20 Ralph, 'The Society 1876–1976', 8; Levine, *Amateur and Professional*; http://www.britarch.ac.uk/baa, June 2006.

21 Sweet, *Antiquaries*, 1–5.

22 J.D. Cantwell, *The Public Record Office 1838–1958* (1991).

23 G.H. Martin and P. Spufford (eds), *The Records of the Nation: The Public Record Office, 1838–1988; The British Record Society, 1888–1988* (1990).

24 J.W. Burrow, 'Victorian historians and the Royal Historical Society', *Transactions of the Royal Historical Society*, 5th series, 39 (1989), 125–40; S. Collini, *Public Moralists: Political Thought and Intellectual Life in Britain 1850–1930* (1991), 216–21.

25 Llewellyn Woodward, 'The rise of the professional historian in England', in K. Bourne and D.C. Watt (eds), *Studies in International History* (1967).

26 *English Historical Review*, 1 (1886), 3; Paul Readman, 'The place of the past in English culture, c.1890–1914', *Past and Present*, 186 (2005), 147–200; idem., 'Landscape preservation, "advertising disfigurement", and English national identity, c.1890–1914', *Rural History*, 12 (2001), 61–83; Catherine Brace, 'Looking back: the Cotswolds and English national identity, c.1890–1950', *Journal of Historical Geography*, 25 (1999), 502–16.

27 H.H. Howarth, 'Old and new methods of writing history, being the opening address of the historical section at the Dorchester meeting', *Archaeological Journal*, 55 (1898), 122–44.

28 Quoted in H.P.R. Finberg, 'Local History', in H.P.R. Finberg (ed.), *Approaches to History* (1962), 111.

29 Wood, 'Fifty Years', 87.

30 Levine, *Amateur and Professional*, 173–4.

31 Levine, *Amateur and Professional*; A. Brundage, *The People's Historian: J.R. Green and the Writing of History in Victorian England* (1994).

32 See J.W. Burrow, *A Liberal Descent – Victorian Historians and the English Past* (1981), 179–80.

33 Anon, 'Proceedings', *Transactions of the Lancashire and Cheshire Antiquarian* Society, 2 (1884), 152, 160.
34 Quoted in A.C. Wood, 'Local history', *Transactions of the Thoroton Society*, 49 (1945), 84.
35 J. Simmons (ed.), *English County Historians* (1978), 1.
36 Levine, *Amateur and Professional*, chapter 2.
37 *ECH*, 56, 66–7, 405–6.
38 Ibid., 160–1.
39 Wood, 'Fifty Years'.

VI *Local history and national history, 1880–1945*

Between the 1880s and the Second World War local history enjoyed something of a schizophrenic existence. The societies flourished, turning out record series volumes and annual transactions, touring their counties (transferring from 'brakes' to motor buses in the process), and attracting new members to join in their research sections. In other words, they continued the associational tradition in the form established during the nineteenth century. Archaeologists maintained links with the societies, participating in, and keeping track of, the local digs organised by the societies. By contrast, historians, mindful of Professor Freeman's suggestion in 1884, maintained a lofty distance, while always hoping that relevant illustrations would be found to help with the business of writing national history. Local history flourished, but at the same time it was frowned upon, hence the schizophrenia. We can identify three consequences. First, professional historians working in a local context had to justify their work in national terms, because their findings could be used only to test nationally conceived ideas and arguments relating to politics, constitutional matters, and the government of the state. Even the Victoria County History had to be justified in terms of the national framework, and researched in the national archives. The exception to this generalisation was in the newly-formed discipline of economic history. The second consequence was that the county societies operated in isolation from the mainstream of academic history, although often with tacit if not implicit support from professional scholars. The third, slightly more problematic consequence, was that the subject made relatively little progress in methodological terms.

The study of the village

Marginalisation made little or no sense, but for reasons which were not necessarily obvious to contemporaries. The first of these was connected to the study of the village. In the late-1870s England entered what turned out to be a long period of agricultural depression, which came to an end only with the Second World War. This posed obvious questions for economists, but equally it raised interesting new questions for historians. Marx, Arnold Toynbee and others argued that from about 1760 England had gone through an agricultural revolution, and that the essence of that revolution had been the destruction of open field farming, the enclosure of commons and wastelands, and the consolidation of small farms into large ones to produce an efficient agricultural sector which fed a growing population. But where and when, it was asked, had the open fields originated, and what was the significance of enclosure both in the sixteenth and nineteenth centuries? If these questions could be answered it might be possible to understand more clearly why a seemingly efficient post-1760 agricultural system had apparently become highly inefficient. The key to unlocking this particular question seemed to be the 'village community'. If this could be properly understood, the longer term development of agriculture might become clearer.

The importance of the village was initially stressed in the 1850s, particularly in relation to European communities. Two early studies were those of Erwin Nasse, first published in German in 1869 and in English in 1877, and Sir Henry Maine's *Village Communities* of 1871. Maine argued that the original form of landownership and cultivation had been the co-proprietorship of self-governing village communes. While some commentators branded him – much to his horror – as an agrarian radical, because his book lent support to the land nationalisation movement, he argued that the study of the English village was vital for an understanding of what had happened to rural society in the later decades of the nineteenth century.[1] His work was closely followed by Frederic Seebohm's *The English Village Community*, published in 1883. Seebohm attended Maine's original lectures, and he also accepted that the village had to be viewed in the long term. Where the two scholars parted company was over origins: Maine argued for the concept of an early medieval village community, while Seebohm traced the communal features of medieval agriculture to the Roman *villa*.[2]

Seebohm saw his work as that of an economic historian: 'to learn the meaning of the old order of things, with its "community" and "equality" as a key to a right understanding of the new order of things, with its contrasting independence and inequality'.[3] Like Maine, and other late nineteenth-century historians, including F.W. Maitland and Paul Vinogradoff, he saw in the study of the village community a way of understanding and coming to terms with the problems of his own society.[4] Vinogradoff worked originally on feudal relations in Lombard Italy after graduating at Moscow University in 1875, but he came to London in 1883, and from his work in England's medieval archives came studies of feudal tenure and the development of the manor.[5]

The work of these historians from Maine to Vinogradoff was not about politics and nation states. Like all good history at the time, it was thoroughly grounded in the sources, but these were often local rather than national records. Similar studies continued in one form or another beyond the First World War, notably in C.S. Orwin's study of Laxton. This Nottinghamshire village had come to be recognised as the only place where open fields survived in the context of a functioning manor court, and consequently it was seen as a suitable subject for investigation in the hope of finding answers to some of the agrarian issues then under discussion.[6] Other historians, recognising that the study of the village was producing useful new insights about the state of rural society more generally, began to look at questions concerning the origins of England's towns and boroughs. Maitland's *Domesday Book and Beyond* was not just a study of medieval Cambridge, but a pioneer of urban history when it appeared in 1897–98.[7]

The irony in all this, was that professional historians in the universities were so concerned with states and nations, that they were marginalising local history just at the time when it was becoming clear that careful study of the locality was an important means of understanding national issues. Of course, this emphasis on the local as the key to understanding broader historical issues, reversed the Freeman doctrine that saw local history only as illustrating the wider issues on which professional historians had pronounced. Not surprisingly, it cut little ice with the professional historical world. The view that local history was useful only in the service of national history had other consequences, of which the most obvious was its absence from the mainstream of higher education history teaching as the university sector expanded in the twentieth century. The first formal act of recognition of local historical studies by a university was at the University of Reading, which in 1908 instituted a research fellowship in the subject for Frank Stenton. Many of the subjects he researched were essentially on local themes and depended on exploring local material, but Stenton did not regard himself primarily as a local historian, and when he was promoted to a chair in 1912 the fellowship was allowed to lapse.[8] Local history developed instead in the context of the new discipline of economic history and, within universities, adult education.

Economic history, local history and adult education

Economic history is often dated from Arnold Toynbee's *Lectures on the Industrial Revolution in England*, published in the 1880s, but until the First World War it was considered to be largely an offshoot of economics. Subsequently, until the 1960s, it developed a stronger orientation towards history through the Workers Educational Association and the extramural departments of universities. R.H. Tawney (1880–1962) contributed to the debate about the English village with his book *The Agrarian Problem in the Sixteenth Century* (1912). He wrote in the preface that in his view economic history should shed light on the presuppositions about social expedience which influenced statesmen and humble individuals alike. His interest in the humble individuals led to a lifelong involvement with the WEA, notably through pioneer classes in Longton in Staffordshire and Rochdale in Lancashire. Partly as a result of his influence, economic history developed with a strong sense of place, whether in relation to local, urban, county, or regional roots.[9] Local people wanted to hear about national history in its *local* context, in contrast to university undergraduates who were taught that local history was relevant only as an exemplar of national history.

The result of this growing interest in economic history at the local level can be seen in studies published during the inter-war years. One of Tawney's students at Rochdale was A.P. Wadsworth, editor of the *Manchester Guardian*, a local man with serious academic credentials. Throughout the inter-war years he was publishing scholarly articles on different aspects of the history of Rochdale and its surrounding area in the *Transactions of the Rochdale Literary and Scientific Society*. Wadsworth's interests ranged through coal mining, the woollen trade, pre-parliamentary enclosure, and the development of industrial workshops in the area.[10] His major book, *The Cotton Trade and Industrial Lancashire, 1600–1780*, was jointly written with Julia de Lacy Mann, Principal of St Hilda's College, Oxford, and published in 1931. G.H. Tupling's work on the agrarian history and industry of Rossendale, Lancashire, was another pioneering local study in the economic history tradition. Tupling wrote the book because he wanted to know why and how a domestic woollen industry was superseded by the factory cotton industry.[11] Like Wadsworth, Tupling was a regular contributor to local journals, particularly articles in *Transactions of the Lancashire and Cheshire Antiquarian Society* on the early modern history of Lancashire, markets and fairs, the early metal trades, and the beginnings of engineering. Another pioneering book to come out of Lancashire was Frank Walker's *Historical Geography of Southwest Lancashire before the Industrial Revolution* (1939) which examined how the different physical geographies of south-west and south-east Lancashire had influenced their histories.[12]

Similar studies in other areas included H. Heaton's *The Yorkshire Woollen and Worsted Industry* (1920), A.H. Dodd, *The Industrial Revolution in North Wales* (1933), and W.H.B. Court, *The Rise of the Midland Industries, 1600–1838* (1938). These scholars tended to be outside of universities, or like Tawney to spend much time beyond their boundaries. L.L. Price, Reader in Economic History at Oxford 1907–22, seems from his surviving papers to have 'spent most of his time either lecturing or examining away from the university'.[13]

When universities were involved, the link was with their adult education tuition. By 1928 there were ten extension courses in local history outside London: four in Nottingham, three in Cambridge, two in Leeds, and one in Oxford. Hull joined this group in 1930. In Nottingham, local history was promoted through the Department of Adult Education, founded in 1920. David (J.D.) Chambers, who graduated in 1920 from the History department, was immediately appointed staff tutor with responsibility for local history. The awkward relationship between traditional historians and local and economic history – Chambers was to become first Professor of Economic History at Nottingham – is neatly summarised in his early career. In addition to being appointed staff tutor, he started doctoral research. His teaching, together with the influence of Tawney and other WEA tutors, led him in the direction of economic history, and he began work on a thesis, which was eventually completed in 1927 as 'Nottinghamshire in the period of the Industrial Revolution'.

Chambers found his inspiration among the amateur scholars who had attracted Tawney, Price and others into WEA lecturing. In particular, two men, both schoolmasters, influenced Chambers: Arthur Cossons and W.E. (Bill) Tate. The three men shared common interests. Chambers recalled having 'many contacts with both of them' during these years. They made contributions to the book which Chambers wrote on Nottinghamshire. Tate compiled the list of Nottinghamshire enclosures, which served as the prototype for studies of each English county that he assembled during his lifetime.[14] Cossons contributed to Chambers' book a map of transport links into Nottinghamshire. His own work on the county's turnpike roads appeared in 1934, the forerunner of a series of studies in years to come compiled on the same principles (although not quite so extensively as Tate's work on enclosures.[15] His son Sir Neil Cossons, formerly

Director of the Science Museum and Chairman of English Heritage, recalls that 'some of my earliest boyhood memories are of interminable Sunday afternoons when my father's smoke-filled study was also full of "J.D", of Bill Tate, or on occasion both'.[16]

By contrast with these easy relationships, Chambers recognised that the academic community was unlikely to look favourably on his chosen topic, and when in 1932 he turned his thesis into a book, *Nottinghamshire in the Eighteenth Century*, he went to some lengths to meet potential critics who might criticise his failure to write national history. He wrote in the preface that the book was 'essentially an attempt to use local history in the service of general history, and it is addressed to those students and teachers who regard local history in the light of a means, not an end'. He acknowledged that 'the general purpose and the method of this book differ somewhat from those of most other books of its kind'. This was, he argued, because 'it attempts to show the movement of local history during the period preceding the Industrial Revolution on the background of national history, and local material that cannot be related to the facts of national history either as an example of, or as an addition to, existing knowledge has been generally excluded'. Here then was a clear statement of intent, followed with the assertion that 'the study of local history has lately made rapid progress . . . because it brings the student into touch with particular aspects of general history'. And to make sure the point was taken, he added, 'finally, it should be said, this work makes no claim to be a contribution to antiquarian lore'.[17]

Despite this obvious attempt to set the record straight in advance of the main chapters of the book, it is difficult to see quite what Chambers meant, or to believe that his heart was in the preface. Which facts, one would like to know, did he omit because they were not relevant to general history? In reality the book is a sound scholarly study of Nottinghamshire, set in the context of economic history as it was understood in the 1920s. What it lacks is any discussion of the towns, and a chapter on transport was omitted for reasons of space, but this hardly amounts to censorship on behalf of national history. Chambers undoubtedly recognised the ambiguity in writing local history purely in the service of general history, doubtless because of the influence on him of amateur scholars.

Nor is it surprising that Chambers seems to have endured an uneasy arrangement with his Nottingham supervisor, the Oxford-trained historian Leonard Owen, who understood history in the context of the nation. Two cultures had developed, and where they came into conflict there was no real meeting of minds. A.C. Wood, another member of the Nottingham History department, edited *Transactions of the Thoroton Society* from the 1920s to the 1950s, and he was aware that fellow professionals might disapprove of his editorial berth. In an article he published in 1945, he inadvertently revealed just how aware he was of the need to protect his back: 'it is a sound principle for the local historian *always* . . . to see that his work fits into the larger frame of national history, *never to forget* that his county or town forms part of a greater unit'.[18] What this meant in practical terms was vividly demonstrated by Wood in his *History of Nottinghamshire*, published in 1947. Although conceived as a single volume history of the county from the Romans onwards, its structure owed nothing to Dugdale or the concerns of economic historians. It was, in fact, no more nor less than national history written in a local context. Consequently chapter headings included 'Baronial Turbulence and the Monastic Revival', 'The Reigns of Henry II and his sons', 'Tudor Nottinghamshire', and 'The Early Georges'. Even more oddly, or so it seems today, the book ended somewhat abruptly with the 1832 Reform Act because, or so Wood claimed, 'it is hardly possible after 1832 to isolate county history for separate treatment'. In his view 'henceforth the history of Nottinghamshire was inseparable from that of the larger unit, nation and empire, to which it belonged'. Wood's version of county history was reflected in the subject matter, with an emphasis on political, religious and administrative issues. There was little on trade and industry, and hardly anything on the lives of the ordinary inhabitants of the county. For Wood national history and professional history were one and the same thing, but the vital point here is not that local history could be seen as contributing to national history, but that it was accepted *only* in this role.

Nor was Wood being oversensitive to the likely criticisms of his fellow professionals. In 1948, giving his inaugural lecture at Leicester University, Professor Jack Simmons argued that 'a true understanding of England's past can be attained only by studying local and national history side by side. It is clearly not useful to embark on a study of local history wholly by itself, with the county or town or village one is examining for one's widest horizon'.[19] Simmons, like Wood, was reflecting a line of thinking that hardly changed before 1945, in which local history was regarded as serving a means to a national end. Wood emphasised this subordinate role when he wrote that 'it enables us, piece by piece, to check or correct the sweeping statements of those who handle the wider field'.[20] Among professional historians, local history was saddled with justifying itself in national terms, if it was to be justified at all.

The Victoria County History

The relationship between local history and economic rather than political history was also apparent with the founding in 1899 of the Victoria History of the Counties of England, known from that day to this as the Victoria County History or, colloquially, the VCH. The VCH was not conceived as local history, but as a contribution to national history through the study of local communities. In turn, this form of study reflected late nineteenth-century ideas about writing a definitive unified account of the history of humanity. These were the years of what we would today call mega-projects, such as the original *Dictionary of National Biography*, started in 1882 under Leslie Stephen's editorship, to write brief biographies of notable British people for what was announced as a *Biographia Britannica*. It was completed by 1900, but supplements were added through the twentieth century until it ran to 36,000 entries and about thirty-three million words.[21] A similar project was the New English Dictionary, sponsored by Oxford University Press. The VCH had similar hopes, including a 'modern Domesday' listing all owners of estates of five acres or more, and architectural descriptions of all the major buildings alongside the topographical histories. In fact, the domesday was never undertaken, and listing of buildings became less significant with the foundation in 1908 of the Royal Commission on Historical Monuments.[22] Yet it is not surprising in this optimistic atmosphere to find the founding fathers claiming that 'owing to the thoroughness of the work, it is safe to say that it is a definite finality in English local history, and that *its value will not diminish*'.[23]

The overall plan for the VCH envisaged two types of volume for each county: general volumes with chapters on natural history (including geology), pre-history, Roman and Anglo-Saxon remains, ethnography, Domesday Books, architecture, natural history and earthworks. They were to include a transcription of Domesday entries, and to have sections on political, ecclesiastical, maritime, economic and social history (including archaeology, education, industry, sport, architecture and population). There were also to be topographical volumes giving accounts of the history of each parish, topic by topic. Each volume was to include maps. This was perhaps a little too optimistic. Ethnography was never covered, and few general articles on architecture were published, but some new subjects were included from time to time, including schools by 1901. The intention was to provide every county, and each parish through the topographical volumes, with an authoritative history, with these histories representing, collectively, the history of England. The driving force behind the VCH, Herbert Arthur Doubleday (1867–1941), suggested that the collective account of the localities would provide 'a National Survey . . . tracing . . . the story of England's growth . . . into a nation which is now the greatest on the globe'.[24]

Doubleday planned a new history of each county, to a uniform scheme, employing professional specialists to write general chapters, and other staff to compile the topographical volumes. The number of proposed volumes ranged from eight for Yorkshire to two for Rutland. London was included within Middlesex. The overall plan envisaged 160 volumes, to be researched, written and published in six years. Somewhat optimistically, Doubleday anticipated a profit of £250,000.

Some counties had their own editors, including the distinguished local historian R.S. Ferguson in Cumberland, founding editor of the Cumberland and Westmorland Antiquarian and Archaeological Society in 1866, and William Farrer in Lancashire. Farrer seems to have agreed to abandon a scheme of his own for a Lancashire history in order to work with the VCH, and eight volumes were produced 1906–14. Ferguson planned a four-volume history, with himself as editor and contributor, although he died in 1900 before any of the volumes were printed, and his place was taken by Canon James Wilson, vicar of Dalston, a medievalist, who saw two volumes into print in 1901 and 1905.[25]

Since it was recognised that the county histories of earlier generations had made mistakes which were all too often recycled, the intention was that these new studies should be written from original sources. Doubleday appointed subject editors to write or organise the writing on topics in which they were specialists, and the intention was that they should contribute on their subject for each county. Hercules Read and Reginald Smith were appointed editors for 'Anglo-Saxon remains'. For the parish studies, the abortive Lincolnshire project, whereby Bishop Wordsworth wanted his clergy to write the individual parish entries, suggested how future schemes might progress.[26] However, in Lincolnshire, Rev. William Oswald Massingberd, Rector of South Ormsby, complained that 'we have a large county, a huge mass of records, very little done, & very few workers', although he subsequently became the driving force behind the VCH in the county, and it collapsed with his death in 1910.[27] Rev. J.C. Cox, whose parochial history guide was the basis of much VCH work in the early years, was a firm supporter of the VCH in Derbyshire, for which two volumes were published in 1905 and 1907. This success may have been to the disgust of another local antiquary, John Pym Yeatman, who condemned the VCH as 'a wild project, doomed sooner or later to utter failure'.[28]

The problem with employing the clergy was that they lacked the money, if not the time, to search the records in London. Those with the means would often employ one of the record agencies which grew up in the capital, and Doubleday decided that record searching needed to be centrally organised if progress on the VCH was to be maintained. He used Hardy and Page, a leading London record agency firm. William Page (1861–1934) was soon brought into the structure of the VCH, partly to supervise and train the female historians and classicists recruited by the agency to search the archives. Once they had done the research it made sense for them to draft parish histories. Not everyone appreciated the role of women in the VCH. In 1904 the Secretary of the Public Record Office wrote to the general editor of the VCH complaining about 'the presence of so many ladies employed on the *Victoria County History* . . . [who were] causing great inconvenience to the general public'.[29] Their potted histories were checked by local editors. In 1904 Page became sole editor, a post he retained until his death.

In a number of respects VCH volumes were progressive, laying considerable emphasis on archaeology, having sections on economic history, and insisting on official records being methodically searched and buildings scientifically examined. At the same time, the project had a distinctly dated feel, seemingly being aimed at 'the country house and parsonage market for local history'.[30] Local committees were set up in each county, and bore all the hallmarks of a Victorian society. They were usually headed by an aristocrat – preferably the lord lieutenant – or a bishop. In Devon the initiative was taken by Sir Roger Lethbridge, who sought out the lord lieutenant, Lord Clinton, at the Hotel Metropole in Cannes, to persuade him to take a lead. An impressive local committee was formed, although few if any of the members were capable of contributing to the project except in the form of cash, which never materialised in any quantity.[31] The role of the local committee was to raise money, seek out local editors and contributors, and 'gain access to private collections of MSS'.[32] As such, the whole VCH scheme was designed to appeal to the local gentry in much the same way that the earlier generation of county historians had done. The 1904 manifesto emphasised how it was a private enterprise founded on an appeal to the local patriotism of those seen as potential sponsors and patrons. By subscribing in advance, they would have their names included in the last volume for the county, to preserve for all time the record of their patronage.[33]

Work on the VCH got off to a flying start. The first volume, on Hampshire, appeared in 1900, eleven had come out by the end of 1904, and a further twenty-seven were published between 1905 and 1907. This was good progress, but counties were not necessarily as pliable as Doubleday and Page might have hoped. In Northamptonshire, the county committee began by arguing that Morton's transcription of the Northamptonshire section of Domesday Book had been 'carelessly executed'; that Bridges' work had been completed before many sources were known and before the advent of a scientific approach to historical development; and of Baker's work they claimed that only a fragment remained. Consequently all the previous histories were discounted, and work started from scratch. Volume 1, published in 1902, dealt with natural history and early man through to the Northampton Survey of the twelfth century. Volume 2, published in 1906, covered ecclesiastical history, religious houses, early Christian art, schools, industries, forestry, sport and ancient earthworks. This was not untypical.

By 1907 the VCH was running into some of the problems which had beset the county historians, particularly problems of finance. Page was forced to look for economies, so he dropped the articles on feudal baronage, and decided to use junior workers to write general chapters, so avoiding the delays of concentrating authorship in the hands of a few experts. The experts were now simply to vet the work undertaken by others. Page still hoped to see around sixteen volumes published yearly, but the project was in trouble and work had to stop. Financial support organised through the publisher W.H. Smith saw a revival in 1910. Eight volumes were issued in 1911 and fourteen more in the three succeeding years, so that 74 were in print by 1914. Among the nine counties completed by 1914 was Bedfordshire, in three volumes 1904–12, with an index 1914. It owed much to the eighteenth-century tradition of the scientific study of the local environment with sections in volume 1 (1904) on geology and natural history as well as prehistory, Anglo-Saxon archaeology, Domesday, ecclesiastical history, and religious houses. The hundreds and parishes were handled in volumes 2 and 3. Berkshire also finished before the First World War.[34]

Although dated to our eyes, in their own time VCH volumes broke new ground with their chapters on economic and social history and industries. They were based on research in public and private archives, and included major chapters written by well-known local antiquaries. For the two Nottinghamshire volumes (1907 and 1910) William Stevenson wrote on earthworks, Rev. J.C. Cox on religious houses and forests, and Frank Stenton on Domesday. Sections were also written by paid research assistants. They were often women, and Miss Hewitt and Miss Locke were acknowledged in the Nottinghamshire volumes. As with Nottinghamshire, a number of other counties also managed one or two volumes before 1914, including Cornwall, Essex (where J.H. Round was prominent in editing and writing the two volumes published in 1903 and 1907), Gloucestershire, Herefordshire, Lincolnshire, Norfolk, Suffolk, and Surrey. Suffolk set up a county committee in 1907 consisting of local nobility, gentry, mayors and leading churchmen together with several practising historians. Two volumes appeared in 1907 and 1911, partly researched by Lillian Redstone, but nothing further has taken place. Surrey managed four volumes 1904–12, with an index in 1914.[35]

Hampshire, the first county to be completed, ran to five volumes when it was finished in 1914, Hertfordshire to four and Lancashire to eight. Buckinghamshire was completed 1905–28 in five volumes.[36] County Durham produced volumes in 1905, 1907 and 1928, the latter covering the city of Durham and the south-eastern portion of the pre-1974 county. Various contributions were complete when publication was suspended. Three general volumes on Kent were published 1908–32, and Northamptonshire produced volumes in 1902, 1906 (two), 1930 – with sponsorship from James Manfield, the shoe manufacturer and local philanthropist – and 1937.[37] Other counties made less progress. In Cheshire work began in 1904 on a series of four volumes. Various chapters were written on natural history, geology, forestry and agriculture, as well as contributions on ecclesiastical history and religious houses, but work was abandoned, some typescripts were returned, and others lost.[38] At one time the whole project seemed in danger, and in 1920 completed but unpublished articles were returned to their authors, which is why Sir Frank Stenton's introduction to the Lincolnshire Domesday eventually appeared in 1924 as part of the Lincolnshire Record Society's edition.[39] Having survived the post-war crisis, in 1932 the VCH became part of London University's Institute of Historical Research.

Huntingdonshire was alone in producing the whole series during the inter-war years, 1926–38. Some general articles were written before 1909, but work restarted only in 1924 when Granville Proby (1883–1947) agreed to underwrite it, and a number of contributors were signed up to bring about a collaborative enterprise. Sussex began with two volumes 1905–7. Four topographical volumes followed between 1935 and 1953. Warwickshire volumes appeared in 1904 and 1908, but not again until in 1935 the county was selected for a pilot project. Subventions from the county and borough councils allowed the appointment of Philip Styles in 1937 as part-time topographical editor. Five volumes followed and in 1969 the series was completed. Five Worcestershire volumes were published 1901–26.[40]

In April 1938 the 100th volume of the VCH appeared, with no sign of Doubleday's anticipated profit. It was sixty volumes short of the original plan, it was already thirty years overdue, and it was suffering the same problems as local history more generally in terms of its acceptance within the community. Since, as far as the academic community was concerned, anyone working within a local context, or a recognisably non-national context, had to justify their approach in terms of the national agenda, the VCH had to adopt an unhappy compromise. It emphasised the importance of the national archives for the study of the parish. Researchers worked in the Public Record Office, and successive editions of Cox's booklet on how to write a parish history emphasised the importance of documents in the *national* archives. The last of these editions, the sixth, appeared in 1954, and was in reality a complete rewrite by R.B. Pugh, the general editor of the VCH. Pugh emphasised the standard VCH way to write a parish history, with significant emphasis on the public and printed record sources. Half of his book was devoted to a commentary on public records, but he did then note that 'the county record office ought to be a frequent place of resort for every parish historian'.[41]

This balance would not have seemed unusual in the inter-war years. H.M. Barron's *Your Parish History: How to Discover and Write it* (1930), took a similarly top-down approach in terms of the records and, like Cox, stopped in the seventeenth century. Joan Wake's *How to Compile a History and Present-Day Record of Village Life* (1925), was 'written for the Women's Institutes of Northamptonshire'. It discussed church and county records, but also included sections on the Public Record Office, the British Library and the Bodleian Library. The stress was on the importance of public records, and in an era when there were still relatively few local record offices this was not entirely surprising. Yet there were signs that local history could stand on its feet without being seen purely contributing to national history. The Historical Association had started producing local bibliographies before the First World War. In 1925 it formed a Village History Committee, and in 1928–29 this became the Local History Committee. It produced a local history bibliography. Then, in 1938, the National Council of Social Service began publishing a series of local history leaflets through a sub-committee which became the Standing Conference for Local History in 1948, the predecessor of the modern British Association for Local History. These green shoots would burst into flower after 1945.

Record publishing

Record publishing flourished between 1880 and 1945. The Hampshire Record Society was founded in 1888, and the Bedfordshire County Records Committee was established in 1898 to take steps to preserve the records then kept in the county muniment room at Shire Hall. Various extracts from these were published in 1907–11. The Thoroton Society began a *Record Series* in 1903 with an edition of seventeenth-century Bishops' Transcripts, but subsequently, and as with similar series in other counties, there has been a particular strength in medieval materials. The Devon and Cornwall Record Society was set up in 1904, record publishing began in the early years of the twentieth century in Middlesex, the Bedfordshire Historical Record Society began publishing in 1913, and the Norfolk Record Society dates from 1930.[42] Professional historians were happy to be associated with record societies, which enjoyed academic respect from the time of their formation in Victorian England. In Lincolnshire, the importance of the Cathedral and the diocese of Lincoln, attracted numerous scholars to active membership of the Record Society, founded in 1910 by Canon Charles Wilmer Foster (1866–1935). He was personally associated with one of the most important volumes produced by the Record Society in the early years, *Lincolnshire Domesday and the Lindsey Survey* (1924). The introduction, written by Stenton, was originally intended for the VCH. Foster was also a driving force behind the establishment of the Lincolnshire Record Office, which involved persuading four independent authorities, the City of Lincoln and the three county divisions, to entrust their records to the dean and chapter, ultimately to become the archives office.[43]

Stenton, as a professional historian, saw his interests in a national context, although he had roots in Nottinghamshire where he had a house at Southwell. But his work on Lincolnshire was important, and Kathleen Major – herself an academic historian with strong Lincolnshire roots and contacts – has written that Stenton's 'continuous interest [as] one of the most eminent historians in the country was of great value to a local society'.[44] Another outsider with academic credentials who played an important part in the Lincolnshire societies was Professor Alexander Hamilton Thomson (1873–1952), who, significantly, had begun his teaching career as an extra-mural lecturer at Cambridge. After the First World War he taught at Newcastle, and then at Leeds, where he held the Chair of History from 1924 until his retirement in 1939.[45] Ultimately these historians had links to record societies because they published material which would be of value to the historian of the nation, even if the records themselves were primarily local.

Although the record societies were the guardians of publishing, many other sources were put into print by private and public bodies. Independent record publishing ventures in Nottinghamshire included Robert White's *Dukery Records*, published in 1904, while Nottingham Corporation took it upon itself to publish extracts from its own records. The first volume of *Records of the Borough of Nottingham*, edited by William Stevenson and covering the period 1155 to 1339, appeared in 1882, and a further five volumes were published before the First World War. The series eventually ran to nine volumes covering the period to 1900. Other authorities also put part or all of their records into print.

A slightly different initiative was that taken by W.P.W. Phillimore. The son of a Nottingham doctor, he took the name Phillimore from the family of his maternal grandmother, and after education at Oxford he became a successful London lawyer. But his passion was records. He was a lifelong campaigner for records preservation. He believed that the original documents should be conserved, but that access should be made easier by the printing of transcripts. To this end he founded the British Record Society in 1888, and wrote a letter to *The Times* advocating the provision of county record offices by the new county councils, the first use of the term. He sent clerks and volunteers around the country to transcribe parish records. At his death in 1914 he had covered 1,200 parishes from many counties in 200 volumes.[46] The best known were the Phillimore Marriage Registers series. Phillimore wrote, edited and published local and family histories for many years before he established Phillimore and Co in 1897. To popularise amateur interest he wrote *How to Write the History of a Family*. The company continued to operate after his death. In the 1960s it was acquired by Dr Marc Fitch, re-financed and re-located in Chichester to provide more space and reduce overheads.[47] Phillimore was also a founder of the Canterbury and York Society.

Between about 1880 and the Second World War, professional historians saw themselves researching and writing the history of the nation from the public records. They might join, and play a major role in the societies, particularly the record societies, but their interest in local history went only as far as searching for suitable examples to illustrate national history. The Public Record Office was their laboratory, and the *English Historical Review* their scholarly journal. Local history stagnated intellectually, and its flag was kept fluttering only through the local societies, and Adult Education and WEA classes. The subject matter of local history was recognised either as national history at the local level, as with Wood's *Nottinghamshire*, or the study of places through their economic history, exemplified in the work of Wadsworth, Heaton, Chambers and others. Moving the subject on was complicated by the problems faced by the would-be researcher. The emphasis on the national archives in the Public Record Office was partly a simple practical issue; indeed, Chambers' work on Nottinghamshire demonstrated the problem of accessing the local sources which were critical to an understanding of local societies. His book was based on a combination of secondary sources, printed records, and some primary sources, but he does not seem to have had access to private papers, and one of the problems facing local historians before 1945 was to locate and gain access to local primary sources. It was not until after the Second World War the great majority of counties had a record office, and it was only when a new range of material became available that local history took on new dimensions and began to escape the stigma with which it had been cursed since the late nineteenth century.

Notes

1 E. Nasse, *On the Agricultural Community of the Middle Ages, and Inclosures of the Sixteenth Century in England* (1872); H. Maine, *Village Communities in the East and West* (7th edn, 1895).

2 F. Seebohm, *The English Village Community, Examined in its Relations to the Manorial and Tribal Systems and to the Common or Open Field System of Husbandry* (4th edn, 1905).

3 Seebohm, *English Village Community*, vii.

4 J.W. Burrow, ' "The Village Community" and the uses of history in late nineteenth-century England', in N. McKendrick (ed.), *Historical Perspectives. Studies in English Thought and Society* (1974), 255–84.

5 P. Vinogradoff, *Villainage in England* (1892); *The Growth of the Manor* (2nd edn, 1911).

6 C.S. and C.S. Orwin, *The History of Laxton* (1935); idem, *The Open Fields* (1938). For subsequent studes: J.D. Chambers, 'The open fields of Laxton', *Transactions of the Thoroton Society*, 32 (1928), 102–25; J.V. Beckett, *A History of Laxton: England's Last Open Field Village* (1989); Philippa Venn, 'Exceptional Eakring: Nottinghamshire's other open field parish', *Transactions of the Thoroton Society*, 94 (1990), 69–97.

7 F.W. Maitland, *Domesday Book and Beyond, Township and Borough* (1897).

8 Stenton's local work included the chapter on Domesday in vol. 1 of the Nottinghamshire VCH, part authorship of the *Place Names of*

Nottinghamshire (1940), J.E.B. Gower and Allen Mawer (eds), and *Documents Illustrative of the Social and Economic History of the Danelaw* in the British Academy Records of Social and Economic History series (1920), as well as vol. 18 of the *Lincolnshire Record Society* series in 1922.

9 R.H. Tawney, *The Agrarian Problem in the Sixteenth Century* (1912); Stephen K. Roberts (ed.), *A Ministry of Enthusiasm* (2003), 43–7, 59–76.

10 A.P. Wadsworth, 'The history of the Rochdale woollen trade', *Transactions of the Rochdale Literary and Scientific Society*, 15 (1923–25), 90–110, idem, 'The early factory system in the Rochdale district'. *TRLSS*, 19 (1935–37), 136–56; idem, 'The history of coal mining in Rochdale district', *TRLSS*, 23 (1947–49), 105–13.

11 G.H. Tupling, *The Economic History of Rossendale* (Chetham Society, 86, 1927). Julia de Lacy Mann was not the only woman researching and writing local economic history in these years. Other examples were Gladys Thornton who, on the basis of a Ph.D thesis, wrote *A History of Clare, Suffolk* (1928), which is an introduction to the Suffolk cloth trade; and Mary Lobel, *The Borough of Bury St Edmund's: A Study of the Government and Development of a Monastic Town* (1935); *ECH*, 373.

12 *ECH*, 226.

13 T.C. Barker, 'The beginnings of the Economic History Society', *Economic History Review*, 30 (1977), 3.

14 W.E. Tate, *A Domesday of English Enclosure Acts and Awards* (ed. Michael Turner, 1978). Tate's county handlists are set out, 4–5.

15 A. Cossons, *Coaching Days: The Turnpike Roads of Nottinghamshire* (1994 edn); idem, *The Turnpike Roads of Leicestershire and Rutland* (2003).

16 John Beckett, 'The guardian of the nation's heritage: Sir Neil Cossons, OBE', *East Midland Historian*, 10 (2000), 18–22. Tate and Cossons published six and five articles respectively in *Transactions of the Thoroton Society*. Tate's were mostly on enclosure, and his first book was his handlist of Nottinghamshire enclosures which appeared in the Record Series in 1935: W.E. Tate, *Parliamentary Land Enclosures in the County of Nottingham during the 18th and 19th centuries (1743–1868)* (Thoroton Society Record Series, 5, 1935).

17 J.D. Chambers, *Nottinghamshire in the Eighteenth Century* (2nd edn, 1966), xxiv.

18 A.C. Wood, 'Local History', *Transactions of the Thoroton Society*, 49 (1945), 86. My emphasis. A.C. Wood, *A History of Nottinghamshire* (1947).

19 J. Simmons, *Local, National and Imperial History* (Inaugural Lecture, University of Leicester, 1948, published 1950), 7. This was the first ever inaugural lecture given at University College, Leicester, and Simmons was the first holder of the chair of History.

20 Wood, 'Local History', 86–8; Wood, *History of Nottinghamshire*. Ironically some of A.C. Wood's own work would now be classified as eco-

nomic history, notably his major article of 1951 'The history of trade and transport on the River Trent', *Transactions of the Thoroton Society*, 54 (1950), 1–44.

21 H.C.G. Matthew, *Leslie Stephen and the New Dictionary of National Biography* (1995); Keith Thomas, *Changing Conceptions of National Biography: The Oxford DNB in Historical Perspective* (2005).

22 R.B. Pugh, 'The Victoria History: its origin and progress', in R.B. Pugh (ed.), *General Introduction* (1970), 3; *ECH*, 28–31.

23 From the 1904 manifesto reproduced in C.P. Lewis, *Particular Places: An Introduction to English Local History* (1989), 55.

24 VCH *Hampshire*, I (1900), vii. These claims were in the advertisement printed in what was the first published VCH volume.

25 *ECH*, 102, 224–5.

26 *ECH*, 251–3.

27 *ECH*, 254–5; C. Sturman (ed.), *Some Historians of Lincolnshire* (1992), 42–3.

28 *ECH*, 113.

29 Lewis, *Particular Places*, 54–7.

30 Ibid., 56.

31 *ECH*, 122.

32 Pugh, *Victoria History*.

33 K. Tiller, 'The VCH: past, present and future', *Historian*, 42 (1994), 18.

34 *ECH*, 38, 51.

35 Ibid., 149, 369, 382–3.

36 Ibid., 58.

37 Ibid., 141, 212, 300.

38 Ibid., 82.

39 C.W. Foster and T. Longley (eds), The Lincolnshire Domesday and the Lindsay survey (*Lincoln Record Society*, 19, 1924).

40 *ECH*, 206–7, 392, 408, 428–9.

41 R.B. Pugh, *How to Write a Parish History* (6th edn, 1954), 25.

42 *ECH*, 38–9, 89, 173, 276, 285–6.

43 A personal account of the setting up of the archives, and the personalities involved, is given in F. Hill, 'From Canon Foster to the Lincolnshire Archives Office', *Lincolnshire History and Archaeology*, 13 (1978), 71–3.

44 Sturman, *Some Historians*, 59.

45 Ibid., 55–66.

46 John Beckett (ed.), *The Thoroton Society* (1997), 12.

47 *LH*, 27/2 (1997), rear cover.

VII W.G. *Hoskins and the founding of modern local history*

In the years prior to the Second World War local history struggled to maintain its credibility with the community of professional historians who concerned themselves with politics, the state, and constitutional matters. Local studies were seen as a means of contributing to the understanding of these issues, but in themselves they were considered to have value only as contributions to antiquarian study. Local history gained acceptance only within economic history. After 1945 much was to change. Methodologically the beginnings of a new way of thinking originated in France in the 1920s, in the work of the *Annales* School, and arrived in England after 1945 for a variety of linked reasons, including the founding of the Department of English Local History at Leicester University, the revival of the VCH from its inter-war doldrums, and the opening of many new archive offices (and with them the making available of records not previously in the public domain). If any one person can be said to have driven the new local history, it was W.G. Hoskins, who founded the Leicester department, and who pressed for the subject to be studied in its own right, not as a contribution simply to national history.

The Annales School

The origin of new thinking about local history began not in England but in France, with the founding of what came to be known as the *Annales* school in 1929. *Annales* was the title of a scholarly journal edited by Lucien Febvre and Marc Bloch, which emphasised the importance of an interdisciplinary approach to history. Febvre attacked the narrow empiricists and specialists who had dominated the history profession since the 1880s. He wanted to see problem-oriented history, and an end to the compartmentalisation in which individual historians focused on a particular issue using a carefully chosen body of sources. In Peter Burke's words, the contribution of the early Annalists can be summed up in three themes:

In the first place the substitution of a problem-orientated analytical history for a traditional narrative of events. In the second place, the history of the whole range of human activities in the place of a mainly political history. In the third place – in order to achieve the first two aims – a collaboration with other disciplines: with geography, sociology, psychology, economics, linguistics, social anthropology, and so on.[1]

Put simply, Febvre and Bloch's idea was to guide French historiography away from the minute scientific style it had adopted in the later nineteenth century, towards a wider and more social scientific approach, sometimes described as 'total history', or *histoire totale*. This approach involved integrating the skills and tools of various disciplines such as economics, geography and statistics. The purpose was to try to understand the structures determining the course of history and the evolution of communities.

Fernand Braudel, who followed the founding fathers as editor of *Annales*, went further in his book *The Mediterranean and the Mediterranean World in the Age of Philip II*, published in 1947. He examined the physical and human geography, the economic and social life of the region, its political structures and so forth, although the failure to integrate the approaches meant that the book left something to be desired. Even so, Braudel's achievement was to demonstrate the significance of the *longue durée*, rather than the short case study, and *histoire totale*. Geography was important, because of French ideas about regions, and *histoire totale* also required a thorough ecological examination of the community. This approach was particularly successful in rural history, and *Annales* was linked with a major methodological breakthrough, the use of parish registers to reconstitute the rural family. But it was also the case that by taking the whole of the Mediterranean as his study area, Braudel pointed to some of the weaknesses of the *Annales* approach. It made far more sense to tackle *histoire totale* at the local level. Perhaps the classic study was Emmanuel Le Roy Ladurie's work on the Languedoc peasantry between the fifteenth and eighteenth centuries, which combined historical geography, demography, sociology and economic history.[2]

W.G. Hoskins

The ideas of the Annales school spread from France to England, and were to be particularly important in the field of local history, but the potential needed to be tapped, and one person stands out in this process, Professor William George Hoskins (1908–92). At the age of 23 in 1931 Hoskins was appointed to a lectureship in economics at the then University College, Leicester. His interests at the time were in Devon; indeed his first book, published in 1935, was on Exeter, and his thesis, completed in 1938, was on Devonshire landowners – both topics which fitted easily within the context of economic history during these years. But he spent much of the 1930s learning about, and beginning to understand, Leicestershire. In the process, he began to use documentary sources which were hardly known at the time, such as probate inventories. He also started to understand the importance of archaeology for an appreciation of local history, of settlement patterns, of topography, and of deserted medieval village sites. All of these themes were new in local history, but they reflected the kind of interdisciplinary approach being developed in France. Although some of these disciplines had been touched on by the county historians, Hoskins' contribution was to bring them back on to the agenda and to do so from an academic position. Perhaps it is not surprising to find that his base at Leicester was in Economics rather than History.

Quite how much Hoskins knew of the *Annales* tradition in these years is not clear. His work closely paralleled many of the ideas being developed in France, particularly perhaps Hoskins' reading of contemporary sociologists such as Lewis Mumford, and the influence on him of George Bourne's *Change in the Village* (1912). The great county historians had been chiefly concerned with the governing classes, and their histories lacked farmers, agricultural labourers, blacksmiths and similar 'ordinary' individuals. Historians and archaeologists alike adopted this top-down approach to the past. R.H. Tawney, as a young scholar, thought that the lives of people could not be recreated because the documentary sources simply did not exist:

> What manner of men these were in that personal life of which economics is but the squalid scaffolding . . . we cannot say. Of the hopes and fears and aspirations of the men who tilled the fields . . . we hardly know more than of the Roman plebs, far less than of the democracy of Athens.[3]

Similar problems occurred in archaeology. Before the 1930s professional archaeologists made little attempt to study the homes of medieval peasants, confining themselves almost entirely to grander buildings such as churches and manor houses. Even the vernacular dwelling-houses they did notice were those of a relatively prosperous class. Medieval archaeology 'was almost entirely concerned with the study of the remains of those buildings, erected by the wealthier sectors of the population: principally churches, abbeys, castles and manor houses'.[4]

Hoskins did not accept these constraints; rather, he grew to believe that local historians should study the lost culture of the countryside. By 1940 he was trying to interest students in how people lived in the past, their homes, furnishings, food and drink, standard of health, education, work and amusement, and these concerns later translated into his conceptualisation of a lost society which he believed the historian could and should try to recreate. There were parallels here with the *Annales* school, which had a certain nostalgia for past and predominantly rural societies rather than urban and industrial ones. Hoskins described a form of peasant civilisation, which included the values of thrift, *local* self-reliance and welfare, and localised decision-making. By contrast, the values of country house life, which had been extensively discussed by the county historians, were quite different.

Like Braudel with his concept of the *longue duree*, Hoskins began to search for the origins of modern civilization not in recent times but in the Anglo-Saxon period. He traced the demise of peasant society to the point where it was swept away by eighteenth-century enclosures, which destroyed what he saw as the 'last great bulwark' of the old society, the open fields. These ideas can be found expressed most tellingly in his study of the Leicestershire village of Wigston Magna, published in 1957. The influence of Mumford and Bourne is apparent from Hoskins's picture of a stable peasant society that was destroyed by the parliamentary enclosure act of 1766.[5] 'The reconstruction of this former society', he wrote, was 'the principal theme' of his book. He set out to portray a village with a large group of what he saw as free peasant landowners in the absence of a resident lord, in which the open fields survived when they were disappearing in villages elsewhere in Leicestershire, and in the Midlands more generally through the fifteenth, sixteenth and seventeenth centuries. Enclosure arrived in 1766, and destroyed the old way of life. By 1901:

> The peasant village had been swamped and then submerged completely, and the tide of industrialism rolled on over it unchecked. Fifteen times as many families now lived and got their living off the same area as had done so in the early fourteenth century, at the height of the medieval boom in farming. But a whole culture, a qualitative civilisation, had perished to bring about this quantitative triumph.[6]

In these words the reader can almost feel Hoskins shudder.

While he was developing these views about past societies, Hoskins was also branching out in other directions in his thinking about the local community. He recognised that documentary sources alone did not tell the full story. As with the *Annales* scholars, he realised that to understand the community in its entirety, a much wider range of sources and ideas was needed. Advances in field archaeology, place-name analysis, aerial photography, and the study of maps, were all vital for local historical studies, and Hoskins recognised that geography and anthropology were just as important as historical documents when trying to understand the local community. The first useable aerial photography images were taken between the wars, and began to reveal ancient remains either invisible or barely visible on the ground, enabling archaeologists to pinpoint the previously unknown sites of, among other features, Neolithic henges, Iron Age farmsteads, and Roman villas. Place-names, recognised as important by scholars at least as far back as Camden, were gradually made to yield up their secrets with the founding in 1923 of the English Place Name Society, with the intention of publishing studies of each county. The study of place-names involved philologists and historians – EPNS still has its base in the English Department at Nottingham University – another example of the cross-disciplinary co-operation which lay behind the development of post-war local history.

Finally, Hoskins recognised the importance of the landscape as an historical source, particularly the sites of Deserted Medieval Villages (DMVs). By the end of the 1940s he, along with Maurice Beresford and others, was particularly interested in lost villages. Hoskins's article on the 'Deserted Villages of Leicestershire' was published in 1945,[7] and Beresford's 'Deserted Villages of Warwickshire' in 1950.[8] It was in DMVs that the possibility of reconstructing the life of the medieval peasant was raised through the DMV Research Group, founded by Beresford and the archaeologist John Hurst in the 1950s, partly to encourage the compilation of lists of deserted villages and to gather information about them. The group conducted excavations at Wharram Percy. It was re-founded in 1986 as the Medieval Settlement Research Group, and today brings together archaeologists, geographers and historians in the study of all types of medieval settlement, particularly rural settlements.[9]

The Making of the English Landscape

By the early 1950s Hoskins was intensely aware of what past landscapes could tell us about the lives of earlier communities. This was the background to *The Making of the English Landscape*, first published in 1955. The book was designed to teach historians to read history from the landscape. Hoskins wrote this:

> The English landscape itself, to those who know how to read it aright, is the richest historical record we possess. There are discoveries to be made in it for which no written documents exist, or have ever existed. To write its history requires a combination of documentary research and fieldwork.[10]

Looking back, we can see that *The Making* was the first serious attempt to study the landscape in a systematic way in order to assess how it has changed and altered through time, and to relate the findings to what it tells us about past communities. As such it enables us to interpret 'the landscape' as an historical document and, perhaps even more importantly, to show that its importance for the local historian is just as great as for the archaeologist and historical geographer. Hoskins' view was that the sentimentality which had marked much writing about the landscape overlooked the fact that what we see today is the remains after generations of manipulation in the interests of mankind. Thus by peeling off the layers we can start to learn a good deal about the past and, by learning to read the landscape as a rich historical record in itself, we have an additional primary source for understanding past society.

Hoskins insisted that landscape historians should be concerned not just with changes in the landscape, or with buildings and standing structures, but with the human background which explained why change took place. His interest in the desertion of medieval villages was just part of his vision of himself as a landscape historian, helping to understand the past layers through examining the development of field systems, or through other issues such as the restructuring of landscape to curb population by the destruction of cottages. His work made it possible to isolate three types of landscape. First, village landscapes, mainly in the Midlands, and created in the late Anglo-Saxon period. Second, landscapes with dispersed farmsteads (rather than nucleated) with a continuity of occupation going back even further, and often called landscapes of ancient dispersal. Third, later dispersed settlement, after nucleation had taken place in the village lands, often known as landscapes of secondary dispersal. The main variables are the type and date of origin of the settlements we see today because these have influenced the layout of roads and fields. Landscapes of ancient dispersal where parliamentary enclosure was not usually needed are sometimes referred to as Britain's 'antique lands'.

Hoskins reached the conclusion that the key to understanding local history was the land, and his views were most powerfully argued in *The Making*. Inevitably there were weaknesses in his analysis; indeed, Hoskins later came to recognise that he had underplayed the importance of the prehistoric and Roman contribution to the past – an omission corrected by Christopher Taylor in a later edition of the book. But the book was to lead to much more, including the editorship of a series of county landscape histories for Hodder and Stoughton, various talks on Radio 3, and a BBC TV series *Landscapes of England* which went out between 1976 and 1978 and turned Hoskins into a nationally known figure.[11]

Hoskins gloried in being descended from 'six centuries of yeomen farmers, churchwardens, constables, overseers, bailiffs of the manor, rarely anything much above that'.[12] As Charles Phythian-Adams has argued, Hoskins identified with a dying provincial culture: he was 'both visionary and poet of that disappearing world to which he saw himself as having just belonged'.[13] Consequently, we find him despairing about design, industrial buildings, and just about everything connected with Victorian England, let alone the twentieth century, of which he wrote that 'especially since the year 1914, every single change in the English landscape has either uglified it or destroyed its meaning, or both'.[14] Hence his real concern, the peasant community described in *The Midland Peasant*, *The Making of the English Landscape*, and again in his book *Midland England*. Hoskins wrote of a 'peasant civilisation' stretching from the Anglo-Saxon period to the twentieth century, but enjoying its greatest importance in the sixteenth and seventeenth centuries: 'for those two hundred years – seven human generations – rural England flowered'.[15] As David Matlass has written, 'the pervading tone of Hoskins' work is a melancholy one of seeking consolation and refuge in the past'.[16]

Post-war developments

As Hoskins' ideas developed, his position at University College, Leicester, became increasingly anomalous. He had been appointed as Economics lecturer in the department of Geography and Commerce, but he disliked teaching economics, and almost from the moment he arrived at Leicester sugared his pill with courses at Vaughan Working Men's College on subjects including the antiquities and archaeology of Leicestershire. His research regularly appeared as articles in *Transactions of the Leicestershire Archaeological Society*, to which he contributed sixteen papers in fifteen years. Even before the Second

World War Jack Simmons, of the History Department, encouraged the College principal, F.L. Attenborough, to create a new department for Hoskins. Initially Simmons made little impact on Attenborough, who thought of local history as one of Hoskins's 'academic hobbies'. When Hoskins returned to Leicester after spending the war in London, Attenborough was more sympathetic, partly because as an Anglo-Saxon historian himself he enjoyed the time he spent with Hoskins exploring and photographing the Midland countryside. As a result, the Department of English Local History was set up in 1948: Hoskins was the only member of staff.

The founding of Hoskins's department at Leicester coincided with other positive developments for local history. The Standing Conference for Local History was set up in 1948 under the auspices of the National Council of Social Service, subsequently the National Council for Voluntary Organisations, as a federation of county committees made up of the new groups which were springing up in towns and villages all over the country, and which were the spearhead of post-war amateur enthusiasm for local history.[17] The idea was to promote history through newsletters and magazines, lectures and research projects. In 1961 the Standing Conference took over the *Amateur Historian*, a journal founded in 1952 and devoted to 'historical enquiry as a popular activity'. It sought to guide the non-specialist through the problems of locating and using evidence. The Standing Conference was succeeded in 1982 by the British Association for Local History (BALH), and the role of county local history organisations has been debated ever since, particularly their relationship to the longer established county history societies.[18]

The *Amateur Historian* was aimed, as its title suggested, at people outside the universities, and with relatively little time to devote to research. It was also local in orientation, aimed at people studying their family or locality. These 'intimate spheres of research' were regarded as the proper object of study for the amateur, but the journal was designed to provide a brief overview of subjects and areas relevant to their work. It began with articles on the VCH and on interpreting the *public* records, in this case feet of fines. The first edition also included an article by Christopher Hill on Cavaliers and Roundheads, and subsequent general articles included contributions on trade union history, popular movements, and the conciliar courts. Unfortunately the 'amateur' image seemed to emphasise what many people saw as the worst aspects of antiquarianism, and in 1968 it changed its name to *The Local Historian*.[19]

The founding of the Standing Conference almost exactly coincided with the post-war revival of the Victoria County History. From 1948 the Institute of Historical Research negotiated partnerships with local authorities to fund a small editorial staff to do the research, writing and editing of future volumes. The IHR provided supervision and technical expertise. It guaranteed the quality of the work, and it oversaw the printing and publication. The cost of printing was met out of revenue from sales. Ten county committees were formed 1948–64, funded from the rates. The Leicestershire and Wiltshire committees were set up in 1948, Oxfordshire in 1949, Staffordshire in 1950, Essex in 1951, the East Riding of Yorkshire in 1953, Middlesex in 1955, Gloucestershire in 1959, Shropshire in 1960, and Somerset in 1964. Leicestershire collapsed in 1958, apparently due to differences of opinion between Hoskins, who had inspired it, and the general editor, R.B. Pugh. However, under Hoskins's energetic leadership the county produced five volumes in ten years, a record for the VCH. The fourth volume, on Leicester, was the first to be devoted to a single town.[20]

Pugh also set about the first major overhaul of the VCH since its inception, reflecting changing values and interests in local history. Articles on natural history were dropped. Pre-history was re-planned, and a gazetteer of archaeological sites published. The ecclesiastical history of the county was treated at greater length with separate chapters for the Church of England, Roman Catholicism, and non-conformity. Social and economic history was divided into articles on agriculture and particular industries. A general chapter on politics was changed to articles on parliamentary and administrative history. Three articles were devoted to communications. Efforts were made also to improve the topographical volumes. Pugh recognised that early volumes 'were not very different from those of Morant and Hasted. It follows that the descent of the manor, rectory or advowson has hitherto formed the backbone of each parish narrative. The VCH therefore has been a rather one-sided compilation.' Cambridgeshire was among the first to benefit from the enlargement of the range of subjects, and the second volume published in the revived series, on the city of Cambridge (1959) contained the first detailed analysis of the university city.[21]

Local history and the parish

These changes at the VCH partly reflected a debate about the subject matter of local history. Hoskins disliked any form of theory. As he noted in his inaugural lecture at Leicester in 1966, 'I have a temperamental allergy to such new inventions',[22] but in the vacuum this left the subject came to be associated with rural and agricultural history. In part, of course, this reflected Hoskins's primary interests, but it was also to do with the people he gathered around him at Leicester. Shortly before he left Leicester in 1951 for Oxford, Hoskins secured funding to appoint Joan Thirsk to undertake a study of Lincolnshire farming. Hoskins himself, Thirsk, and Hoskins's successor Herbert Finberg were leading lights in the founding of the *Cambridge Agrarian History of England and Wales*, and the setting up in 1953 of the British Agricultural History Society with its journal the *Agricultural History Review*.[23] This rural tone coloured the Leicester image, despite Hoskins's interest in urban history from his days in Exeter, and his editorial work for the VCH volume on Leicester in 1958, or indeed the work of subsequent scholars at Leicester including Alan Everitt and Charles Phythian-Adams. Ironically, perhaps, the VCH volume on Leicester is considered to have set new standards for the study of urban history.[24]

Hoskins may have been able to ignore theory, and to work where his interests took him, but Herbert Finberg, Hoskins' successor at Leicester in 1951, was well aware of the hostile environment in which the Department of English Local History existed. In an intellectual sense the subject had hardly moved forward since the days of William Lambarde, but Finberg understood that once local history became an academic rather than an extra-mural subject it needed a methodology. In an inaugural lecture delivered at Leicester in 1952, Finberg suggested a methodology designed to bridge the divide between local and national history. The distinction he drew was between 'national history localised' – the study of national history at the local level, which was in effect what professional historians did – and 'local history *per se*'. This latter definition was much more controversial. Finberg was suggesting that each community was worthy of study in its own right – as the county historians and the VCH had long believed – and not only as part of the wider whole – the approach of the professionals. Finberg saw the local community as the parish, and he argued that the study of the parish should be seen in terms of its life-cycle from origin to ending: 'the business of the local historian, then, as I see it, is to re-enact in his own mind, and to portray for his readers, the Origin, Growth, Decline, and Fall of a Local Community'.[25]

For Finberg this definition was to become something of a straitjacket. Victor Skipp has written that Finberg was 'so intent on establishing that the local community is "a social entity that has a perfectly good claim to be studied for its own sake", that he simply refused to acknowledge that it could be studied with any other purpose in mind'.[26] That may be so, but Finberg's definition opened a debate which had largely been avoided in the past. Whatever Hoskins's allergies when it came to theory, the subject rapidly moved in new directions, under-pinned by different theoretical bases, and stemming from three contri-butions, all of which were, coincidentally, published in 1957.

The Midland Peasant

The first of the three books was Hoskins's own study of Wigston Magna, *The Midland Peasant*. Despite his antipathy to theory, Hoskins accepted that an academic study needed to develop ideas about the relationship between local and national history. Con-sequently, at one level he characterised *The Midland Peasant* as 'a con-tribution to English economic and social history, and not a history of the village as such'. But this was only part of the story, because Hoskins also believed that local historians should develop concepts which would lead to the nationalisation of locally conceived themes – turning, in other words, on its head the view of professional histori-ans that local history could contribute to national history only in the form of case studies. He saw local studies as throwing light on com-monly conceived ideas about national history, and therefore the study of Wigston Magna was designed to offer parallels for the Midlands more generally. Consequently the title was deliberate: *The Midland Peasant* was designed not merely to document in great detail the history of a single Leicestershire village, but also to formulate ques-tions, particularly about the farming community, which would be more widely applicable. It was to be 'a study of the Midland peasant-farmer and of the open-field system in which he worked all his life . . . a study of a peasant culture, of the way it was built up (as far as we can discover it), of the way it worked, and of the way in which it was finally dissolved'.[27] There were echoes here of Finberg's origins, rise, decline and fall of the individual community.

Hoskins may have wanted to avoid theory, but he recognised that local history needed to have direction. As he noted in his inaugural lecture after he returned to Leicester as Hatton Professor of English History (1965–68), 'we should be studying living communities and their reaction to their environment, and to change in that environment over the past 2000 years'. Local history should be 'a science of Human Ecology'. Here were echoes of one of the central *Annales* themes. Hoskins also commented that 'the local historian must learn to ask sociological questions', and that he needed 'to be a little of everything – a physical geographer, a geologist, a climatologist, a botanist, a medical man, a builder, as well as an historian'. Hoskins recognised that local history needed to develop new ideas if the subject was to escape from its antiquarian image. Like the *Annalists* he recognised the need for intellectual breadth, and he was well aware that local historical writing had too easily been 'preoccupied with facts and not with problems'.[28]

Farming regions

If Hoskins recognised that local historians needed to broaden their intellectual horizons to understand the context of individual events and – primarily rural – places, he was less concerned with boundaries, and this brings us to the second contribution of 1957, Joan Thirsk's *English Peasant Farming*. Thirsk was, for many years, research fellow in the Department of English Local History at Leicester, and she eventually followed Hoskins to a Readership in Economic History at Oxford University. In *English Peasant Farming* she was trying, like Hoskins, to examine a national theme in a local context and so, as with *The Midland Peasant*, the real subject matter was more accurately described in the sub-title. Hoskins' had sub-titled his book *The economic and social history of a Leicestershire village*, while Thirsk's book was subtitled *The Agrarian History of Lincolnshire from Tudor to Recent Times*. While, in theory, both books were 'local history nationalised', Thirsk was much more interested than was Hoskins in boundaries. As she recalled forty years after the book was published:

> Lincolnshire's agrarian history greatly sharpened my perception of local differences, and they have remained ever since a central interest in all my research and writing. In contrast, when working on the county of Leicestershire, Hoskins had not separated out any regions. Admittedly the differences within that county are not as striking as in Lincolnshire, but I am sure that, if I had been working in the same area, I would have made distinctions between its forests, wolds and vale.[29]

The message here is unmistakeable, and it suggested that local historians had not only to tackle themes, but also geography.

The county and parish historians, and even the early town historians, had assumed that the parish or the manor was their area of study, but as local historians widened the scope of their intellectual interests they ran up against questions relating to regions. These were already familiar to geographers, and H.C. Darby brought the issue sharply into focus with an article he published in the second volume of the *Agricultural History Review*. Darby noted how county historians and topographical writers had struggled to classify the countryside, because it could not easily be squeezed into the administrative boundaries imposed for convenience by earlier generations. He pointed to what for a geographer was the obvious fact, that any study of the rural community could make little progress if it was constrained by county and parish boundaries. Even the great county historians, he argued, despite their emphasis on antiquities, natural history and local description, occasionally strayed into regional issues. He cited Dugdale's efforts to distinguish land around the River Avon as the North Woodland and South Felden.[30] As early as the 1670s Richard Blome had distinguished two main types of soil, 'champain and woodland', and added 'yet commonly about the towns [of Norfolk] it is clayey, chalkey, and fat earth, and not destitute of wood. The sea-coast "champain" land afforded plenty of corn; the heaths fed great stocks of sheep and an abundance of coneys; the woodland grazed cattle, yet also provided corn ground.' By the eighteenth century there was, Darby argued, already a 'general preoccupation' among agriculturalists 'with differences in soil and in the face of the countryside'.[31]

From here it was only a short step to the conclusion drawn in 1796 by the agricultural writer William Marshall that 'Natural, not fortuitous lines, are requisite to be traced; agricultural not political distinctions are to be regarded'. In his view a 'natural district' was marked by uniform or similar soil and surface (i.e. marsh, vale, mountains), and an 'agricultural district . . . is discriminated by a uniformity or similar practice' such as grazing or arable.[32] Subsequently, in his 1818 review and abstract of the Board of Agriculture's county reports, Marshall pointed repeatedly to the unsatisfactory nature of the county as the unity of study, since this was both 'irrational and unscientific'. Thus, 'to prosecute an agricultural survey by counties, is to set at naught the distinctions of nature'.[33] The Royal Agricultural Society, founded in 1838, sponsored prize essays in the form of county surveys. These were mainly concerned with agricultural practice, but this was related to physical circumstances, and they were written with a geological basis. Some authors linked geology with land utilisation, and stressed the weakness of county boundaries in soil formation and treatment. In his prize essay on Nottinghamshire in 1846, R.W. Corringham bisected the county into east and west, and described the local variations of farming practice in each soil division, while emphasising the impracticability of making a regional division based only on soil types.[34]

Darby's point was that any study of agriculture had to be linked to a discussion of place. Hoskins understood this, writing in 1954 that 'the history of farming must be studied on a regional basis. England may be a small country, but no country in the world has such a diversity of soils, climates, natural resources and topography, in such a small space . . . . We must get down to earth, to crops, animals, soils, buildings, implements.'[35] But it was Thirsk who developed the argument. In her Lincolnshire book, she emphasised the variety of experience within the county as a result of the different types of farming appropriate to different soils and working conditions. From this beginning she went on to look more generally at English agricultural history, working from regional and local examples to construct a map of English farming regions. She established without any doubt the importance of regional variation in agricultural history, and all agricultural historians now work in the light of her arguments.[36] Implicitly she also pointed to more general issues in regard to the study of local history, particularly the significance of agricultural differences in terms of settlement patterns and other long established 'local' variations. She recognised as well the possible significance in England of the French concept of *pays*, to which Darby pointed in 1954.[37]

Regions without boundaries

A third influential publication in 1957 was David Chambers's *The Vale of Trent, 1670–1800*. From 1946 until his retirement in 1964 Chambers was head of the sub-department of Economic History at the University of Nottingham. With his own department, he was able to move away from the rather stilted position he had adopted in his study of Nottinghamshire when it was published in 1932 to describe his approach to the locality as that of the regional historian. Thus *The Vale of Trent* was subtitled 'a regional study of economic change'. In the introduction Chambers wrote that

> The regional historian is closer to the field of action, he can see, and may know intimately, the places where the events of the story took place; and since the volume of evidence is on a regional and not a national scale he can examine, or at least sample, all that is physically accessible.[38]

The Vale of Trent, Chambers suggested, was a region with an economic life of its own. Agricultural and mineral products were exchanged across the region, often by way of the River Trent and its tributaries. But what was the region? To overcome the pressing problem of boundaries, Chambers included in his work a map which had no boundaries. After his death, one of Chambers' former students and collaborators described him as 'a path-breaker in relating detailed regional knowledge to the broader problems of the economy at large'.[39]

The three books published in 1957 made this an important year for the methodology of local history. Hoskins's *Midland Peasant* adopted the traditional approach by accepting that the administrative boundary shaped the individual community, which was the bedrock of local history. Broadly speaking, the county and the parish have remained old favourites for local historians. The VCH continues to operate under these assumptions, and has successfully modernised its approach to understanding and interpreting the past without needing to question the basic unit of study (the parish) from which it operates. Yet the studies by Thirsk and Chambers raised important new concerns about the concept of community, and in looking for elements of cohesion or contrast using boundaries based on soil and agricultural type, they were asking important questions about the relationship of different village types through time. Furthermore, all three books began from the assumption that what were essentially local studies had significance in themselves. Hoskins sought to raise questions about village types in the Midlands, Thirsk used Lincolnshire as a stepping stone for appreciating the wider issues of regions, and Chambers depicted the Vale of Trent as reflecting 'most of the contemporary currents of economic change', and raising 'the same kinds of questions with which the student of the national economy is confronted'.[40] If Thirsk's study has underpinned much thinking about the agricultural history of England, Chambers' work is the spiritual starting point for subsequent work on regional economic interaction, to which we shall return in chapter VIII. The real danger in these debates was that professional historians such as Hoskins, Thirsk and Chambers, operating in universities, would set an agenda that the societies, with their more eclectic and less sharply focused interests would simply ignore. In this sense, what might be termed the professionalisation of local history after the Second World War left it still under attack from 'real' historians, and at the same time in danger of being isolated from the amateur community.

Notes

1 Peter Burke, *The French Historical Revolution: The Annales School, 1929–89* (1990), 2.

2 E. Le Roy Ladurie, *The Peasants of Languedoc* (1966; English translation

1974); John Tosh, *The Pursuit of History* (3rd edn, 2000), 107–9.

3 R.H. Tawney, *The Agrarian Problem of the Sixteenth Century* (1912), 121.

4 M. Beresford and J.G. Hurst (eds), *Deserted Medieval Villages* (1972, reissued 1989), 76.

5 The most obvious of Mumford's works to affect Hoskins was *Technics and Civilization* (1934).

6 W.G. Hoskins, *The Midland Peasant: The Economic and Social History of a Leicestershire Village* (1957), 282.

7 W.G. Hoskins, 'The deserted villages of Leicestershire', *Transactions of the Leicestershire Archaeological Society*, 22 (1944–45), 241–64.

8 A revised version of Hoskins's original article appeared in *Essays in Leicestershire History* (1956); M.W. Beresford, 'Deserted villages of Warwickshire', *Transactions of the Birmingham and Midlands Archaeology Society* (1950), 49–106.

9 M. Beresford, *The Lost Villages of England* (1954, reissued 1998); Beresford and Hurst, *Deserted Medieval Villages*, 77; *Rural History Today*, 7 (July 2004); M.W. Beresford and J.G. Hurst, *Wharram: A Study of Settlement on the Yorkshire Wolds* (1990); M.W. Beresford and J.K. St. Joseph, *Medieval England: An Aerial Survey* (1979); Chris Dyer, 'Maurice Beresford and local history', *LH*, 36/2 (2006), 128–30.

10 W.G. Hoskins, *The Making of the English Landscape* (1955), x.

11 Joan Thirsk, 'William George Hoskins 1908–92', *Proceedings of the British Academy*, 87 (1994), 339–54. More than 250 scholars attended a conference in 2005 to celebrate the fiftieth anniversary of the book's first appearance. See also W.G. Hoskins, *Fieldwork in Local History* (1967), 94.

12 W.G. Hoskins, *The Age of Plunder: King Henry's England, 1500–47* (1976), xiii.

13 C. Phythian-Adams, 'Hoskins's England: a local historian of genius and the realisation of his theme', *Transactions of the Leicestershire Archaeological and Historical Society*, 66 (1992), 143–59.

14 Hoskins, *Making*, 231.

15 Hoskins, *Making*, 126.

16 David Matlass, 'One man's England: W.G. Hoskins and the English culture of landscape', *Rural History*, 4 (1993), 187–207.

17 *ECH*, 193–5, 213–15, 287–9.

18 David Hayns, 'County local history organisations in England and Wales: a report on the recent BALH survey', *LH*, 22/2 (1992), 89–96. The first edition of the *Amateur Historian* was for August–September 1952.

19 *Amateur Historian*, 1/1, 8 (October–November 1953); 4/3 (Spring 1959); 4/5 (Autumn 1959); 4/6 (1959–60); Alan Crosby, 'The Amateur Historian and The Local Historian: some thoughts after fifty years', *LH*, 32/3 (2002), 146–55; L. Munby, D.H. Owen, and J. Scannell (eds), *Local History Since 1945: England, Wales and Ireland* (2005), 19–20.

20 *ECH*, 30–1, 240, 334–5, 346–7, 446.

21 R.B. Pugh, *How to Write a Parish History* (6th edn, 1954), 22; *ECH*, 69–70. Cambridgeshire has now been completed in ten volumes.

22 W.G. Hoskins, 'English local history: the past and the future', in Richardson, 137.

23 Joan Thirsk, 'The British Agricultural History Society and *The Agrarian History of England and Wales*: new projects in the 1950s', *Agricultural History Review*, 50 (2002), 155–63. Ironically, the rural image was further fostered with the launch in 1990 of the journal *Rural History*. Keith Snell, one of the founding editors, holds a chair in the department.

24 C.R.J. Currie, 'The history of the VCH series', in C. Sturman (ed.), *Some Historians of Lincolnshire* (1992), 88–92.

25 Richardson, 115; capitals in the original.

26 V. Skipp, 'Local history: a new definition', *LH*, 14/6 and 7 (1981), 394.

27. Hoskins, *Midland Peasant*, xviii–xix.

28 Richardson, 128, 136. In much the same way, Hoskins wrote in *The Midland Peasant* that 'I have rejected a considerable amount of material that would ordinarily have gone into a local history as generally understood and which would doubtless have interested the people of Wigston and its neighbourhood': xviii–xix.

29 Joan Thirsk, 'From farming to food: forty years in Lincolnshire history', *Lincolnshire History and Archaeology*, 32 (1997), 9.

30 H.C. Darby, 'Some early ideas on the agricultural regions of England', *Agricultural History Review*, 2 (1954), 31.

31 Ibid., 34.

32 William Marshall, *Rural Economy of Western England* (1796).

33 Quoted, 'Some early', 38.

34 R.W. Corringham, 'Agriculture in Nottinghamshire', *Journal of the Royal Agricultural Society of England*, 6 (1845), 1–43; Darby, 'Some early', 47.

35 W.G. Hoskins, 'Regional Farming in England', *Agricultural History Review*, 2 (1954), 11.

36 Joan Thirsk (ed.), *The Agrarian History of England and Wales* (vol. 4, 1500–1640, 1967, vol. 5, 1640–1750, 1984–85); idem, *England's Agricultural Regions and Agrarian History* (1987). The importance of these ideas can be seen for example, in H.C. Prince's chapter, 'The changing rural landscape, 1750–1850', in G.E. Mingay (ed.), *The Agrarian History of England and Wales, vol. VI (1750–1850)* (1989).

37 Darby, 'Some early', 31.

38 J.D. Chambers, The Vale of Trent, 1670–1800: A regional study of economic change, *Economic History Review*, Supplement 3, 1957, 2.

39 G.E. Mingay, 'The contribution of a regional historian: J.D. Chambers, 1898–1970', *Studies in Burke and His Times*, 13 (1971), 2002–10.

40 Chambers, *Vale*, 2.

VIII New approaches: the region and the community

The developments of the 1950s had various results. First, they produced a vigorous methodological debate about the purpose and function of local history. Under the wing of economic history, local history had flourished, and in the 1960s it was to be just as significantly affected by the rise of social history. Second, through the rapid spread of interest in the subject at all levels, new questions were raised about access to the sources, and the use of the data. In 1957 it was still possible to walk into one of the smaller record offices and be the only searcher on that particular day. Half a century after Hoskins, Thirsk and Chambers stamped a significant imprint on the nature of local history, that is a world which has long passed away; indeed, in many record offices it is crucial to book a place beforehand. Local history, in one form or another, is now one of the fastest growing and widest ranging pastimes in this country. It engages professional historians and amateurs alike; it has entered several key stages in the national curriculum; it is taught in many university history degree courses; and it is discussed at local society meetings up and down the country every night of the week. In this chapter we look at the evolution of thinking since the days of Hoskins, Thirsk and Chambers, and in subsequent chapters we examine the fragmentation (and related specialisation) of the subject, the development of the sources, methodological advances, and what it means to us now. Inevitably there will be overlap, but local history was invigorated in new ways in the post-war years, and since the 1960s it has gone off in so many directions that tying it down in a coherent fashion is by no means straightforward.

Counties and parishes

It was obvious by the end of the 1950s that using local history simply as a means of illustrating themes in national history was short-sighted. Each community had a history of its own, which was worthy of study, and each study helped to shed light on the broader issues with which 'proper' historians concerned themselves. The 'local' clearly had much to say about the 'national', as was apparent from a series of studies of county communities in the English Civil War.[1] The county evidently had a life of its own as a significant social and political reality in the seventeenth century, and this remained the case well into the nineteenth, if not the twentieth century.[2] To give an example, by the late eighteenth century Lincolnshire had developed a county 'season' focusing on Lincoln race week with plays, balls and concerts. The annual Stuff Ball could draw up to 300 people from across the county.[3] This, of course, was the county as a social entity for the county elite, but local newspapers also offered a county context and the county was also a political entity – sending MPs to Parliament – and an administrative and judicial area through Quarter Sessions, transformed into County Councils in 1888.

Counties were, in this sense, a cultural entity, and the efforts of the Church of England to break down the boundaries between them when it created new dioceses in Victorian England revealed some of the entrenched prejudices which survived. Derbyshire and Nottinghamshire, brought together in 1884 as the Diocese of Southwell, both resented the 'marriage', which had to be dissolved in 1927.[4] When C.B. Fawcett set out a blueprint for regional government in 1919 he was careful to stress in reference to the ancient counties that 'it seems to be generally true that local patriotism, in so far as this feeling exists and is associated with the counties, bases itself on these older divisions'. For Fawcett, in trying to bring some coherence to regions, 'county patriotism becomes a factor of great weight in the delimitation of the provinces', although this was

> very much stronger in those counties which approximate to natural regions than elsewhere. Thus Yorkshire, Lancashire and Devonshire are counties in which it is strong; while in Surrey, Hertfordshire, and Rutlandshire, it appears to be far less important.[5]

He might have mentioned Cornwall in this list. Part of the debate surrounding the establishment of the new diocese of Truro in 1876 to serve the county, was expressed in terms of racial, social and occupational differences. In turn, this introduced the notion of the Celtic-ness of the Cornish in contrast to the supposed Saxon stock east of the Tamar.[6]

Parishes were also significant units of identity and, for the local historian, of study. Here the approach, following in the wake of *The Midland Peasant*, was to understand the parish as a microcosm of wider and more significant trends. Hoskins had seen this mechanism primarily in economic terms, but was this sufficient? In her book *Contrasting Communities*, published in 1974, Margaret Spufford implicitly took issue with this view:

It has . . . been a source of surprise to me that local historians have almost always interpreted [their] initial brief in economic terms. We have many studies now of the gentry, landowners, tenants, village economies, open fields, of the way, in fact that most ordinary people, in ordinary villages before enclosure earned their bread-and-butter, or rather lard. What we have not got are studies of the way the ordinary villager before enclosure thought and felt.[7]

This was at least in part aimed at Hoskins's approach to Wigston Magna:

the local historian is not dealing with communities whose interests, in the sixteenth and seventeenth centuries, were confined to the bare economic necessities of life, even though the materials he has at his disposal on the economic life of any community are often so much richer than any others.[8]

This move away from the economic structure of the community towards its social dynamics was partly a consequence of changing ideas in the study of history, notably the development of a distinctive social history. The publication in 1963 of E.P. Thompson's book *The Making of the English Working Class* created a seismic shock through the history profession, which subsequently rubbed off on to local history. Thompson refused to accept the argument that history was about the 'successful', about those who left a written record of themselves and their doings, about politicians and governments, about landlords and businessmen. Instead, he set out to rescue 'the poor stockinger, the Luddite cropper, the "obsolete" hand-loom weaver, the "utopian" artisan . . . from the enormous condescension of posterity'. For the first time, a historian was arguing that it was simply not good enough to dismiss the great mass of humanity as being beyond historic reach. These people were not just economic units, they were people, and as such needed to be given back their real identity – hence the birth of social history as a discipline distinct from economic history. The implications for local history were to be equally profound. Thompson wrote the book when he was an adult education tutor, and he acknowledged that 'it was written in Yorkshire and is coloured at times by West Riding sources'.[9] It was possible to think of trying to understand the mentality of communities and thereby to escape the accusation of economic determinism.

A pioneer study, in this context, was David Hey's reconstruction of the Shropshire village of Myddle, which included the expected source-based analysis but took as its centrepiece Richard Gough's contemporary study of his own community.[10] David Levine and Keith Wrightson wrote similar studies on the Essex village of Terling, and the south Tyneside village of Whickham.[11] Whickham is a study of a village transformed from agricultural to industrial enterprise by the development of the Newcastle-based coal industry, but it is microhistory in the sense that it covers virtually all aspects of identity and experience within the community, as well as wider contacts and influences beyond the parish. Similarly significant in this context are Marjorie McIntosh's two books on Havering, Essex, and David Underdown's study of Dorchester. Underdown looks in detail at the religious development of Dorchester in the lead up to the Civil War, and emphasises the significance of community-based festivals, recreations, sports, and the moral order, to establish what he saw as the cultural unity of the area. Other microstudies have taken a broader canvass, such as David Rollason's study of early modern Gloucestershire, in which he even managed to recreate something of the early modern languages of class and power.[12]

Microhistory

This form of writing has interesting parallels with Hoskins's idea of local history nationalised, and often draws on concepts from the *Annales* School, as well as ideas from historical anthropology to concentrate on a micro issue as a way of studying broader ideas about how societies work.[13] Microhistory, as it has come to be called, is concerned not with the empirical study of the community for its own sake, but as an analytical tool for studying local communities, which is also an antidote to macro-level ideas and theories.[14]

Perhaps the most obvious development of microhistory has been in relation to demography. The early work of the Cambridge Group for the History of Population and Social Structure (CAMPOP, founded 1963) was concerned with establishing national population aggregates, with national and even international trends in the study of the history of the family and of social relationships.[15] It was soon clear that the work with parish register data being undertaken at Cambridge had local dimensions. These were disseminated through the Local Population Studies Society, founded in 1968. Its journal, *Local Population Studies*, concentrates on assessing demographic data in individual places and on techniques in such a way as to add a great deal to our understanding of population trends at the local level.

The way in which material collected for a national purpose influenced thinking about the locality can be demonstrated through the Devon village of Colyton. This small community first shot to academic fame in 1966 when E.A. Wrigley used the data collected from the parish registers as an indication of the trends of family size and structure in pre-industrial England.[16] Subsequently he recognised that the data had important implications for the evolution of the village.[17] Colyton became a much debated village in academic circles when Pam Sharpe used the parish register data to look at the position of women in the village.[18] In the wake of these studies the analysis of local population has provided an excellent basis for investigating other variables such as village type, patterns of occupation, economic development, class and social structure, food supplies and diet, climate, famine, price movements and similar factors.[19]

We now understand that the demographic behaviour of communities varied according to the dominant employment type. In turn, this suggests that the way in which local communities responded to economic change needs to be understood in terms of their own priorities, not in terms of the broader trends identified, perhaps fairly crudely, in relation to the national aggregate. Barry Reay's book *Microhistories* had as its more explicit subtitle: *Demography, Society and Culture in Rural England, 1800–1930*. He tackled three parishes in Kent to undertake a 'total reconstitution' including class analysis and cultural context. What separated this from what we might call traditional local history was his use of the parishes as sites 'for a consideration of much wider issues'.[20]

Regions

The county retained residual significance for the cultural life of the local community, and no one questioned the significance of the parish and the town as study areas, even if the methodology, aims and intention changed as the range and appreciation of the sources and methods developed. But what of the region? Were the agricultural differences emphasised by Thirsk reflected in other ways? Were wolds communities different from fenland and marsh communities? How did upland communities, with their emphasis on pastoral farming, sit alongside lowland areas where open field farming was practised? Comparative questions like these led to broader questions. Why did some regions industrialise, while others seemed to go backwards in terms of manufacturing and output? And how far were cultural issues responsible for a broadening or narrowing of industrial interests, or political consciousness, or physical differences?

These questions emerged in the context of the broader issue of how the country had changed from a predominantly rural-agrarian to a largely urban-industrial society. This had occurred, but at different rates and in different ways across the country. The county and the parish might be of limited value when discussing industrialisation, just as it bore little relationship to agricultural regions, and so the local historian had to think in terms of the similarity and contrasts between different areas, increasingly defined as regions. These were not necessarily questions being asked in meetings of county societies, but many members, through participating in archaeological digs and attending excursions, understood the issues relating, for example, to stratigraphy, building types and materials, and vernacular housing types. While each community was worthy of study in its own right, it was the comparative perspective which soon started to pay dividends in terms of our understanding of the locality.

The problem was to decide on the nature of regionalism. England has no equivalent of the kingdoms or principalities of France, Germany or Italy, and few of the Anglo-Saxon tribal divisions had any real meaning after 1066, although cross-border affinities declined only slowly.[21] We can point to the Danelaw, or the Association movements during the seventeenth century, or the brief reign of the major-generals during the Commonwealth of the 1650s, or the regional divisioning of 1803 during the Napoleonic war scares, but these were more or less the only use of regional rather than parish or county boundaries before recent times. England has no regions in the French sense, and even today, despite the introduction of a Scottish Parliament and a Welsh Assembly, there is no desire for regional devolution in England – as was witnessed in November 2004 when in a referendum the north-east decisively rejected any form of regional government. Although England is divided by the government into clearly defined regions, and each region has a regional development agency, government office, regional cultural consortia and so forth, there is little sense of regional awareness or regional consciousness, except perhaps in areas where language and accent determine place. Obviously we can talk about regional culture, of fenlanders and Cornishmen, of Yorkshiremen (and women) and Cumbrians, to name only a few, and it may be that regional consciousness is most clearly developed at the margin such as Tyneside and especially Cornwall.[22]

Geographers have divided the country into provinces or regions which suit their purposes, although from time to time they have been concerned about the relevance of these divisions for their discipline.[23] Simply deciding the boundaries in what might occasionally appear to be a rather arbitrary way remains alien to historians. When, in the 1980s, the publishing house Longman announced a new 'Regional

History of England' series, devised under the general editorship of Professors David Hey and Barry Cunliffe, one local historian was outraged at what he perceived to be the arbitrary division of the country into ten regions to suit the demands of the publisher.[24] Regional history, it seemed, could not be written to geographically-determined boundaries: as one would-be contributor put it in 1990, the early volumes in the series had 'avoided any initial confrontation with the problems of regional boundaries and common experience, indeed [they] sometimes appear uncomfortable with the idea of a regional dynamic'.[25] Neither Joe Bettey on Wessex, the first post-AD1000 volume to be published, nor David Hey (on Yorkshire) made any real attempt to discuss the nature of their regions, while Marie Rowlands admitted in 1990 after the publication of her West Midlands volume (in 1987) that she was 'increasingly conscious that I don't know how to write regional history'.[26]

Yet, as the series progressed, and as authors came to grips with the problems of writing regional history, some interesting ideas were discussed. John Broad, in preparing the volume on the south Midlands and the Upper Thames – sadly never published – claimed that he was being careful not 'to try to forge some false regional identity',[27] while one of the last volumes to appear, by Brandon and Short on the southeast – Kent, Surrey and Sussex – addressed the 'personality' of the area rather than its regionality, although, as we shall see, that reflected a change in the direction of thinking about regions by the 1990s.[28] An alternative approach was to see regional history as the study of communities, within a regional context which related to geographically defined areas, or to functional areas defined according to economics, trade, agriculture, industry or politics.[29]

If such approaches, limited as they are to geographically determined regions, seem inadequate, they do at least recognise some of the problems. By contrast, scholarly journals devoted to the academic study of local and regional history, notably *Northern History* (1966), *Midland History* (1971), *Southern History* (1979) and, in similar vein, *The London Journal* (1975), tend to publish contributions relating to places and issues within the region, rather than to address regional issues. Arguably they have done little for the theoretical development of regional history. Even so, the importance of the approach is reflected in the setting up of regional history centres at universities from East Anglia through Bristol to Exeter, Manchester, Lancaster, Keele, Kingston, Hull, Teesside and Nottingham. Each of these centres seeks to bring together local historians of all denominations, professional and amateur, scholar and enthusiast, but it is the

geography of the region, not the subject matter, which is all-encompassing.

Pays

As a result of this uncomfortableness with regional ideas, the
approaches to regionalism among historians have gradually come to
concentrate less on geography and more on community. The concept
of *pays*, borrowed from French geographers and based on features of
physical geomorphology, was first debated in the 1950s. It suggested
that different parts of the country might exhibit characteristics more
in keeping with areas of similar soil type and farming method rather
than with places which might just happen to be in the same administrative area.[30] Alan Everitt, who succeeded Hoskins as Hatton
Professor of English History, used his inaugural lecture at Leicester in
1970 to assess the importance of this comparative dimension. He suggested that areas of the countryside might continue to show locally
distinctive characteristics which can be traced back to their earliest
settlement history.[31] He developed this in his book *The Pattern of
Rural Dissent* (1971), and more fully in 1979, when he wrote that

> the basic regional pattern in this country has in many ways not
> remained constant: it has been an evolutionary pattern. Not only
> have regional boundaries changed: at a more fundamental level,
> new kinds or types of region have from time to time come into exis-
> tence and overlaid or transformed the old.[32]

County and other administrative boundaries, he suggested, were of
little use to the local historian, because of the 'pattern of sharply-
localised contrasts . . . more closely resembling the geological map
than that of our modern regions or our ancient counties and kingdoms'. A rough and ready division of the countryside into 'the fielden
or "champion" areas, the forest areas, the fell or moorland areas, the
fenland, the marshlands, the heathlands, the downlands and the wold
or wald countrysides', provided a framework for studying connected
patterns within different kinds of countryside from the earliest days
of settlement onwards.[33]

Everitt was moving the local historian's attention in the direction of
regional societies with contrasting rates of evolution: towards a
country, in other words, which 'has never been a monolithic community but an incomplete amalgam of differing but related societies, of
differing but related pays'. Like Hoskins, he was using the local view-
point in a national context; in effect, to offer a local historian's view

of national society as the product of its separate parts.[34] Thus localities needed to be studied not simply for their own sake, but for the light they shed 'on English society as a whole . . . we need to pay greater attention than we have done . . . to the indigenous life of the local communities of England, and to the fact that it stemmed ultimately from different roots from that of the community of the realm'.[35]

Settlement

The various ideas being debated at Leicester led backwards towards patterns of settlement. Harold Fox argued that there is a distinctiveness about 'wolds' societies over several centuries, and through each stage of development. He looked for parallels and similarities in the way of life among the wold villages spread through several counties. Wolds were essentially woodland areas within the Midland Plain where the intensification of land use took place in the early Middle Ages. The subsequent history of such places from the Black Death onwards shows a series of remarkable similarities. A similar type of argument was advanced by Brian Roberts in proposing that the diversity of rural landscapes can be traced back to a time when local differences in habitat were linked to contrasts in culture, economy and society. Detailed mapping of several Midland counties suggested strong connections between types of field system and the presence of villages and hamlets. Settlement clearly had considerable significance for our understanding of regional and local character and culture over time.[36]

Charles Phythian-Adams, Everitt's successor at Leicester, pursued this thinking further, to suggest that because 'no local society can be regarded as situated in glorious isolation in relation to the centre', spatial context is all important. The difficulty is to find places and areas which were meaningful to the people in them, and which also had distinguishable cultural traits. Phythian-Adams suggested that the areas which best suit this definition are the 'great centrally-focussed river-drainage basins', and those 'decentralised but localised groups of broadly parallel or slightly convergent rivers that are delimited in each case by the same watershed line, and which share an identifiable stretch of coastline at their points of outlet'. This led him to conclude that

definable groups of counties have more features in common internally than they have with neighbouring groupings, since they are separated . . . by both physical and political boundaries (of considerable antiquity) . . . . It can be no accident that down even to this century, dialect features have probably accorded more with this geographical feature [drainage basins] than with any other.

Drainage basins, in other words, are 'the most relevant spatial entities through which culture, economy and even population movements may be understood'. These 'cultural provinces' Phythian-Adams sees as 'generally focused arenas of influence and regional interaction', without being in any way prescriptive, although he was sufficiently confident to outline fourteen cultural provinces, while rejecting any accusations which might be offered of 'geographical determinism'.[37]

Doctoral students at Leicester sought to test some of these ideas. Work on Lutterworth and Melton Mowbray suggested that they were centres for an identifiable area in the early modern period, and that Lutterworth's influence stretched beyond the county boundary into Warwickshire.[38] The focus of several studies was on a hierarchy of geographical areas from the parish, through the 'neighbourhood area' (a handful of adjacent or interlinked parishes), the *pays*, the county, and finally regions consisting of several counties – Phythian-Adams's cultural provinces. Family reconstitutions using parish records suggested it was possible to show local inter-linkages which crossed parish and even county boundaries for business and marriage purposes. Local communities, in this sense, were the product of networks of friendship, business and family, with extended kinship networks drawn from a number of 'dynastic families' which provided the stable core of particular communities.[39]

Regional flexibility

A different approach to the region has been associated very largely with the work of Dr John Marshall, and builds on the idea of regional flexibility originally developed by J.D. Chambers. In his study of the Vale of Trent, Chambers simply left off the boundaries. He recognised, in other words, that geographical determinism offered little help when it came to understanding the way in which communities might develop through time, and that communities need not be tied into particular places. Marshall, who at one time studied under Chambers, developed this argument by suggesting that 'an historic region relates to some kind of large, extended community of interest and people. Boundaries do not tell us much about the inter-related groups of people who make up wider communities than the purely local.' Administrative boundaries, in other words, were not critical considerations for the local historian: 'the region . . . is a term of convenience, located specifically in time as well as space, with no promise of more than temporary existence'.[40] The local historian, he suggested, was also the regional historian:

> He has to be prepared to study whole patterns of historical development across large tracts of the English countryside. He has to show how whole groups of industries developed, for economic life defines its own arbitrary boundaries, and tells us much of what happened in the town or village; he has to trace the larger communities which have been mentioned; he has to study types of farming and the administration of large estates; he has to examine entire market areas . . .[41]

In Marshall's regions the boundaries are drawn not according to spatial limits, but to the purpose for which they were required. He recognised the arbitrary nature of these regions:

> if we are to talk of regions, we must have bricks with which to build them, and these building-bricks must consist of areas that can, at a variety of levels be seen as coherent or homogenous, but which relate to the whole of the region, perhaps rather more tenuously, but which nevertheless show some kind of identification with a greater unity. Very often this quest will result in uncertainties, and the explorer will find himself lost in a jungle of trends, factors, variables and movements.[42]

The problem of the physical boundaries is never far from the surface here: 'One's region', Marshall has written, 'which need not be a county per se, must often be taken as given, and may be examined from differing standpoints, or be given an historical identity as one reveals layer after layer of its history: demographic, extractive, administrative, ecclesiastical, economic, social and cultural'.[43]

In this sense the region is not something to be sought since it already exists 'whether in the form of a county or in that of a developed industrial region'. Equally it may be a pays, or an area with some sort of hallmark of tradition and self-awareness such as Merseyside, the Lake District, or Cornwall. It could be the north-east, although ideas as to what constituted this region have changed through time. The area dominated in the nineteenth century by the mining and export of coal was not an obvious region in the Middle Ages. Even today the idea of a single homogenous 'north-east' is an oversimplification because within the general term are a range of smaller or sub-regions, which are significant for local people even if they are meaningless to those beyond the area.[44] What the region should *not* be, in Marshall's view, is a rigidly defined area imposed for some arbitrary reason. Thus James Obelkevich drew the boundaries for his study of religion in South Lindsey, Lincolnshire, in the nineteenth century, on the basis that although it 'did not coincide with any administrative or ecclesiastical unit . . . its geographical and social boundaries were clear'.[45]

Others who have worked from similar principles were Marie Rowlands in her study of the metalware trades of the west Midlands, Victor Skipp on the Forest of Arden,[46] and Marshall himself in a study of the Lake Counties written jointly with John Walton. Marshall and Walton's book takes as its starting point the 'discovery' of the Lake District, and the realisation which went with this that the ancient county boundaries divided a region which possessed many common interests. Even so, they emphasise the importance of geographical considerations, and the distinctive physical characteristics of the area reflected in its human destiny and development. Marshall and Walton also stress the cultural coherence of their region, as reflected in the foundation of the Cumberland and Westmorland Antiquarian and Archaeological Society in 1866.[47]

Regions and industrialising society

If the region was a dynamic, rather than a static, geographically-determined area, how does this affect our understanding of industrialising society? The emphasis in many local studies has been on rural society and the pre-industrial period, but what happened with industrialisation? Just as microhistory seeks to understand how individual communities evolved through the Industrial Revolution, and then to look at what this meant for society more generally, so the regional approach looks at different experiences of different parts of the country.

Since, in theory, we would expect regional differences to become less significant during industrialisation, economic historians traditionally wrote of the nature and impact of industrialisation primarily in macro-economic terms.[48] Once questions were asked about the nature of industrialisation in different regions, it was soon clear that the process varied significantly, from south Lancashire and the West Riding of Yorkshire, which industrialised early and fully, the west and east Midlands which came later and took a different form, and southern England where it was possible to think in terms of de-industrialisation.[49] The same was true more broadly of Europe where, in different regions the industrial experience was quite distinctive and, as in England, often associated primarily with marginal territories.[50] Not only were regional experiences quite different, the early phases of industrialisation tended to increase rather than decrease regional differences. Langton argued that because much early industrial development depended on canals and water-borne traffic, for which the network was fragmented, regional differences tended to be emphasised rather than to disappear.[51]

Langton's argument produced a spirited debate,[52] but these new approaches led to a redirection of thinking about the nature of industrialisation. It had seemed by the 1980s that the economic explanations developed in the context of local studies since the 1930s, had been swept aside by the rise of econometrics and other hard-edged statistical and theoretical approaches. These national overviews were concerned primarily with measuring the timing, pace and scale of industrialisation, but failure to pay attention to the varied regional experience had produced the same type of generalisation that had been true of demographic studies. Langton's argument reminded the scholarly community that national trends are only the sum of the parts, and led to a rethinking of the nature of industrialisation at a local level. Pat Hudson's collection of papers, published in 1989, attempted 'to understand the Industrial Revolution as an economic, social and political process', and to do so 'with the regional perspective at centre stage'. The book set off lively debate attacking aggregate studies in favour of a disaggregated or regional approach. In turn, this highlighted the spatial limitations of industrialisation. As Hudson reflected, 'regional studies may be of more value in understanding the process of industrialisation than studies of the national economy as a whole .... Industrialisation accentuated the differences between regions .... Macroeconomic indicators fail to pick up this regional specialisation and dynamic which was unique to the period and revolutionary in its impact.'[53]

Once we start to approach the Industrial Revolution in terms of local and regional history we begin to see the process in a very different light. The majority of migratory moves in the eighteenth and early nineteenth centuries took place over short distances, and this is important in explaining how the industrial workforce came together. Economic opportunities were opened up for those people ready to migrate towards industrial work, and in many cases individuals moved together with their family and friends. The coal mining district of south-west Lancashire supplied most of its labour needs from a relatively definable surrounding region. Many people were simply moving to a new job in the same area, and short-distance migration often took place in order to maintain bonds with home and family. Almost inevitably it tended also to reinforce custom and kinship links.[54] As a result, regional coherence was founded on connections between different places involved with the same industry, networks of branches of a particular society, or information networks on which the regional press and regional social protests were based. At the root of many of these connections was the movement of people, and with people went cultures, partly reflected in an interest in the dying folk-lore customs, proverbs, pastimes, games and modes of speech. The regional cultural identity of Roman Catholicism in south Lancashire was also significant between the sixteenth and nineteenth centuries.[55]

Organisations of industrialists were almost all regional, because their market, economic interests and their power were based at regional not national level. Industrialists obtained finance through a localised network of commercial, social and familial links, since face-to-face contact and trust were important. Banking transactions were denser within regions than beyond them, interest rates varied between regions, and many commercial crises and waves of bankruptcies were regional in intensity. Pressure groups were regionally based: the successful movement for factory reform was based in the West Riding of Yorkshire, while the Anti-Corn Law League originated in Manchester. Social protests, such as Luddism, were regional, reflecting the stresses and strains of rising prices, falling wages, and unemployment. Trade unions tended to be fragmented, as a reflection of the specific working conditions in different regions, which made it difficult to mobilise national responses when employers posed threats to wages or working hours.[56]

The movement of goods clearly reflected the connections which existed between and within different areas, and the linkages were probably strongest during the canal era as transport developments helped to foster intra-regional connections. Most industrial regions were located around networks of canals. As a result, separate canal-based regional economies developed, and in the early phases of industrialisation this served to protect local specialisms. Regions began to look limited only when the railway arrived from the 1840s and gradually transformed the pattern of local and national communications.[57]

Connected to this notion was the idea of large towns at the centres of integrated local and regional economies. This, of course, was a geographers' concept, but it has been employed in the context of industrialisation. Stobart has argued that the success of north-west England in the eighteenth century was the result of a dynamic and interactive urban system. Without such a system, as in areas like the Weald, Shropshire, Cornwall and elsewhere, sustained growth did not take place.[58] In the absence of a dynamic network of towns a critical mass of industries did not develop. If this was so in the eighteenth century it was even more apparent in the nineteenth. Manchester, at the hub of a network of linkages, was described by Faucher in 1844 as 'like a diligent spider [which is] placed at the centre of the web, and sends forth roads and railways' to its industrial outposts. Cotton would arrive in Manchester, before being spun, woven and dyed in the towns and villages of Lancashire, then returned to Manchester for finishing and packing. A network of transport links radiating out from the city enabled the whole process to be completed in less than eight days. Modern regions are, of course, almost always defined in terms of their central urban focus, which has both an administrative and a trading function. They tend to be at the heart of transport services and local newspapers, of professional and entrepreneurial services, and the focal point of cultural and leisured life.[59]

This rather generalised conclusion may overlook differences of focus within the town. The county borough of Stoke-on-Trent was formed in 1910 as the result of an amalgamation of the six Potteries towns of Burslem, Fenton, Hanley, Longton, Stoke and Tunstall, and given city status in 1925. Yet cultural identities continue to be with the local towns of the conurbation rather than the city. According to Ray Johnson, 'the city is made up of many small community units, and people identify with these rather than the conurbation as a whole'.[60] By contrast, the cutlery trade of Sheffield transcended the town boundaries, hence David Hey's vivid depiction of Hallamshire.[61] Regional affinities were not necessarily the same for all social groups: John Marshall has shown how contrasting perceptions of a region can be held by people of different social status, in this case in the Furness district of Cumbria.[62] Cultural considerations, in other words, often overrode any sense of economic or political unity.

Cultural identity

This notion of cultural identity can be taken further. David Fischer's work on communities migrating from England to the United States has suggested that Puritans moving from East Anglia to Massachusetts, and Quakers migrating from the Midlands to Delaware, took with them their cultural patterns, and the differences have survived from the seventeenth century to the present day.[63] Much the same thing happened among emigrants to Australia.[64] Of course, we recognise cultural patterns in terms of regional distinctiveness in architecture, food, spoken accent, religion (with strong areas of Catholicism surviving to the present day), and perhaps something even as apparently neutral as body language. Similarly the attachment to place that people felt in the past can be read from the language of gravestones as a symbol of local attachment.[65] For some commentators, however, this very attachment is breaking down: as Michael Ignatieff has written, 'we think of belonging as rootedness in a small familiar place yet home for most of us is the convulsive arteries of a great city. Our belonging is no longer to something fixed, known and familiar but to an electric and heartless creature eternally in motion'. Snell has even suggested that cremation, rather than burial, followed by the scattering of ashes, is a sign of our basic rootlessness in modern society.[66]

Postmodernism

Finally, is any of this of value? The role of postmodernism has been to raise some interesting and complex issues, which are worth debating even if they appear not to help the subject along greatly. George and Yanina Sheeran started the ball rolling with an article in the *Local Historian* in 1999, in which they argued that local history had been under-theorised, and specifically that there had been no proper engagement with the post-modernist debate which was at that time engaging the attention of many academic historians. They pointed out quite rightly that there had been no real attempt to isolate the distinguishing characteristics or discipline of local history, that discussion over definition was rare and was often taken for granted, and that as a result local historians were failing to appreciate the extent to which historians generally were struggling to come to terms with the idea that much of the past has already been lost, or was never recorded, leaving us with only a residue. The Sheerans suggested that the position implicitly adopted by local historians was that of the realist or modernists who built on the tradition of British empirical research in the form of a detective trail, searching for the 'truth' about the past. Local historians, they suggested, had hardly begun to explore the philosophical problems of using primary sources to 'reconstruct' the past: 'we might be re-inventing it [the past of any locality] in our own image for our own time'.[67]

The Sheerans' article was controversial, but readers of the *Local Historian* were at least presented with some of the issues which had been around for a long time, even if they have scarcely been acknowledged outside of the universities (and, sometimes, within them). In this context, Professor Edward Royle drew attention to the distinction between 'empirical' and 'scientific' history, or the accumulation of facts which would speak for themselves (antiquarianism in local history terms) and the expectation that the past is capable of structure and rational interpretation. Good local history, Royle maintained, can reach out beyond the simplistic belief that the past can be known, which has frequently been the inspiration for local historians, 'without yielding to the intellectual despair of postmodernist relativism'. In this context Royle cited the influence of the *Annales* School.[68] At its logical extreme, postmodernism more or less assumes we cannot reconstruct the past, whereas most local historians would simply take the more reasonable view that we try to come as close as we can to doing so.

In this debate, perhaps for the first time, professional and amateur local historians were being challenged in a journal read by both constituencies to think clearly about the viability of the subject. This was not about the unit of study, whether the parish, the county or the region, but how successfully the existing methodological tools enable us to interpret the past. Local historians might be hostile to the postmodernist canon, but there are areas where it has made a significant difference to the approach by all historians, in particular perhaps the understanding of landscape not purely in terms of the economic and social approach favoured by Hoskins, but in a cultural sense, a recognition that it is at one and the same time a geological construct and also a 'narrative', because of what it can tell us of generations of human history.[69] It is a distinction drawn less rigidly, but tellingly by Christopher Taylor, when he argues that

> local history, by its very nature, is primarily the study of localities, as is much landscape history. Equally important, local history is concerned with the community, either collectively or as individuals. That is, local history is the study of people and places, as is landscape history. Both are concerned with the relationship of people to their actual or perceived world, whether physical, social, economic, political or aesthetic.

But landscape history is still different from local history even if the two enjoyed a symbiotic relationship, because 'unlike local history, landscape history is the study of the landscape itself. That is, the landscape is the main source of evidence for its own history, and has to be read in the same way as are books, documents, maps and photographs.' We cannot, as Hoskins might have done, attribute the modern landscape purely to human intervention because that overlooks the role of nature, and the interaction of man with his environment in the past.[70]

How we study the landscape is just one of the issues which, as I have tried to suggest in this chapter, have become intrinsically interwoven with an ongoing debate about the very nature of local history. Is it about parishes, regions, *pays*, communities, regions – however defined – or what? Should it be studied by taking a parish, a manor, a village, or even a single individual, as a way of recreating the cultural and social identity of places? Is it about total history, as the *Annales* School originally proposed and microhistory seems to support, narratives of events, history from below, or even somewhat nebulously the routines of 'everyday life, perhaps best explained in the German term 'alltagsgeschichte'? Or, perhaps even more controversially, is the study of local history entirely a misnomer because it diverts us from broader issues and takes us down byways where we lose our way? Frank Furedi has argued that because local history disaggregates the totality of experience, it leads to 'the destruction of historical thinking', which becomes fragmented when communities are studied for their own sake. He has argued that local history has 'a disposition for portraying history as a series of unconnected events that exist in accidental relation to each other', and that 'developments are explained not as a result of wider social forces, but of accidental local details', so that there is a 'permanent danger of equating the banal with major developments'.[71]

To many local historians, this *angst* among the professionals must seem remote from the business of archival research, let alone landscape, archaeology, and oral testimony. Surely, they are entitled to suggest, local history is about reconstructing past communities, in ways which make sense, rather than worrying about issues linked to postmodernism and other theoretical constructs which seem to approach the wider issues in a negative rather than a constructive manner. Local history was traditionally the study of a particular local community, or group of communities (in the sense of a county) without specific reference to the broader range of events, forces and processes impinging on those communities. Many practitioners might argue that this is still what it is, but since the 1950s it has evolved in numerous ways, and has itself been rethought in different historical contexts. Until the 1950s it was viewed either as having nothing to say of relevance to the national past, hence the marginalisation endured before 1945, or as relevant only in terms of providing examples to fit preconceived ideas about the national past.

The rethinking of this position, inspired by Hoskins, brought a recognition that the past needed to be studied not purely through administratively defined units such as counties and parishes, but by understanding the regional linkages which affected ordinary life. But the rethinking went further than this, as a result of *Annales*, the emphasis on recreating societies not simply economic constructs, the importance of ethnography and other disciplines as well as, most recently, gender distinctions. As historians have broadened their perspective on how the past should be viewed, moving away from narratives of political events to take in economic and most recently societial concepts relating to everyday life, local history has necessarily been forced to adapt. Some of the more detailed arguments of scholarly studies in the microhistory tradition may have passed the wider community by, or at least some of the nuances within these studies may have done – how may local historians in Kent appreciated the subject matter of Reay's book from his title? – there has, inevitably, been a spin-off, reflected, for example, in articles published in *The Local Historian*, although some of the more intangible interests of the microhistorians have yet to feature on its pages.[72]

Within this shifting emphasis, perhaps the most widely debated issue has related to the unit of study. As local history has become embedded in academic study, scholars working in the area have sought ways of understanding the relevant levels of definition. Traditionally local historians worked within existing boundary structures, but the recognition that county and parish boundaries are of relatively little value in studying anything other than the rural – and then not even the farming – past, produced a debate about the breadth or otherwise of the boundaries to be employed in local research, particularly the past of an industrialising society. In this context the 'region', however loosely defined, has become the significant organising concept, but it is not the only one: the VCH continues to offer a reassuringly stable agenda as volume after volume of high quality local history written in the finest tradition of English archival research, addresses essentially the questions laid down in 1899 and subsequently refined, on a parish-by-parish basis. Yet even the VCH is changing, with new emphasis on outputs published on the world wide web, and studies which transcend parochial boundaries. Local history, like all history, moves on and, in doing so, it diversifies, as we shall see in chapter IX.

Notes

1 Among these were Alan Everitt's *The Community of Kent and the Great Rebellion, 1640–60* (1966), but a number of vigorous younger scholars who went on to write national history cut their teeth with such studies, notably Clive Holmes, *Seventeenth-century Lincolnshire* (1980), John Morrill, *Cheshire, 1630–60: County Government and Society During the*

English Revolution (1974), and Anthony Fletcher, *A County Community in Peace and War: Sussex 1600–60* (1975). The doctoral thesis, as a local study designed to tease out and illustrate a national picture, particularly when the constituent parts were added together, showed just how far, and how quickly, the subject had developed.

2 C. Phythian-Adams, 'Re-thinking English local history' (*University of Leicester, Occasional Paper*, 4th series, 1, 1987), 30, 47; C. Phythian-Adams, 'Local history and national history: the quest for the peoples of England', *Rural History*, 2 (1991).

3 R.J. Olney, *Rural Society and County Government in Nineteenth-Century Lincolnshire* (1979), 13–14.

4 John Beckett, 'Derbyshire and the establishment of the diocese of Southwell in 1884', in P. Riden (ed.), *Essays in Derbyshire History* (2006), 115–33.

5 C.B. Fawcett, *Provinces of England* (1919, reprinted 1960), 42, 68–9.

6 Philip Payton, *Cornwall* (1966), 223; P.S. Morrish, 'History, Celticism and propaganda in the formation of the diocese of Truro', *Southern History*, 5 (1983), 248–54.

7 Margaret Spufford, *Contrasting Communities: English Villagers in the Sixteenth and Seventeenth Centuries* (1974), xix. The book was based on a Leicester doctoral thesis supervised by Finberg.

8 Ibid., 352; J.D. Marshall, 'Communities, societies, regions and local history, perceptions of locality in High and Low Furness', *LH*, 26 (1996), 36–47.

9 E.P. Thompson, *The Making of the English Working Class* (1968 edn), 13–14.

10 David Hey, *An English Rural Community: Myddle Under the Tudors and Stuarts* (1974). Hey was a student and for four years a member of staff of the Leicester department, and his book was published by Leicester University Press. See also Alan Macfarlane, 'The study of communities', *Social History*, 5 (1977).

11 Keith Wrightson and David Levine, *Poverty and Piety in an English Village: Terling, 1525–1700* (1979); idem, *The Making of an Industrial Society: Whickham, 1560–1765* (1991).

12 M.K. McIntosh, *Autonomy and Community: The Royal Manor of Havering, 1250–1500* (1986); idem, *A Community Transformed* (1991); D. Underdown, *Fire From Heaven: Life in an English Town in the Seventeenth Century* (1994); David Rollason, *The Local Origins of Modern Society: Gloucestershire 1500–1800* (1992); Albion Urdank, *Religion and Society in a Cotswold Vale: Nailsworth, Gloucestershire, 1780–1865* (1990).

13 Peter Burke, *New Perspectives on Historical Writing* (1991), 1–23; Pat Hudson, 'Regional and local history: globalisation, postmodernism and the future', *JORALS*, 20 (1999), 5–24.

14 Pat Hudson, 'Industrialisation in Britain: the challenge of micro-history'. *Family and Community History*, 2/1 (1999) 5–6.

15 This risks simplifying the enormous output from CAMPOP since the 1960s, which includes E.A. Wrigley and R.S. Schofield, *The Population History of England, 1541–1871: A Reconstruction* (1981), which used results from a survey of 404 parishes (relying mainly on material collected by amateur scholars); Peter Laslett, *The World We Have Lost* (3rd edn., 1983); idem, *Household and Family in Past Time* (1972), idem, *Family Life and Illicit Love in Earlier Generations* (1977), and many others.

16 E.A. Wrigley, 'Family limitation in pre-industrial England', *Economic History Review*, 19 (1966).

17 E.A. Wrigley, 'The changing occupational structure of Colyton over two centuries', *Local Population Studies*, 18 (1977), 9–21.

18 Pam Sharpe, 'Literally spinsters: a new interpretation of local economy and demography in Colyton in the seventeenth and eighteenth centuries', *Economic History Review*, 44 (1991), 46–65.

19 Pam Sharpe, 'The total reconstitution method: a tool for class specific study', *Local Population* Studies, 44 (1990), 41–51.

20 Barry Reay, *Microhistories: Demography, Society and Culture in Rural England, 1800–1930* (1996), xxi–xxii; Hudson, 'Industrialisation in Britain', 5–16; Christopher French, 'Taking up "the challenge of micro-history": social conditions in Kingston upon Thames in the late nineteenth and early twentieth centuries', *LH*, 36/1 (2006), 17–28.

21 Charles Phythian-Adams, *Land of the Cumbrians: A Study in British Provincial Origins, AD400–1120* (1996); Christopher J. Brooke, *Safe Sanctuaries: Security and Defence in Anglo-Scottish Border Churches, 1290–1690* (2000).

22 Mark Stoyle, *West Briton: Cornish Identities and the Early Modern British State* (2002) The idea of Cornish identity has been discussed at length by historians of the county, which now has an Institute of Cornish Studies (an adjunct of Exeter University) to look in detail at what this meant. *Cornish Studies*, 11 (2003), reflected this preoccupation with articles on A.L. Rowse and the writing of British and Cornish History, the Celtic Revival and Anglicanism in Cornwall 1870–1930, and on where and when Cornish was spoken. Each of these contributions was concerned with the cultural distinctiveness of the county, but it was recognised that even within Cornwall the western part of the county was more regionally committed to Celtic values than other areas.

23 E.W. Gilbert, 'The idea of a region', *Geography*, 45 (1960), 158; G.W.S. Robinson, 'The geographical region: form and function', *Scottish Geographical Magazine*, 69 (1953), 51; P.L. Garside and M. Hebberet (eds), *British Regionalism, 1900–2000* (1989); R. Johnston, J. Hauer and G. Hoekveld (eds), *Regional Geography: Current Developments and Future Prospects* (1990).

24 The regions were carefully chosen by the editors, but Dr John Marshall, the founder in 1978 of the Conference of Regional and Local Historians (*CORAL*), was particularly annoyed. As a result, the Longman series was dismissed by *CORAL* (newsletter no 12 undated c.1981) with a reference

to 'arbitrarily divided portions', and *CORAL*'s journal, the *Journal of Regional and Local Studies (JORALS)* was reluctant to review the books.

25 *JORALS*, 10/2 (1990), 5.

26 Ibid., 41; J.H. Bettey, *Wessex from AD1000* (1986); David Hey, *Yorkshire from AD1000* (1986); Marie B. Rowlands, *The West Midlands from AD1000* (1987).

27 *JORALS*, 10/2 (1990), 6.

28 Peter Brandon and Brian Short, *The South East from AD1000* (1990).

29 J.V. Beckett, *The East Midlands from AD1000* (1988), 1–10; Evelyn Lord, 'The boundaries of local history: a discussion paper', *JORALS*, 11 (1991), 75–87, is an attempt to contextualise the different approaches.

30 H.C. Darby, 'Some early ideas on the agricultural regions of England', *Agricultural History Review*, 2 (1954), 30–47; Joan Thirsk, *Fenland Farming in the Sixteenth Century* (1953), the first of a series of occasional papers published by the Department of English Local History at Leicester which explored the different issues under debate; idem, 'Industries in the countryside' in F.J. Fisher (ed.), *Essays in the Economic and Social History of Tudor and Stuart England* (1961).

31 Richardson, 10–11, 139–59.

32 A. Everitt, 'Country, county and town: patterns of regional evolution in England', *Transactions of the Royal Historical Society*, 29 (1979), 81.

33 Ibid., 83.

34 A. Everitt, 'River and wold: reflections on the historical origin of regions and pays', *Journal of Historical Geography*, 3 (1977), 1–20.

35 A. Everitt, *Landscape and Community in England* (1985), introduction. Other articles by Everitt addressing similar issues included 'Place Names and pays', *Nomina*, 3 (1979), 95–112, and 'The making of the agrarian landscape of Kent', *Archaeologica Cantiana*, 92 (1976), 1–31.

36 H.S.A. Fox, 'The people of the wolds in English settlement history', in Michael Aston, David Austin and Christopher Dyer (eds), *The Rural Settlements of Medieval England* (1989), 77–101; Charles Rawding, *The Lincolnshire Wolds in the Nineteenth Century* (2001); B.K. Roberts, 'Rural settlement and regional contrasts: questions of continuity and colonisation', *Rural History*, 1 (1990), 51–72.

37 Charles Phythian-Adams (ed.), *Societies, Cultures and Kinship, 1580–1850: Cultural Provinces and English Local History* (1993), 9–10, 13, 14.

38 *ECH*, 243–4; John Goodacre, *The Transformation of a Peasant Economy: Townspeople and Villagers in the Lutterworth Area, 1500–1700* (1994).

39 Phythian-Adams, *Societies*, 59.

40 J.D. Marshall, 'Local and regional history – or both? A dialogue', *LH*, 13/1 (1978); E. Royle (ed.), *Issues of Regional Identity* (1998), 1.

41 Marshall, 'Local and Regional'.

42 J.D. Marshall, 'Why study regions? (1)', *Journal of Regional and Local Studies*, 5/1 (1985), 23.

43 J.D. Marshall, 'Why study regions? (2): some historical considerations', *Journal of Regional and Local Studies*, 6/1 (1986), 2–3. The overall context

of Marshall's intellectual thinking is given in Elizabeth Roberts and Oliver M. Westall, 'J.D. Marshall: the making of the identity of a regional historian', in Royle (ed.), *Issues*, 226–39. Marshall did not comment on this chapter of his festschrift when, somewhat incongruously, he reviewed it for *Journal of Regional and Local Studies*, 18 (1998), 49–60.

44 Norman McCord, 'The regional identity of north-east England in the nineteenth and early twentieth centuries', in Royle (ed.), *Issues*, 102–17; W. Stokes, 'Regional finance and the definition of a financial region' in ibid., 118–53; Robert Colls, *The Pitmen of the Northern Coalfield: Work, Culture, and Protest, 1790–1850* (1987).

45 J. Obelkevich, *Religion and Rural Society: South Lindsey 1825–1875* (1976), 2–4.

46 M.B. Rowlands, *Masters and Men in the Small Metalware Trades of the West Midlands* (1975); Victor Skipp, *Crisis and Development: An Ecological Case Study of the Forest of Arden, 1570–1674* (1978).

47 J.D. Marshall and J.K. Walton, *The Lake Counties from 1830 to the mid-Twentieth Century* (1981), ix.

48 P. Deane and W.A. Cole, *British Economic Growth, 1688–1959* (2nd edn, 1967); Peter Mathias, *The First Industrial Nation, 1700–1914* (1969).

49 M. Palmer (ed.), *The Onset of Industrialisation* (1977).

50 Sidney Pollard, *Peaceful Conquest: The Industrialisation of Europe, 1760–1970* (1981); idem, *Marginal Europe: The Contribution of Marginal Lands since the Middle Ages* (1997), 221–54; Royle (ed.), *Issues*.

51 J. Langton, 'The Industrial Revolution and the regional geography of England', *Transactions of the Institute of British Geographers*, new series, 9 (1984), 145–67.

52 G. Turnbull, 'Canals, coal and regional growth during the Industrial Revolution', *Economic History Review*, 40 (1987), 537–60; D. Gregory, 'The production of regions in England's Industrial Revolution', *Journal of Historical Geography*, 14 (1988), 50–8; J. Langton, 'The production of regions in England's Industrial Revolution: a response', *Journal of Historical Geography*, 14 (1988), 170–6.

53 Pat Hudson (ed.), *Regions and Industries: A Perspective on the Industrial Revolution in Britain* (1989); Maxine Berg and Pat Hudson, 'Rehabilitating the Industrial Revolution', *Economic History Review*, 45 (1992), 38–9; John Beckett and John Heath, 'When was the Industrial Revolution in the East Midlands?', *Midland History*, 13 (1988), 77–94.

54 J. Langton, *Geographical Change and Industrial Revolution: Coalmining in South-West Lancashire, 1590–1799* (1979); Colin Pooley and Jean Turnbull, *Migration and Mobility in Britain since the Eighteenth Century* (1998), 82–5; Langton, 'Industrial Revolution', 157.

55 John Langton, 'The continuity of regional culture: Lancashire Catholicism from the late sixteenth to the early nineteenth century', in Royle (ed.), *Issues*, 82–101. See also Hudson, 'Regional and Local History', 5–24, especially 13–16.

56 D. Gregory, 'The production of regions in England's Industrial Revolution', *Journal of Historical Geography*, 14 (1988) 54; Hudson (ed.), *Regions and Industries*, 21; P. Hudson, *The Industrial Revolution* (1992), 104; R.A. Butlin, 'Regions in England and Wales c.1900–14', in R. Dodgshon and R.A. Butlin (eds.), *Historical Geography of England and Wales* (2nd edn, 1990), 223; Pollard, *Peaceful Conquest*, 34; Langton, 'Industrial Revolution', 151–4.

57 Langton, 'Industrial Revolution', 162–3; Jon Stobart, 'Regions, localities and industrialisation: evidence from the East Midlands, circa 1780–1840', *Environment and Planning A*, 33 (2001), 1305–25.

58 J. Stobart, *The First Industrial Region: North-West England, c.1700–60* (2004), 223; Brian Short, 'Deindustrialisation of the Weald', in Hudson (ed.), *Regions and Industries*, 156–74.

59 Langton, 'Industrial Revolution', 156–7; Everitt, 'Country, county and town'.

60 VCH *Staffordshire*, 8 (1963), 252–71; *The Times*, 6, 8 June 1925; M.W. Greenslade, 'The Potteries: a question of regional identity', in A.D.M. Phillips (ed.), *The Potteries* (1993), 164–76; Ray Johnson, 'Cultural traditions in the potteries', in Phillips (ed.), *The Potteries*, 282.

61 David Hey, *The Fiery Blades of Hallamshire: Sheffield and Its Neighbourhood, 1660–1740* (1991).

62 Marshall, 'Communities', 36–47.

63 David Hackett Fischer, *Albion's Seed: Four British Folkway in America* (1989).

64 Dennis Hitch, 'Cambridgeshire emigrants to Australia, 1842–75: a family and community perspective', *Family and Community History*, 5/2 (2002), 85–97.

65 K.D.M. Snell, 'Gravestones, belonging and local attachment in England, 1700–2000', *Past & Present*, 179 (May 2003), 97–134.

66 Michael Ignatieff, *The Needs of Strangers*, unreferenced quote in Keith Robbins, 'Local history and the study of national history', *The Historian*, 27 (1990), 15–18.

67 George and Yanina Sheeran, 'Reconstructing local history', *LH*, 29/4 (1999), 256–62; idem, 'Discourses in local history', *Rethinking History*, 2 (1998), 65–85.

68 *LH* 30/2 (2000), 125.

69 For other responses see *LH* 29/3 (1999), 187, 259. See also K. Tiller, *English Local History: The State of the Art* (1998), 22–3.

70 Christopher Taylor, 'People and places: local history and landscape history', *LH*, 32/4 (2002), 234–49.

71 F. Furedi, *Mythical Past, Elusive Future: History and Society in an Anxious Age* (1992), 230, 235–9.

72 Alan Crosby, '*The Amateur Historian* and *The Local Historian*: some thoughts after fifty years', *LH*, 32/3 (2002), 152.

IX *New approaches: family history, towns, landscape and other specialisms*

In the nineteenth century antiquarianism was an umbrella which sheltered a variety of specialisms connected with what we would today call local history. Eventually some of these specialisms ducked out from under the umbrella to make their own way in the world as separate disciplines, notably archaeology and history. Unfortunately, what was left tended to be seen as the parts no one else wanted, and 'antiquarian' gradually became a pejorative term. The image was perpetuated by the seemingly unbreakable fascination of county journals with church bells, family pedigrees, heraldic bearings, and other relatively esoteric interests, which were written up with little reference to a wider context. This was part of the reason why local history suffered from an image problem. We have seen how some of the difficulties were eroded through the growing association from the 1920s with economic history – itself a new discipline living in a relatively hostile environment – and from the 1960s, social history. Yet even as local history has blossomed in the years since c.1960, the process of fragmentation has continued as separate disciplines have developed with ever greater specialisation. Family history, urban history, landscape studies, and place-name analysis, all turned into specialist subjects with their own methodologies and outlets. Consequently some of the key issues which were once the province of the local historian are now disciplines in themselves, with more, or sometimes less good relations with the original subject. In this chapter we look particularly at the way the study of the family has become a separate area of interest, and at how the study of towns is now often seen as separate from local history. We shall look also at some of the sub-disciplines which now have a separate but related existence, including landscape studies, industrial archaeology, and place-names. The list is not exhaustive, and any split with local history is more apparent than real. After a storm, we put down the umbrella and go our separate ways, but that does not mean we lose contact; indeed, the specialisms we shall be looking at in the following pages can be seen as an enrichment of the whole process of studying local history.

Family history

The interest in family history has been one of the most remarkable stories of post-war Britain, but it was hardly a new development. Family history, although associated in the public mind with a leisure pursuit developed only in recent times, has a long and distinguished past. As we have seen, much of the commercial basis for earlier local history revolved around family pedigrees and manorial descents, and similar subjects populated the pages of early county society journals; indeed, they are still reflected in the manorial descents outlined in some volumes of the VCH. Nor has family history been driven only by curiosity. In the wake of the Norman Conquest, establishing a pedigree gave a family legitimacy and credibility in land ownership, hence the lengthy statements of descents found on the Plea rolls, the records of actions brought under the common law in the courts of Common Pleas, Exchequer, and Kings Bench. In these early days much depended on orally transmitted knowledge, but in the course of time the need to establish the legitimacy of descents led to more sophisticated methods of recording and establishing pedigrees.

The great topographical studies in the sixteenth and seventeenth centuries raised the profile of individual families, and Lambarde, Dugdale and Thoroton pieced together genealogies partly because of the leading local role played by gentry families, and partly for straightforward commercial reasons. This period saw the first systematic interest in pedigrees, with searches of Chronicles and deeds, and in the records of Chancery and the Exchequer. The rise of many new gentry families in the sixteenth century into a landed society which placed considerable emphasis on ancient blood and lineage, encouraged the process. The Heralds' Visitation from the 1560s recorded many pedigrees, some of them probably fabricated, but by the 1580s and beyond, and in keeping with the stricter approach to records more generally, greater emphasis was laid on the use of record evidence. Augustine Vincent, who had studied under Camden, and who entered the College of Arms in 1597, had previously worked in the Tower Record Office. He brought a knowledge of the public records to the study of genealogy. John Smyth (d.1640) of Nibley, Gloucestershire, steward of the Berkeley family, wrote their history and genealogy partly from the public records and partly from their family papers and charter at Berkeley Castle.

As in so many other areas, it was really Dugdale who made the major breakthrough, in both his *Antiquities of Warwickshire* (1656) and his *Baronage of England* (1675–76). Both studies showed his skill in compiling evidence and drawing conclusions citing contemporary record evidence for every statement made – a principle still followed by the VCH. From this lead came a range of new interests, and particularly the use of sources such as parish registers to supplement the usual dependence on church monuments. Registers had begun in the 1530s, although they became more commonly available from the 1560s. County histories from Dugdale onwards contained numerous pedigrees of the landed gentry, but not all were as honest as Dugdale and some undoubtedly included a number of highly dubious material simply because of the need to attract subscriptions.

Towards the end of the eighteenth and into the nineteenth century the publication and improved arrangement of the public records aided genealogists, while the growth of the middle-class saw the development of several large commercial genealogical practices. The Burke family, John Burke (1787–1848), his son Sir Bernard Burke (1814–92) and grandson Henry Farnham Burke (d.1930), set up a major research and publishing practice which spawned Burke's *Peerage* from 1826, *Commoners and Landed Gentry* from 1837, and *General Armory* (1842–84). The books were far from faultless, and they were particularly apt to recycle family myths. J. Horace Round (1854–1928) launched an attack on pedigrees which 'preserved like flies in amber the follies and errors' of earlier generations. Professor E.A. Freeman also attacked what he considered to be the numerous fictions in Burke's publications. Without doubt many published family histories from the nineteenth century, including those in early volumes of the county societies, have to be treated with care if not outright scepticism, although the best series is probably the thirty-five volumes published 1893–1921 by J.J. Howard and Frederick Arthur Crisp under the title *Visitation of England and Wales*. The temptation to slide over awkward linkages was, in any case, encouraged by the standard landowner practice of adopting a male heir, perhaps a nephew, in the absence of a direct descendant, but insisting on a name change if he was to inherit the property. In this way the line was ostensibly maintained.[1]

By the end of the nineteenth century the interest in pedigrees and family history was rapidly expanding, and a number of guides was published to help individuals and families with the process of compiling a family history. Among the more impressive of these was W.F.W. Phillimore's *How to Write the History of a Family* (1897 and 1900) and his *Pedigree Work* which was revised and reissued down to 1936. The Society of Genealogists was founded in 1911 'to promote, encourage and foster the study, science and knowledge of genealogy by all lawful means', and one of its main aims was to bring together in one place the various indexes and transcripts which were then being made, an aim it continues to fulfil.[2] In 1925 it began publishing *The Genealogists' Magazine*. Much emphasis was still being laid on good lines and royal descents, and little attempt was made to link the history of individual families to the times through which they lived. The genealogies of ordinary families were virtually ignored, although a notable exception was William Miller Giggs's *A History of the Higges or Higgs Family* (1933).

The transformation of family history from the pursuit of leisured gentlemen with plentiful time on their hands, to a popular interest shared by thousands of people across the country, was still to come after the Second World War. The first of a new generation of guides for beginners was Arthur Willis's *Genealogy for Beginners*, published in 1955. In 1961 the Society of Genealogists staged an exhibition on the theme 'The Ancestry of the Common Man', and it was from around the early 1960s that interest began to grow. Anthony Wagner, Garter King of Arms 1961–78, wrote a number of books exploring the nature of the subject and the possibilities of extending pedigrees into the past,[3] but the real development of a mass interest was taking place through what was increasingly termed 'family history'. Many local family history societies were formed in the early 1970s, and the subject was boosted in 1979 by a popular BBC television series called 'Family History'.

By the end of the 1970s family history societies had been founded in most counties, usually with members who had no formal academic background or training, but whose main interest was in their ancestors. The societies brought like-minded people together, and they formed a Federation in 1974, which did a good deal to publicise and assist the subject through regular conferences and numerous publications. A popular commercial magazine, 'Family Tree', was founded in 1984. Research was also helped by developments abroad, notably the role of the Mormon church through the Genealogical Society of Utah. This has made its materials available through Family History Centres across the country. Its International Genealogical Index (IGI) became available in England in 1977, and in 1985 the British Genealogical Record Users' Committee was formed to support its microfilming programme.

This was just one of the many developments relating to the availability of sources. Parish register printing began in the nineteenth century. In 1894 Phillimore, in conjunction with Thomas Matthews Blagg, produced the first of 233 volumes containing transcripts of marriage registers of about 1,650 parishes. The Society of Genealogists collected printed, manuscript, and typescript copies of registers, while the Parochial Registers and Records Measure (1978) ensured that the majority of parish records over 100 years old have been deposited in county record offices where they have often been transcribed by local family history societies, and in many cases made available over the web.[4] The societies have also been active in transcribing tombstones. The 1920s saw the College of Arms and other groups collecting directories on a systematic basis to identify streets and houses in which family members may have lived. Indexes were, and are, prepared for census returns, directories, and post-1837 civil registration. The gradual release (under the 100 year rule imposed on sensitive documents) of nineteenth-century census enumerators' books, together with the availability of probate material, has greatly boosted the materials available to searchers. Such was the scale of demand that in 1997 TNA and Office for National Statistics opened a new Family Records Centre in London.[5]

Interest in genealogy is now international, with migrant families across the globe taking an interest in their roots. When, on 1 January 2002, the 1901 census became available online, TNA's carefully developed system was overwhelmed by the huge demand, and it was nine months before it was working again. The increasing availability of source materials on the internet is making family history ever more accessible to individuals of limited means and with limited time. Modern family history, or family tree history, remains indisputably a part-time or retirement occupation for individuals and families, an interest which has developed from a combination of source availability, greater leisure time, and an increasing life span. It is also easy. It takes only a few hours to learn by experience the basics of researching the census materials online, and then to branch off into many other interests. Family tree courses are readily available for those needing a starting point,[6] and books and guides are available in abundance either through local bookshops, or family history societies. The National Archives, in addition to being instrumental in establishing the Family Record Centre, has produced various guides to records which are largely aimed at the family history market, but which have significant spin-offs for local historians more generally. Its popular guide to finding your ancestors among the records of The National Archives is now in its seventh edition.[7] Computer software has been designed specifically for the purpose of recording family trees.

The real difficulty is to decide what status we can place on modern family history. As in the seventeenth century, so today family historians tend to be fascinated by their own backgrounds, and wholly uninterested in anyone else's or, indeed, in broader issues connected with family development including employment, poverty, and other issues. None of them is likely to aspire to publish in the academic *Journal of Family History* established in the United States in 1975, and sub-titled 'Studies in Family, Kinship and Demography', or the online family history journal started in 1996. They might just take an interest in *Family & Community History*, established in 1998, but they will find the articles far more concerned with academic study of the family, with the household, kinship groups, and the interaction of the family with other institutions and social processes, not with individual families. In this sense academic family history parallels urban history in being interested less in individuals and more in concepts and ideas about families.

In England the first attempts to write a rounded history of the family as a social institution began in the wake of E.P. Thompson's *Making of the English Working Class*, and during the 1970s studies such as Peter Laslett and Richard Wall's, *Household and Family in Past Time* (1972), and Michael Anderson's *Family Life in Nineteenth-Century Lancashire* (1971) began the process of analysing the family in detail. Since then a great deal of effort has gone into the study of the family at all social levels from the aristocracy through the middle-class to the poor, and taking in the particular role of women and the distinctive position of children. As a rule, family tree historians have not been particularly interested in these wider issues, but the substantial audiences for the BBC's 'Who Do Think You Are?' series suggests a turning of the tide. Much of the emphasis has been on contextualising families, which may also explain the growing popularity of VCH parish studies mounted on the website British History Online.

Yet linking work on individual families into the wider context of local history remains a challenge. Professor David Hey has made particular efforts to create the idea of family history leading into the study of the wider community. Professor Hey, with a background in adult education, and with the title of Professor of Local and Family History, has been ideally placed to develop these linkages, which he has done in a series of books aimed partly at the family history market.[8] Hey's work was specifically developed with a view to beginning a dialogue with family historians, in the hope of integrating their work within local history more generally through the study of surnames, mobility and family structures, in an attempt to bridge the perceived gap. Recently Hey has published *Journeys in Family History* (2004), a

National Archives guide to exploring one's past and finding one's ancestors. The book encourages people to explore their own past through searching out their ancestors, and shows them how to work backwards to make family links into the nineteenth century, the early modern period (1550–1800), and even, for the most hardy, the Middle Ages, before 1550. Each of the main chapters includes a section on the appropriate sources. As such the book leads them through family history into the study of the wider 'family' community.

Hey has not been entirely alone in his quest to link family and local history together in fruitful collaboration. A similar approach was adopted in the 1990s by the Open University in a series of publications entitled 'Studying Family and Community History, 19th and 20th Centuries', and linked to a course designed to offer practical suggestions for research projects, exercises for honing the relevant skills, and help with using the relevant sources, written, oral and visual. The material was set within the context of demography, social and economic history, sociology, historical geography, and anthropology in an effort to bring family history within the broader scheme of historical studies. Attention was paid to population movements across borders, and to migration, work and occupations, social mobility, elections, religion, culture and leisure.[9] The possibilities, in other words, for using family history within the broader context of local history are recognised, and already there is published work on migration using data compiled by family tree historians.[10] It remains the case, even so, that many of those searching for their roots think of the subject as an amusing and absorbing hobby, and they have no obvious interest in producing a documented family history. Nor do they see their work as of any value beyond their own immediate family.

Urban history

Antiquarians studied towns just as they did counties and parishes, and some of the town biographies of the eighteenth and early nineteenth centuries were classics in their own right. For all sorts of reasons, they were often gilded, celebratory accounts, which tended to emphasise politics and politicians, local government, the manorial court, the borough, and other overtly 'political' issues. In the twentieth century the growing link between local history and economic history had a significant impact on urban studies. W.G. Hoskins's, *Industry, Trade and People in Exeter, 1688–1800* (1936) was, in many senses, a prototype study indicating the potential for economic and social analysis of an eighteenth-century town. As such it moved away from the earlier tradition of urban celebration, and pointed local historians in the direction of an economic framework for urban studies. David Chambers also wrote urban history, in his case on Nottingham, and he supervised Roy Church's study of the same Victorian town, which was essentially a piece of modern economic history in an urban context with little 'social change' of the type which developed following the publication of Thompson's *The Making of the English Working Class* in 1963.[11] An unusual, but extraordinarily impressive contribution to urban history in the post-war years was Sir Francis Hill's four-volume study of Lincoln. Sir Francis (Frank) Hill (1899–1980) was a Lincoln solicitor, and his work occupied forty-five years. What impressed commentators was the way in which he used 'in a systematic and coherent way, very rarely seen before this time, the available techniques of archaeology, topographical description, place-name studies, and genealogy'.[12]

Town biographies fell out of favour with the academic community when a new approach to urban history reached England from the United States in the 1960s. The emphasis came to be placed not on individual towns and cities, but on the demographic, social and spatial processes of urbanisation generally. The new practitioners were dismissive of 'urban biographies' as antiquarian, simply because they were 'case' studies without a comparative perspective. The pioneer text in an English context was Jim Dyos's study of the London district of Camberwell, published in 1961, but the movement towards a separate academic discipline was institutionalised two years later when an Urban History Group was formed.[13] It was officially launched in 1966, and its publishing arm, the *Urban History Yearbook*, appeared for the first time in 1974. Around 700 scholars were recognisably urban historians by 1974, and the *Yearbook* was devised as a forum for discussing 'both the direction in which the subject may be seen to be moving and its general content'. An introductory editorial to the first edition reflected the new thinking: urban history was expected to be 'likely to be dealing with processes that extend beyond the boundaries of a particular community or region to embrace the whole population'.[14] By 1979 it seemed reasonable to conclude that 'urban history and local history have developed in totally different spheres . . . Urban history is local in scale but curiously distanced from the object of its investigations.'[15]

This divorce was possible because the new urban history was concerned with the processes which drove and determined urban life, and its practitioners studied individual towns not in their own right – as earlier generations had done – but as examples of urban growth or other economic and social 'urban' issues.[16] Even so, case studies continued to dominate the bibliographical listings carried by the main academic journal, *Urban History*, which succeeded the yearbook in 1992. Richard Rodger, who became editor in 1992, sensibly adjusted the focus of interest to stress that city biographies were recognised as 'essential' by modern urban historians.[17] This did not satisfy all the professional urbanists: as Lynn Holles Lees expressed it in 1994, 'urban biographies have absorbed all too much of urban historians energies'.[18] The problem with processes was that they distanced the study from the towns with which they were dealing: urban historians, in other words, were no longer men and women seeking to boost civic pride via a celebratory account of the history of a particular town, but passive, distant, commentators using data about places to demonstrate wider arguments about economic and, increasingly over time, social change. In this process there was also a tendency to cherry-pick case studies, and much more attention was paid to cities and great towns, than to middle ranking and smaller towns. As an academic discipline, in which individual cases were subsumed entirely within the general arguments, urban history came fully of age with the publication of the three-volume *Cambridge Urban History* in 2000.[19] London is the only city or town named in any of the chapter headings.

The rise of 'professional' urban history has, perhaps ironically, left the study of towns as places to local historians in a manner we would probably not have anticipated.[20] Local historians, less encumbered by a methodological purity, can study towns as places, concentrating on the site, the buildings, size (both in terms of street pattern and population), and issues of civic administration, culture, religion, education and leisure.[21] This in turn has led to some major urban histories, often collective ventures, as with recent studies of Sheffield, Glasgow, Norwich and Nottingham. A similar volume for Liverpool is currently in preparation. In these volumes the history of the city is discussed in both a chronological and thematic form, using the full range of available source materials, and employing the skills of archaeologists, local historians, and others, both professional and amateur. The cities themselves are examined within the wider urban historical issues, and the result is an urban biography which covers the town's history from settlement to the present, but without the laudatory accounts which typified an earlier generation of such studies.[22]

From a different perspective, the VCH has also had to face up to the implications of the new urban history. The parochial structure of counties creates problems for studying towns, which are usually multi-parished. This may mean that some urban activities were governed by parish considerations, at least until the municipal reforms of the 1830s. Until then, the poor rate, and highways, which were parochial responsibilities, could be separate responsibilities within towns. For the VCH the limitations of the parochial approach were considerable. St Helens, Lancashire, was treated as a district within the township of Windle in the parish of Prescot. Consequently, the history of this important manufacturing town in south Lancashire was dismissed in fifteen column inches neatly hidden within an account of a township within a parish. Histories of south London suburbs in VCH Surrey virtually ignored their urban growth.[23] This, of course, was in the early days before the First World War, and the VCH began to treat towns in a systematic manner in the 1960s and 1970s, just as urban history was assuming a separate identity. But the VCH combined the study of a particular town, using its well honed standard framework, usually within the context of surrounding parishes, especially where these had been partially or completely integrated via a borough extension. As a result, since the 1970s the VCH has produced topographical volumes devoted to Beverley, Gloucester, Coventry, Hull, Oxford, Stafford, Telford and parts of the West Midlands conurbation. Eight volumes cover parts of Essex and Middlesex that have become London suburbs, and ten include the histories of towns of local importance including Banbury, Brentwood, Bridlington, Crawley, Devizes, Harlow, Horsham, Marlborough, Stroud, Woodstock, and Worthing. York (1960) was the first single volume of a city. Recent urban studies have included Witney in Oxfordshire, and Burton-upon-Trent in Staffordshire.

Landscape history

Landscape history progressed rapidly following the publication of Hoskins's *The Making*. Various developments from Hoskins's original views were set out by Christopher Taylor in his 1988 edition of the book. Taylor pointed out, in particular, that Hoskins had modified his views as new methods of analysis became available. We now accept that the origins of nucleated settlements in village landscapes should be placed towards the end of the Anglo-Saxon period, rather than at the beginning where Hoskins located them. It is also recognised that some villages were subjected to a second or even third wave of change, producing a regular plan, hence the appearance of two parallel rows of farmhouses facing each other across a street with tofts of equal size within a regular plan. A good example of this type of village is Laxton, Nottinghamshire.[24] Brian Roberts's work has enabled us to understand more clearly than Hoskins did the emergence of village forms and patterns across time, and the limited role of parliamentary enclosure in landscape change has become increasingly apparent.[25] Another modification post-Hoskins was the greater understanding we now have of changes to landscape and their social repercussions towards the end of the Middle Ages, especially in the thirteenth, fourteenth and fifteenth centuries. Colonisation and reclamation in the thirteenth century helped to create a more urban economy.[26]

These changing priorities have been more than matched by an expansion in the range of landscape history, which now covers physical landscape, particularly in relation to settlement patterns, land use, planned or organic change, standing buildings and artefacts. Where Hoskins was able to contain the whole range of study within the covers of a single book, since the 1950s there have been specialist works on different types of landscape, including urban and industrial, and studies of village types, field types, boundaries, hedges and so forth. We have been reminded as a result that relict features in the landscape tell us that past societies had priorities we may have almost entirely lost, notably portrayed through fish ponds and rabbit warrens. Rabbits have effectively disappeared from our landscapes and our consciousness of them – except as furry semi-domesticated animals – has more or less disappeared. They were once raised in vast numbers for the dining table, and their fur was used for clothing.

Landscape history has grown rapidly as a discipline, partly because of the threat to historic landscapes which is apparent to us all. In recent years the grubbing up of hedgerows has raised questions about their function and usefulness, while considerable acreages of ancient woodland have been destroyed since 1945 as a result of the subsidised agri-business. Today landscape history encompasses a range of disciplines including archaeology, anthropology, art, poetry and cultural geography.[27] As Christopher Taylor has expressed it, his life-long interest in landscape history has 'necessitated working with a variety of scholars in many disciplines, including archaeology, geography, geology, botany, vernacular architecture and art history', although he much regretted 'an increasing number of publications on landscape history involving modernism, structuralism, phenomenology, retrogressive analysis and so on'.[28] A journal, *Landscape Studies*, was founded in 1970, to bring together the practitioners of the subject, archaeological, architectural, and historical. A second journal, *Landscapes*, was founded in 2000. Richard Muir has emphasised the contribution by amateurs to landscape studies, writing that 'the powerhouse of landscape history lies with the unsung field-workers . . . the men and women with the muddy boots and aching joints'.[29]

Vernacular architecture

Landscapes also meant buildings. At one time no real distinction existed between the study of documents, monuments, and landscape features. As archaeology came to represent a separate discipline in the nineteenth century, this situation began subtly to change. Initially, archaeologists confined themselves to prehistory, but from the late Victorian years they gradually moved forward in time to the medieval and, by the 1950s and 1960s, post-medieval periods, hence the founding of *Post-Medieval Archaeology* in 1967.

Alongside this movement, although not strictly in tandem, architectural historians broadened their interests away from a diet of churches, manor houses and public buildings, to take in the homes of ordinary people, including farmhouses and cottages, from about the sixteenth century. This shift can loosely be characterised as a concern with vernacular architecture, the buildings put up by local craftsmen who were not influenced by conventions associated with 'polite' design. Although the term 'vernacular architecture' has been used since at least 1839 to describe the minor buildings of town and countryside alike, the study came of age in the 1950s with the setting up of the Vernacular Architecture Group in 1954 (annual journal, *Vernacular Architecture* from 1970). The formation of the group followed the publication the previous year of an influential article by Hoskins on what he termed the great rebuilding of rural England between 1570 and 1640. Maurice Barley joined the Group in 1955, and his experience led not only to his book *The English Farmhouse and Cottage* (1961), and two substantial chapters in volumes of the *Cambridge Agrarian History of England and Wales*, but to his purchase of a weekend cottage in Brecon where he could put into practice some of the principles he learnt in the Group.[30]

Industrial archaeology

While archaeology has been a separate discipline since the late nineteenth century, with continuing and significant overlap in areas such as landscape history, a new discipline arrived in the 1950s and 1960s, known today as industrial archaeology. The study of industry, and of industrial technology, has a long history which includes several pioneer local and regional studies,[31] and the study of technology has flourished since the founding in 1919 of the Newcomen Society. In the post-Second World War years, as many of Britain's industries ran into economic difficulty, a group of interested amateurs became concerned with the fate of what was increasingly seen as a major archaeological heritage. They soon discovered a community of interests with archaeologists, who were now studying the post-medieval period. It was a logical step further to examine the archaeology of industrial Britain, and this interest really took off in the 1960s with the founding of industrial museums, the setting up of the Ironbridge Gorge Museum in 1967, and of the Arkwright Society in 1971.[32]

Industrial archaeology took over where traditional archaeologists left off, at the onset of the Industrial Revolution. It was primarily concerned with the study of tangible evidence of social, economic and technological development of the past 250 years. Although many of the early practitioners were enthusiasts, whose standards of recording were reminiscent of the eighteenth-century antiquaries, much good work was done, and buildings saved, among them Papplewick Pumping Station in Nottinghamshire, and Moira furnace in Leicestershire. In 1973 the Association of Industrial Archaeologists (AIA) was set up to promote the study of industrial archaeology and to encourage improved standards of recording: 'there is a world-wide concern for the conservation of industrial monuments . . . outstanding relics of the industrial past', as the first edition of the dedicated journal put it in 1976.[33] The efforts of the Ancient Monuments Commissions in England, Scotland and Wales also helped to raise standards in the investigation, recording and publishing of industrial artefacts. Also important has been the work of the Ironbridge Institute.

Two experienced industrial archaeologists, Marilyn Palmer and Peter Neaverson, have set down principles for industrial archaeologists to follow. In their view, it should be set firmly within mainstream archaeology, although they accept that conventional techniques and concepts need modifying to take account of the physical evidence, and the availability of documentary sources. Their work is a further sign of the maturing of a discipline which was once subject to significant criticism for its neglect of careful recording standards.[34] Nor did it do the subject any harm when Sir Neil Cossons, once the curator at Ironbridge, became chairman of English Heritage in 2000. For obvious reasons, industrial archaeology is strongly identified with landscape studies, as well as buildings, structures and machinery. As such it contributes to our understanding of individual communities, hence the relationship with local history.

Oral testimony

So far, we have looked in this chapter at disciplines which began under the umbrella of local history, but which have come to be seen as significant subjects in their own right. We turn now to two which have developed separately, but are integral to our understanding of past communities: oral testimony, and place-name analysis.

The origins of oral testimony lie in social anthropology, particularly the study of societies which do not have a literary tradition. Much early work on oral testimony was linked to the recapturing of experience in past events, either ordinary daily events, or significant historical moments such as the experiences of soldiers on the western front in the First World War.

As recording equipment has improved there have been important spin-offs for students of dialect, folklore and linguistics. Early recording was haphazard, partly because of a lack of understanding of how memory (and prejudice) might work, but the growing availability of good quality tape recorders coincided with the work of George Ewart Evans (1909–88) whose *Ask the Fellows Who Cut the Hay* (1956) used memories of people born in the last quarter of the nineteenth century and living in the village of Blaxhall, Suffolk. A series of further books in the 1960s and 1970s helped to capture the mentality of rural communities in the age of horse power and hand tools. His work inspired others: in 1960, for example, the Nottinghamshire Local History Council held a competition entitled 'The Memories of a Villager'.[35]

With the publication of the first edition of *Oral History* in 1971, a methodology was gradually developed for recording and using memory.[36] From the perspective of the local historian the challenge has been to move from description, to oral testimony as a way of analysing past societies.[37] Some vital research has been undertaken using the testimony of people whose voices would not otherwise have been heard. Elizabeth Roberts's *A Woman's Place: an Oral History of Working Class Women, 1890–1940* (1984) offered an outstanding example of the use of oral testimony in local studies, and of the importance of women and children in the way local history is now researched. Similarly important has been Carl Chinn's *They Worked All Their Lives: Women of the Urban Poor in England, 1880–1939* (1988). Locally organised projects have been particularly useful for recording and conserving material. Nottingham Local Studies Library, for example, holds a substantial collection of oral records (tapes and transcripts) as a result of projects in 1982–84 and 1986–87, with subsequent additions from different, usually smaller, projects, most recently the Nottinghamshire

Living History Archive. A major research oral testimony exercise undertaken at the millennium produced a range of oral recordings from across the country, now deposited in the British Library Sound Archive.

Not surprisingly, there are significant by-products of oral history, including photographs, artefacts and memorabilia which frequently feed into the process of recording and interpreting the past. No one seriously doubts that the testimony of individuals, treated with care, should take its place alongside the landscape and other non-documentary sources in helping us to understand the past. It does, after all, provide a dimension we cannot reconstruct from any other source, but this has led to some concern among historians as to its validity. Hoskins was not an enthusiast, writing somewhat sceptically that provided 'oral testimony is treated as rigorously as written evidence it can make a real contribution to the study of neglected aspects of local history', but adding that it was 'not to be dismissed altogether merely because it is difficult to check its complete authenticity'. The historian at home with documents and landscapes speaks volumes through the words left unsaid in this sentence.[38]

Place-names

A second separate discipline which has contributed greatly to local historical studies is the study of names – place, field and surnames in particular. The meaning of place-names has concerned chroniclers and antiquarians since the days of Bede. Medieval chroniclers occasionally commented on place-names, and the county historians frequently offered etymologies, some more fanciful than others. It was not until the late nineteenth century that place-names came in for systematic study. The survey of English place-names was founded in 1922, to be followed in 1923 by the English Place Name Society (EPNS), which was set up originally to raise funds to conduct a county-by-county series. Thereafter the work went on with support from scholars concerned with the English language, and historians, notably Sir Frank Stenton. Today the Institute of Name Studies is part of the School of English at Nottingham University. Place-name students were once thought of as mainly interested in linguistic analysis, but modern specialists appreciate the importance of topographical features, as well as of working backwards as far as possible through documentary sources – and that means using local record offices. Place-names are now known to follow local and regional patterns, and the most reliable results are gained by examining topography together with the linguistic history of a particular name.[39]

In 1965 the English Surnames Survey was set up at Leicester through the generosity of Dr Marc Fitch. This project grew out of discussions between Hoskins and Fitch, who was one of the Royal Heralds. Also involved were Sir Anthony Wagner, and the archivist Dr Francis Steer. Important work on surnames is taking place also at the National Centre for English Cultural Tradition at Sheffield. Camden was the earliest scholar to take an interest in surnames, but many others have come to recognise that they tell us something of interest about our origins. Once introduced surnames were widely adopted. They were usually based on either place-names (toponyms) derived either from particular places or from landscape features, occupations (smith, thatcher and many others), or some form of nickname, of which the origin has now almost certainly been lost.[40]

Heritage

Finally we come to heritage, a word which is now integral to our understanding of past societies. Heritage is probably no more than a catch-all for a great many popular ideas about the past. Since the listing of buildings was introduced in 1947 there has been a commitment to conservation and preservation of the built environment, which can easily be interpreted in relation to heritage. Certainly among country house enthusiasts, 'heritage' has been a real and important concept since it is deemed to be a good thing, largely as a result of the growth of leisure time and finance, which has seen state resources pumped into the upkeep of what are essentially the private homes of the very rich.[41] Interest in heritage has also arisen through membership of the National Trust and English Heritage, and the popularisation of local history by the media. But heritage is more than this. It is often promoted by local councils and tourist authorities, who use the past to legitimate what is, in fact, usually an economic interest catering for tourists, for whom local history has to be provided in an easily digested form.[42]

Local historians are, inevitably, caught up in this, either through civic societies, heritage organisations, museums and visitors' centres, all of which rely heavily on an input from local history. In 1990, 79 million out of 349 million visits to tourist attractions in this country were to historic properties, and 74 million to museums and galleries. For local historians the challenge is to ensure accurate and honest interpretation, so that the subject is presented accurately to avoid what Robert Hewison called 'bogus history, the creation of something which never happened to satisfy the tourist industry'.[43]

What we have seen in this chapter is that localities can be studied through various disciplines which are related to, but separate from, local history, including family history, urban history, and landscape history. These are some of the major disciplines which have come out from under the umbrella, and we could also have mentioned specialisms such as folklore, with its emphasis on collecting information relating to past local societies including Plough Plays and similar community information.[44] Specialist subjects also spin off from local history such as railway and canal history. Consequently, what we once might have labelled 'local history' is now a rather different concept, one sometimes frowned upon as relatively backward because of what is sometimes perceived to be its emphasis on rural issues in a modern urban-industrial society and, in practice if not in (Leicester) theory, with places rather than processes. Those sections of 'local history' more interested in processes have, as it were, slipped out from under the metaphorical umbrella with which I began this chapter, to follow their own agendas. Since it seems as if almost every subject now has its dedicated followers, with their own societies, newsletters and journals, local history is an amalgam of a great many disciplines and specialities working together to uncover the past. Since it involves both professionals and amateurs, dedicated scholars and enthusiasts, it is something of a motley bunch, but collectively they are all contributing to the greater understanding of past local societies.

Notes

1 L. Stone and J.C.F. Stone, *An Open Elite? England 1540–1880* (1984), 105–47.
2 A.J. Camp, 'Society of Genealogists', *LH*, 22/2 (1992), 68–73.
3 A. Wagner, *English Genealogy* (1960); idem, *Pedigree and Progress* (1975).
4 The best modern site, which relies on voluntary contributions, is http://freebmd.rootsweb.com (June 2006).
5 S. Colwell, *The Family Records Centre* (2nd edn, 2002).
6 C.D. Rogers, *The Family Tree Detective: Tracing your Ancestors in England and Wales* (new edn, 2006).
7 E. Higgs, *Making Sense of the Census Revisited: Census Records for England and Wales 1801–1901* (2005); A. Bevan, *Tracing Your Ancestors in the National Archives* (7th edn, 2006).
8 D. Hey, *Family History and Local History in England* (1987); idem (ed.), *The Oxford Guide to Family History* (1993); idem, *Family Names and Family History* (2000); idem, *Oxford Companion to Local and Family History* (1996); idem, *Journeys in Family History* (2004).

9 R. Finnegan (ed.), *Studying Family and Community History: 19th and 20th Centuries* (4 vols, 1994): Vol. 1: Ruth Finnegan and Michael Drake (eds), *From Family Tree to Family History*; Vol. 2: W.T.R. Pryce (ed.), *From Family History to Community History*; Vol. 3: John Golby (ed.), *Communities and Families*; Vol. 4, Michael Drake and Ruth Finnegan (eds.), *Sources and Methods: A Handbook*. *The Family and Local History Handbook*, an annual publication of BALH and FFHS, also points to developing linkages between local and family history.

10 C. Pooley and J. Turnbull, *Migration and Mobility in Britain Since the Eighteenth Century* (1998).

11 J.D. Chambers, *Modern Nottingham in the Making* (1945); idem, *A Century of Nottingham's History, 1851–1951* (1952); idem, 'Population change in a provincial town: Nottingham, 1700–1800', in L.S. Pressnell (ed.), *Studies in the Industrial Revolution* (1960), 97–124; R. Church, *Economic and Social Change in a Midland Town: Victorian Nottingham, 1815–1900* (1966). The book was primarily an economic history of Nottingham, with only two of the fourteen chapters devoted to municipal affairs.

12 D. Owen, 'Sir Francis Hill', preface to the reprint of *Medieval Lincoln* (1990); Sir Francis Hill (J.W.F. Hill), *Medieval Lincoln* (1948); *Tudor Lincoln* (1956), *Georgian Lincoln* (1966) and *Victorian Lincoln* (1974), all of them published by Cambridge University Press.

13 H.J. Dyos, *Victorian Suburb: A Study of the Growth of Camberwell* (1961).

14 *Urban History Yearbook*, I (1974), 3–6.

15 R. Samuel, 'Urban history and local history', *History Workshop Journal*, 8 (1979), iv–vi.

16 J.R. Kellett, *The Impact of Railways on Victorian Cities* (1969); F.M.L. Thompson, *Hampstead: Building a Borough, 1650–1964* (1974); D. Cannadine, *Lords and Landlords: The Aristocracy and the Towns, 1774–1967* (1980). The best summary of many of the urban debates, although now dated, is in H.J. Dyos and M. Wolff (eds.), *The Victorian City: Images and Realities* (2 vols, 1973).

17 R. Rodger, 'Urban history: prospect and retrospect', *Urban History*, 19 (1992), 8.

18 L.H. Lees, 'The challenge of political change: urban history in the 1990s', *Urban History*, 21 (1994), 9.

19 D. Palliser (ed.), *The Cambridge Urban History of Britain, I, 600–1540* (2000); P. Clark (ed.), *The Cambridge Urban History of Britain, II, 1540–1840* (2000); M. Daunton (ed.), *The Cambridge Urban History of Britain, III, 1840–1950* (2000).

20 Samuel, 'Urban history and local history', iv–v.

21 S. Porter, *Exploring Urban History: Sources for Local Historians* (1990); F. Grace, *The Late Victorian Town* (1992)

22 T.M. Devine and G. Jackson, *Glasgow I, Beginnings to 1830* (1995); W.H. Fraser and I. Maver, *Glasgow II: 1830–1912* (1996); C. Binfield et al. (eds),

The History of the City of Sheffield 1843–1993, Vol. 1: Politics, Vol. II: Society, Vol. III: Images (1993); C. Rawcliffe and R. Wilson (eds.), Medieval Norwich (2004); idem, Norwich since 1550 (2004); John Beckett (ed.), A Centenary History of Nottingham (1997).

23 VCH Lancashire, 3 (1907); C.R.J. Currie, 'The history of the VCH series', in C. Sturman (ed.), Some Historians of Lincolnshire (1992), 88–92.

24 J.V. Beckett, A History of Laxton: England's Last Open Field Village (1989).

25 B.K. Roberts, The Making of the English Village (1987); Richard Muir, Reading the Landscape (1981), completely rewritten in 2000 as The New Reading the Landscape: Fieldwork and Landscape History to reflect 'the growth of serious interest in landscape history/archaeology that has occurred in the last couple of decades and the contribution that recent research has made to our understanding of the evolution of countrysides'. (xiii).

26 M.W. Beresford, New Towns of the Middle Ages (1967).

27 O. Rackham, Trees and Woodland in the British Landscape: The Complete History of Britain's Trees, Woods & Hedgerows (2001); S. Daniels, Fields of Vision: Landscape Imagery and National Identity in England and the United States (1992).

28 C. Taylor, 'People and places: local history and landscape history', LH, 32/4 (2002), 234–49, especially 234–45. J. Thirsk (ed.), Rural England: An Illustrated History of the Landscape (2000) includes chapters on all the major types of landscape, and five case studies.

29 Muir, The New Reading, xiii.

30 Maurice Barley, The Chiefest Grain (1993), 108–14.

31 B. Trinder, The Making of the Industrial Landscape (1982, 1987); M. Palmer and P. Neaverson, Industry in the Landscape, 1700–1900 (1994). Local and regional studies include G.H. Tupling, The Economic History of Rossendale (Chetham Society, 86, 1927), and A.P. Wadsworth and J. de L. Mann, The Cotton Trade and Industrial Lancashire, 1600–1780 (1931).

32 M. Rix, 'Industrial archaeology', Amateur Historian, 2/8 (1955), 225–9; R.A. Buchanan, Industrial Archaeology in Britain (1972).

33 Industrial Archaeology Review, 1 (1976).

34 M. Palmer and P. Neaverson, Industrial Archaeology: Principles and Practice (1998). For criticism of the early phases of industrial archaeology, see J.D. Marshall, The Tyranny of the Discrete: A Discussion of the Problems of Local History in England (1997), 32–3.

35 G.E. Evans, The Horse in the Furrow (1960); idem, The Pattern Under the Plough (1966); idem, The Farm and the Village (1969) were followed by several other studies. His reflections on his lifetime of work were discussed in G.E. Evans, Spoken History (1987). For the Nottinghamshire study: Nottinghamshire Archives Office, DD 121/1; Arthur Cossons, 'The villagers remember', Transactions of the Thoroton Society, 66 (1962), 67–82.

36 S. Caunce, Oral History and the Local Historian (1994); P. Thompson, The Voice of the Past: Oral History (2nd edn, 1988); T. Lummis, Listening

to History: The Authenticity of Oral Evidence (1987); D. Marcombe, Sounding Boards: Oral Testimony and the Local Historian (1995); K. Howarth, Oral History: A Handbook (1999).

37 A. Howkins, Poor Labouring Men: Rural Radicalism in Norfolk, 1870–1923 (1985).

38 R. Samuel, 'Local history and oral history', History Workshop, I (1976), 191–208; W.G. Hoskins, Local History in England (3rd edn, 1984), 39.

39 K. Cameron, English Place Names (new edn, 1996); M. Gelling, Signposts to the Past: Place-Names and the History of England (1978); M. Gelling, Place Names in the Landscape (2000); G. Redmonds, Surnames and Genealogy: A New Approach (2002); idem, Christian Names in Local and Family History (2004); P. Hanks, et al. (eds), The Oxford Names Companion (2002).

40 D. Hey, Family Names and Family History (2000).

41 P. Mandler, The Fall and Rise of the Stately Home (1997); J. Beckett, 'Our green and pleasant land', Journal of British Studies, 38 (1999), 252–61.

42 R. Hewison, The Heritage Industry: Britain in a Climate of Decline (1987); R. Samuel, Theatres of Memory (1994).

43 Guardian, 2 December 1991; Hewison, Heritage; M. Hunter (ed.), Preserving the Past: The Rise of Heritage in Modern Britain (1996).

44 C. Phythian-Adams, Local History and Folklore: A New Framework (1975).

X *The sources revolution*

One of the key problems for local historians in the past was access to the sources. Dugdale, Thoroton, and other county historians succeeded because their social standing among the county gentry enabled them to spend long hours in their neighbours' muniment rooms. Various classes of public records were available for consultation, but as we saw in chapter V these were widely scattered, and would-be researchers required plentiful resources of both time and money. The desire to improve access to research materials was one of the reasons that record publishing became popular in the nineteenth century. Every published edition of a source extended the range of possibilities for both national and local historians, but it was the principle of public responsibility for records which really stimulated change. The founding of the Public Record Office in the mid-nineteenth century improved access to the national archives, and from 1889 the principle of local responsibility for archives was enshrined in the legislation creating county councils. In this chapter we look initially at the growth of access to records, and then at the way research has developed as a result of the consequent growth in the quantity and quality of records available to the local historian.

The National Archives

The principle of public responsibility for archives began with the founding in the nineteenth century of the Public Record Office, renamed in 2001 as The National Archives, or TNA. The PRO, as it used to be known, was, and in some senses still remains, the home of the professional scholar. The university historians of the late nineteenth and early twentieth centuries could not envisage the subject being researched anywhere other than the PRO, unless it was an occasional foray into the accumulating collections of the British Museum, or even more occasionally – and with permission – into the archives of a great house, or the parish chest. The professionals may still find their natural habitat at The National Archives in Kew, but they have been joined by large numbers of amateurs, aware that TNA houses a vast array of documentation that every local historian is likely to need to access.[1] In 1991 half the readers in TNA were involved in local and family history, and the founding in 1997 of the Family Records Centre as a joint venture between TNA and the General Register Office was an acknowledgement of the use now being made of public records by the amateur community.[2]

The importance of TNA to the local historian has, if anything, increased over time, because it houses documentary sources which have become available only in recent years. Some of the best known records which fall into this category are, of course, the census enumerators' books, now available for 1841–1901, but other classes used by local historians include enclosure awards, tithe files, and tax records such as the late seventeenth–century hearth tax returns. In many cases, records in TNA supplement locally available sources. For the post-1834 Poor Law, for example, the local historian will usually find Union records in the county archives, and correspondence between local Poor Law officials and the Poor Law Board and Poor Law Commission in class MH12 at TNA. The two sets of records need to be used in conjunction to piece together the full story of the Poor Law in any particular Union, but so important is the MH12 material that, used alongside local newspaper accounts of meetings of the Board of Guardians, it is a more than adequate substitute where the union records have been lost. TNA sponsors books and guides aimed at local and family historians.[3]

County archive offices

At the local level, in 1889 the newly formed county councils were granted powers to make provision for their own records, and those of Quarter Sessions from which county councils had evolved. These powers were not invoked very quickly although several English counties set up record offices during the 1920s and 1930s, among them Northamptonshire and Lincolnshire.

County and city record offices were primarily designed for the archives of local authorities, but the muniments of landed families were often accepted on long term deposit when the country house was being vacated or even demolished. A survey in 1980 revealed that from a sample of 500 country houses in 1880 only 381 (76 per cent) were occupied or capable of being occupied, and of these 169 were in public and institutional ownership.[4] The closure and demolition of this built heritage raised numerous questions for bodies such as the National Trust, and threatened the loss of archive collections built up over centuries. In these circumstances a trend developed for local authorities to accept the estate papers of landed families as country houses were abandoned by their owners and either transferred to other uses or demolished.

In either case the records had to go somewhere, and while bonfires, rubbish dumps, and municipal skips were not unknown, many were deposited for safe keeping in archive offices. Initially, county archive staff were not always very welcoming when potential researchers came through their doors. In Northamptonshire, where Sir John Habakkuk, later vice chancellor of Oxford University, worked as a young scholar in the 1930s, the formidable Miss Joan Wake held sway at the Record Office, then at Lamport Hall. After she had treated one unfortunate searcher in much the way that a medieval landowner might have treated a troublesome peasant, Habakkuk discovered via a surreptitious glance in the search room register that this was no less than Lord Spencer of Althorpe, who had been trying to read the medieval Latin script of some of the family papers he had deposited for safe keeping.[5] The deposit of private archives in public repositories has gradually been formalised with the decision of central government in recent times to accept selected deposits in lieu of inheritance taxes. They are, in other words, now regarded as a national asset.

Gradually the principle of public responsibility for archives filtered through into research, and in the years after 1945 the pioneer inter-war record offices were joined by many more local repositories. Between 1946 and 1950 fifteen new county or county and borough joint archive services joined the seven pre-war pioneers. The 1958 Public Records Act confirmed the government commitment to local public archive services, and the Local Government (Records) Act of 1962 gave statutory backing to this trend. By the time of local government reorganisation in 1974 the West Riding of Yorkshire was the only English county council not to be running an archive service.[6] In addition, the Church of England records measure of 1978 required each diocese to nominate an archive repository for the deposit of the records of the bishopric and individual parishes. Usually this was the county archives office, thus bringing together parish records, with local authority records, with the papers of landed families.

Today there are record offices in every part of the United Kingdom, staffed by experts in record management, conservation, and production. The Historical Manuscripts Commission, part of TNA, oversees and maintains standards. It maintains the National Register of Archives, and in June 2006 listed 2,003 record repositories in the United Kingdom, as well as institutions elsewhere in the world, which have substantial collections of manuscripts recorded in the NRA index.[7]

The principle of public responsibility for archives helped to make research easier. Apart from the need to pay visits to country houses – sometimes very cold country houses – researchers found when they arrived that the records were seldom boxed, listed or catalogued. W.G. Hoskins spent many hours in the 1930s clambering up ladders at Leicester Castle to rummage through boxes of dusty uncatalogued records in the search for what he wanted. At least he had some idea where the archives were. The extensive records of the Archdeaconry Court of Nottingham shed considerable light on the court's supervision of parish life in Nottinghamshire from the mid-sixteenth to the mid-eighteenth centuries. The records were known to and used by local historians in the inter-war years. A number of articles and even a record series volume were based on them, but one of the authors saw only a sample of the Act Books, and A.C. Wood seems to have borrowed several volumes of the documents when compiling his record series volume. The papers were deposited by a local solicitor in Nottingham University Manuscripts Department in 1943, and many years later Wood's widow returned the papers her late husband had retained.[8] Similar stories can be told for many other collections of material.

Public repositories, with properly defined access, were preferable to the ad hoc arrangements Hoskins had encountered in Leicester, and certainly preferable to the difficulties faced in persuading some organisations that they even had records. Hoskins, as we have seen, was also a pioneer user of probate inventories, as was Maurice Barley, who began research using probate inventories when he became adult education tutor for local history at Nottingham in 1946. In 1950 probate records were still kept in the district registries to which they had been transferred in 1853. It was necessary to obtain a licence from Somerset House to be permitted to see the documents, and even when Barley had gone through these formalities he found that registry clerks sometimes refused to admit that the documents existed.[9] These were not the conditions under which research flourished with any ease.

Gradually, access to documents has been formalised through county and other archive services. Since most record offices have also collected microfilm and microfiche copies of regularly used TNA documents, notably the nineteenth-century decennial census enumerators' books, a substantial body of material is usually available under one roof, which is itself likely to be rather more leak-proof than some country house muniment rooms. Digitisation is already pointing in the direction of a world in which many of the most commonly used documentary sources are available on the internet.[10] Meantime one of the most serious problems facing modern archive repositories is the sheer bulk of material coming in their direction, hence the development of records management with its emphasis on selective destruction.

Even the VCH came to recognise that its staff no longer needed to be in London, and that it made sense for them to reside in the counties they were researching, and to work in the local record office. R.B. Pugh, the general editor, wrote in 1970 that 'it was often said in the past that the parish histories were based too much upon sources available in London. Recently a great deal more reliance has been placed on manuscripts in local custody, *though these are of course regarded as additional to and not substitutes for the centrally-preserved sources.*'[my emphasis] In an attempt to make life more straightforward county check-lists were compiled on to which were entered the minimum sources, printed and unprinted 'which it is expedient to search for each parish in the county'.[11] Despite this rather grudging acceptance of local records, the revival of the VCH post-1945 was partly possible because the professional staff were located in the counties that employed them, often with offices in the archive repository.

The growing availability of records in a secure environment, coming as it did with the expansion of universities in the 1960s and 1970s, created exactly the conditions for which Chambers and the other pioneer economic historians working in a local context during the 1930s must have yearned. Research students, no longer shackled by the need to write national history, could instead research local issues with a view to commenting on the wider context. Where Chambers had been embarrassed about the way he presented his study of Nottinghamshire, the growth of doctoral research in the 1970s and 1980s increased the detailed research going into local history. In 1981 more than half of all post-graduate historical theses in British universities were devoted to studies of counties, towns, villages, regions, or other localised units of study. In 1990 by my calculation, ninety-six of the 207 theses (46 per cent) completed on topics relating to post-1485 Britain and Ireland can be identified from their title as containing a local theme, while in 2004 eighty-six of the 198 completed theses was recognisably 'local' (43 per cent). Local studies, in other words, are being used unashamedly in the service of national history, with an expectation not that they will simply provide an example but, as Hoskins argued, that they will help to illuminate and shape the national picture. The main danger is that research students select their study area without much attempt at understanding the problems of locality or region, and with little appreciation of Hoskins's dictum that local studies might uncover entirely new themes and issues, not just illustrate pre-conceived ideas.

Record Offices were not conceived as a local authority funded means of enabling research students to undertake their work without the need to visit TNA. Their primary function was in terms of archive conservation and record keeping. The public were, in this sense, let in on sufferance, but it was clear from the number of local history societies around the country that they were likely to give a significant boost to research. The would-be local historian no longer had to spend hours tracking down the local vicar to examine his parish records, or to crave access at the back door of a country house in order to see the family records. The microfilming and microfiching of TNA documents, including the census enumerators' books, further relieved them of the necessity of travelling to Kew, and acted as a sort of modern equivalent of record publishing. Most recently, digital imagery is providing yet a further means of providing easy access to documentary sources. Local history has been democratised: it is open to all, at a reasonable price. This process was encouraged by the development of local studies libraries.

Local studies libraries

The availability of archives in local record offices was parallelled by the growth of local studies libraries. A free public library service was introduced gradually as a result of legislation in the 1850s. From the outset, particularly in towns, the new libraries collected local material. A mutually convenient arrangement developed over time whereby libraries concentrated on collecting printed source materials such as local newspapers and trade directories, and archive offices collected primary manuscript material. The distinction was never formalised, so that some libraries have manuscript collections and many archive offices have copies of trade directories and proceedings of local authorities (such as printed reports to councils). Collections of recent material, notably photographs and oral recordings, tend to be deposited in libraries rather than archive offices, but again there is no set pattern.[12]

As material came available through public repositories, whether it was located at TNA, funded by the state, or record offices and local studies libraries funded by county and municipal authorities, new questions arose about how the collections might best be used. The county and parish historians of earlier generations had researched and written their studies from a relatively limited corpus of material. With more sources easily available, new questions could be asked about researching and writing the history of a community by local historians. To demonstrate how the sources revolution has affected the study of the local community, we can look at a number of issues which have been opened up in new and interesting ways. The examples are the family, the land, and the house. These are selected as representative of many others, but in each case the documentary materials are split between local archives and TNA. Finally, in this chapter, we shall look at how the sources revolution has impacted on the VCH.

The family

The study of population has a long and varied history, perhaps most interestingly reflected in the work of seventeenth-century, political arithmeticians such as Sir William Petty and Gregory King. Considerable resistance was mounted to the idea of a census, which was introduced only in 1801 since which time it has taken place every ten years with the exception of 1941. It has grown from five questions in 1801, to 41 in 2001. More importantly, the release into the public domain of census data has taken place at much the same time as a rise in interest in social and family history. For many years historians had available only the grossed up population data in the printed returns, issued after each census. The data itself dated only from the first census of 1801, although contemporary projections based on parish register data undertaken by the Rev. John Brownlee gave an indication of population trends in the eighteenth century. None of this was of much value for the local historian, although the VCH printed a population table for 1801–1901 in the second volume of each county set of red books, which at least made the figures widely available.

The census enumerators' books for 1841–2001 are now the stock-in-trade of family historians, and can be consulted on microfiche or via the internet. Their survival, let alone their release to the public, was debated at some length between 1912 and 1962. It was only really after the 1861 returns were saved in 1962 that microfilm copies started to become widely available. Until then researchers needed to access the originals in the Public Record Office on Chancery Lane. Family trees were more easily pieced together from parish registers which were, of course, still in the parish chest, but it was soon clear that they contained a wealth of data relating to families that rapidly increased the demand to consult them. In turn, this impinged on the work of the clergy, and helped to speed the deposit of parochial records in local archive offices. Meantime, to conserve the documents and to meet demand, TNA began to provide microfilm copies of the enumerators' books, which were deposited in local record offices. It was soon clear that a whole new source of data was becoming readily available.

Professional historians were primarily using demographic data in the service of urban history, hence the towns they studied were less important than the comparative examples they sought to draw. Demographic studies of towns using census and parish register data all too easily became statistical exercises lacking actual people. Knowing about household shape and size does not tell us anything of the social reality of personal relationships and daily life. So much was clear, for example, in Alan Armstrong's study of nineteenth-century York, with its chapters on population, mortality, marriage and fertility, household and family structure, or Michael Anderson's study of early Victorian Preston.[13]

By contrast, local historians could begin to reconstitute individual families, using census enumerators' books, and for the period pre-1841 they could turn to parish registers. They could also use the census enumerators' books to disaggregate the grossed up population numbers published by the VCH into families and individuals. Nor did the possibilities end here, as they began to appreciate the value of taxation records for counting the population in pre-census times, and for identifying family members. Interest grew in the late seventeenth-century hearth tax returns because they provided parish listings of tax payers, and were susceptible to manipulation for population counts. Again, they were microfilmed by TNA and deposited in local record offices. Subsequently many have been published as record society volumes.[14] For similar reasons interest developed in the seventeenth-century Protestation Returns, and the land tax assessments of the eighteenth and early nineteenth centuries. Family history, as the study of individual family trees, was now a real possibility for everyone, built on foundations underpinned by census, parish register and taxation data. As we saw in chapter IX, the difficulty has been to bring the two together, since many family historians are spiritually the successors of the county historians, with an interest in pedigree and genealogy – usually their own.[15]

The land

Our second example of how the availability of sources has thrown new and interesting light on issues which had previously received only limited attention from local historians relates to land and, in particular, tithe and enclosure. Tithes were collected in England for about a thousand years. During that time they were the heaviest direct tax on farming, and the most repugnant. As a tax on the land to support the Church of England they were offensive to the poor, to dissenters, and to farmers forced to part with some of their produce to a parson who had put nothing into their business and had taken none of the risk. They were so contentious that any opportunity to be rid of them was usually taken, either by conversion to a straightforward money payment, or commutation at the time of parliamentary enclosure.

Parishes which had not achieved a formal commutation were subject to the Tithe Commutation Act of 1836. Under this legislation any remaining tithe was converted to a money payment. An original and two copies of the survey (the map and apportionment) were made, which had to be signed and sealed by the Tithe Commissioners. They retained the originals which are now in TNA, but sent the copies to the registrar of the diocese and the incumbent and churchwardens of the parish. Copies of subsequent altered apportionments were supposedly deposited in the same manner. For most parishes, as a result, the tithe documentation was placed in the parish chest, and has been transferred to the local archive office. In cases where it has been damaged, or when it has not survived, it is usually possible to consult the registry copy, or the original apportionments and maps in classes IR29 and IR30 at TNA.[16] Although the maps were not drawn to a uniform scale, they are often the earliest surviving large-scale map of a particular place, and can often usefully be compared with the first edition OS map.

Less well known until the 1960s were the 14,829 tithe files, one for each tithe district, also to be found in TNA (IR 18). Where tithes had been commuted prior to 1836 these are usually not of great value, but for other districts they are the working papers of the assistant commissioners sent around the country to implement the legislation, and consequently they are informative about the process of commutation, and the extent of tithe still payable as well as the farming practice of the area. From the files we can understand something of the conflicts still taking place in English society as late as the 1840s and 1850s, and the difficulties many districts found in reaching an agreement.[17] Taken together with the maps and apportionments, particularly when they can also be related to the 1841 (or, for very late commutations, 1851) census enumerators' books, they give us a mine of information for reconstructing the English village c.1840, establishing the pattern of land and building ownership, and investigating field names.[18]

Parishes took the opportunity to commute tithe whenever the opportunity arose, and one of the best opportunities was at the time of parliamentary enclosure. Contemporaries clearly knew about the process and progress of enclosure as it impacted on their communities, but historians initially concentrated only on those enclosures which took place by Act of Parliament. The Act itself was likely to be available as a printed record, or in manuscript in the House of Lords Record Office, but the award, drawn up by commissioners and implemented by law, was usually deposited among the records in the parish chest. It represented the final authority in matters relating to footpaths and other issues. But what did enclosure represent at a regional or national level? No one really knew, but the question became pressing at the beginning of the twentieth century. Enclosure was held to have been a key feature of the agricultural revolution, but various historians claimed it had also brought about the disappropriation of the peasantry, and that the adverse consequences of this became apparent in the agricultural depression at the end of the nineteenth century.[19] Clearly there was a need to establish what had actually happened.

W.E. Tate set about compiling a comprehensive list of enclosure acts and awards county by county. The first fruit of his labours, on Nottinghamshire, was published in 1935, and after his death the complete series was edited and published by Michael Turner.[20] What Turner showed in his own book on the subject was that to treat enclosure simply as *Parliamentary* enclosure was to miss the fact that land was being taken out of communal use and transferred into private use over centuries, not simply the seventy or eighty years associated with the parliamentary phase.[21] It was soon clear that the search for enclosure documentation needed to be spread much more widely than the parish chest. From the mid-sixteenth century enclosures were commonly enrolled by decree in one of the equity courts, usually Chancery or the Exchequer.[22] As a result, these cases can be found in TNA, although they are often difficult to locate.[23]

In some areas the material is sufficiently complete for significant conclusions to be drawn about the process of enclosure prior to the parliamentary phase.[24] But, without much doubt, the material for the parliamentary period, c.1760–c.1830, is both fuller and more accessible. A few of the awards can be found in TNA but they are mainly available locally and have been deposited in record offices. From 1801, under the terms of the General Enclosure Act passed that year, they were enrolled locally by the clerk of the peace, while the General Enclosure Act of 1845 established a permanent Enclosure Commission with authority to issue awards without submitting them to Parliament for approval. As a result there is some material in various MAF classes in TNA. Commissioners' minute books occasionally survive in local record offices and can provide details of the process from act to award.[25]

The results of all this work which has taken place both to find and interpret the documents is that we now know more than in the past about the process and timing of enclosure, we can unravel the different types of enclosure and their impact on different soil types, and in turn this enables us to look at individual enclosures and to interpret them in the context of particular communities.[26] We can say more about the impact on particular communities both in terms of landscape – notably hedging and stone walling – and in social structure. Early historians of enclosure emphasised the social impact, with cottagers and small farmers driven off the land to become the new industrial proletariat, but by studying individual enclosures in the light of our wider knowledge of the subject we now know that any generalisation is hazardous. In parishes where substantial commons survived, enclosure probably had a devastating impact on the small owner, farmer and squatter,[27] but where the commons had long gone (as in many areas of the Midlands most affected by Parliamentary enclosure) enclosure was often little more than a formal agreement between the existing farmers to try to ensure their economic futures.[28]

Tithe and enclosure documents provide an unrivalled opportunity to piece together important aspects of the local community around the period 1760–1850, but what happened after that? One of the oddities is that we do not know who owns England, because there has been no repeat of Domesday Book. An effort to track down ownership was made in the 1870s in the form of what was often referred to as a new Domesday, the *Return of Owners of Land in England and Wales 1872–74*, published in 1876. This was soon found to be seriously flawed because it depended on information derived from rate books rather than a full study of who owned what. But another study was subsequently carried out, and again the sources are split between TNA and the county archive office. This was the so-called Domesday of 1910.

David Lloyd George's 'People's Budget' of 1909 included proposals for a number of land duties, which in turn required a valuation of all land to be carried out by the Inland Revenue. Initially the budget was thrown out by the house of Lords, precipitating a constitutional crisis, but eventually it reached the statute book and resulted in a survey of every parcel of land across the country. Land valuation offices were required to copy into a pro forma book a description of each property, with the names of owners and occupiers, and information on extent and rateable value. Until 1979 these books were held in TNA's out store at Hayes, Middlesex, but they were then transferred to county archive offices, where they can still be found. From these valuation books, information was collected and checked before being entered into Field Books, of which 95,000 survive in TNA (IR 58). In the field books each parcel of land was recorded in a detailed four-page entry. Additionally, two sets of the largest available OS sheets were sent to District Valuation Offices for the boundaries of each property to be marked, and each unit to be filled in with a colour wash. One set of the OS sheets was regarded as the permanent copy, and is now in TNA (IR 121–35). The other was the working copy, and these have mostly been in local archive offices since 1968.[29]

The land survey was short lived; indeed, in 1914 a legal ruling declared that the basis on which the valuation of agricultural land had taken place was invalid. The duties themselves lasted only until 1920, and most of TNA material became available in 1979. The split between TNA and local archive offices, and the sheer volume of material, has meant that so far research has taken place only on a microscale. At the street, village or parish level, the material can be analysed to provide evidence about houses, agricultural land, and other parcels of property, but in towns the level of detail creates immense difficulties for the historian.[30] Individual entries in the field books are not necessarily consecutive houses, and for a parish of only c.600 people there may be as many as six field books, as I found in using the field books for the parish of Chilwell, Nottinghamshire.[31] The researcher needs to work with these and the related maps, which means the originals in TNA because photocopies lose the all-important colour wash. The detail can be remarkable, and although it takes time and effort to identify properties in both sources and to link the information, it is possible to reconstruct the local community in great detail, especially when linked to the 1901 census enumerators' books and parish registers.

The house

The third example of how the availability of sources has thrown new and interesting light on issues which had previously received only limited attention from local historians relates to individual houses. Until recently, the history of a particular house was locked up in its deeds, which might be known to the owner or, in the case of properties mortgaged to building societies and banks, might not. Now, with

legal transfer of properties dependent only on the land registry documents, older deeds are in danger of being thrown away, although they
will usually be accepted by archive offices.

More importantly, our interest in heritage means we are interested
in our houses, hence BBC television's *House Detectives*, which shows
us how to find out about our houses and, more importantly, the previous occupants. Julie Myerson's book *Home: The Story of Everyone
Who Ever Lived in our House* (2004) which, despite its apparent
parochialism, was widely reviewed in the press, produced some interesting responses. Myerson was accused by a reviewer in the *Times
Literary Supplement* of 'wanting to collect more and more facts for
their own sake without reference to an overall pattern of significance'.
The implication is that such a pattern could have been established, but
usually the national press is interested in a house only if it has a good
story – a past resident who was famous or infamous, or perhaps
both.[32]

Most people will not find such a person, since the majority of
houses were lived in by ordinary people. Yet, just as interest in families has mushroomed with the availability of parish registers and
census data, so interest in individual houses has increased as people
search for what we might call a personal heritage. As with family
history, the danger is that we pile up data about individuals who occupied the house, or extensions and alterations, types of decoration, the
installation of a bathroom and so on. While this may be interesting to
current and future residents, Nick Barratt of TNA stresses the need to
'put your house in a wider context' by asking questions about the local
community, local events through which past inhabitants lived,
employment in the area and so forth.[33] Learning to 'read' a building
when the documentary sources are thin is also important.[34] Even a
single house is likely to involve research in a variety of places, including not only the local studies library and the record office, but TNA
(particularly the 1910 Domesday, but also a range of possible documentary sources for much older houses). The key point is that the
availability of sources will provide information about a particular
house and its inhabitants, make record linkage possible, and encourage micro-studies from which we can branch out into understanding
more fully our local communities: it is, in short, local history from
below.

Let me give an example of how this works. I live in a house which I
bought some years ago because it seemed right for my family needs,
and has a pleasant setting. It is on a straight, narrow road, with a
variety of architecture, which local people find attractive. None of this

really struck me when I acquired the house: I was primarily interested in selling my previous house, negotiating a price I could afford, making sure the property was in sound repair, and moving in. It was only after I had lived in the house for a while that the local historian in me began to ask questions: when was it built, why is the street as straight and narrow as it is; why is there a mixture of older and newer houses in the area? I found from the deeds (which my building society made available to me without charge) that my house was built about 1900. Unfortunately, the archive office had no building plans from which I could date it more specifically, but I also began to find more interesting issues. I soon discovered that I lived in an area of thirty acres, bought by a consortium of Nottingham businessmen in 1846 with the intention of laying it out as allotments. In fact, they changed their minds, and in 1847 turned it into a freehold land society estate. The intention was to make available plots of land of one-third of an acre for working men to buy (thus giving them the vote in county elections), and to use either as an allotment, or to build a cottage with a substantial garden for vegetable cultivation. Originally the intention was that the working men would spend their days in the lace factory at the end of the road, but the plan went awry after a few years, the plots were bought up by the owners of the lace standings, and the working men banished to much smaller properties elsewhere. Today, an estate intended for working men and their families is a middle-class enclave.

I discovered all this by using simple principles. I asked neighbours what they knew, and was pointed in the direction of clauses in the deeds of the area, and of a contemporary map which had been published in local history journals. I found out more by looking in detail at the tithe map, by checking material in the family papers of the major landowners, the Charltons of Chilwell, and by using trade directories. I used the 1910 Domesday records, census enumerators' books, rate and poll books, and parish registers. But having repopulated my house, and many of my neighbours' homes, I went further, to the literature on freehold land societies, allotments, and other forms of communal landholding dating from around the time of the Chartist movement in the 1840s. I am a professional historian, and so perhaps I had an advantage over people living around me, but I was able to discover a good deal in a relatively short time, and I quickly discovered an astonishing level of interest in my work among people living in the area. Everyone, it seemed, wanted to know about their house and their street. The fact that it turned out to be of particular historic interest as an early example of a freehold land society, and one which largely failed in its original intentions, added to the interest value.

Source materials and the VCH

The developments we have described in relation to sources presented the VCH with a challenge, particularly the need to confront and handle the ever growing volume of sources. In an attempt to make life more straightforward, county check-lists were compiled detailing the minimum sources, printed and unprinted 'which it is expedient to search for each parish in the county'.[35] Not surprisingly the parish histories also grew in length. They were conceived originally to be 800–900 words, but by 1910 had increased to a little over 2,000, and by 1968 to nearly 10,000 words.

During R.B. Pugh's tenure of the general editorship of the VCH (1949–77) new topics were added, and the scale of parish histories increased fourfold, with additional information required on land use, and landscape changes, evolution of settlement and communications, social and cultural activities, public services, local government, church, schools, industry and trade. Nor did the escalation stop there: in Christopher Elrington's measured words, writing in 1990, 'the tendency to enlargement did not cease [in 1970]'. In these circumstances it is hardly surprising that the number of volumes also increased. Hampshire, the first county to be completed, ran to five volumes. Modern studies easily reach twenty or more, and there are good reasons for thinking that counties completed many years ago should be re-founded because so much more can now be said about individual parishes. As the project has mushroomed, Elrington was careful to point out that no one any longer thinks of a VCH entry as exhaustive, 'readers are intended to treat it as a starting point for further inquiry and research'.[36]

Unfortunately for the VCH the reform of local government 1972–74 led to the disappearance of some historic counties, and to some county councils dropping out, although in the old East Riding of Yorkshire funds were found to continue the project despite the disappearance of the area. In place of county links the VCH began instead to forge connections with universities. Staffordshire's first volume appeared in 1908 but it was a further forty years before anything more was done. In 1950 a committee was established with representatives of the county council, the county boroughs of Burton-upon-Trent, Smethwick, Stoke-on Trent, Walsall, West Bromwich and Wolverhampton, and the following year Margaret Midgley was appointed editor. In 1993 the

Staffordshire project was transferred to Keele University, with financial support from the county council, and the current staff are members of the History department. A link with the University of Northampton allowed Northamptonshire to be re-started. Volume IV had been published in 1937, but research resumed in 1996 with a partnership between the Institute of Historical Research, a county trust, and the college. Volume V appeared in 2003.[37]

The original target of 160 volumes has long been overtaken by events. As of Spring 2006, 219 volumes have been published. Of the thirty-nine ancient English counties, eleven, together with the North Riding of Yorkshire, have been completed; twelve, together with the East Riding of Yorkshire, are in progress, while fourteen are dormant – in several cases since before the First World War – and three (Westmorland, the West Riding of Yorkshire and Northumberland) have never started. Inevitably, with a project designed to last seven years, and now 107 years old, there have been changes. To try to maintain consistency certain basic sources, published and unpublished, have to be checked for each parish, the notes are arranged from the outset under the same standard headings as the final text of the parish account (in eight sections, all of them divided internally in several ways), and this format facilitates writing up of the text of each section. Today the eight main sections are an introduction containing basic information about the parish and topics not dealt with elsewhere, manors and other estates, economic history, social history, religious life, local government, local politics, and buildings. In general far less space is now given to architectural descriptions of parish churches and great houses.

Modern VCH volumes continue to provide a mass of useful and detailed historical information on a parish-by-parish basis, but the nature of the parish history has changed. Out has gone the basic concentration on the descent of the manor, the church and the parish charities, and in has come economic history and local government, nonconformity and education. Potentially hazardous is the fact that new sections can be added but to maintain continuity old ones cannot be removed. Different editors have added their own preferences, including local government (R.B. Pugh), and local politics and social history (Anthony Fletcher), and the *Handbook for Contributors* was entirely revised in 2003 and again in 2006. More attention is now given to photographs, maps and text figures, and the books tend to be slimmer and to deal with fewer parishes. Yet the words of Dr Christopher Lewis (now the Sussex county editor), written in 1989 remain an accurate portrayal of what the VCH is:

The account of any place must record systematically the main features of its history: the fluctuations in population, the succession of principal landowners, how the inhabitants have made a living and in doing so altered the environment around them, how they have worshipped and how their life as a community has endured over hundreds of years. It must draw attention to what is different and what is typical about that one place in relation to its neighbours, to wider regions, and to the county at large. It must be a store of references for the national historian who may be interested in the career of only one landowner or the growing of a single crop, but satisfying for the local historian who is a native or resident of the place. It must be accurate in every respect.[38]

Lewis was reflecting on the way the VCH had needed to adapt to meet the revolution in local history in the later twentieth century. As the former Staffordshire county editor, Michael Greenslade, once commented, the founding fathers would have been astonished to find a volume of the VCH for Staffordshire discussing the closure of the Ebenezer Congregational chapel in West Bromwich in 1971, and its reuse from 1973 as a Shree Krishna Temple. The VCH format may be similar to that of the earlier county histories, but the style is that of a modern-day 'scholarly work of reference', and no other country has produced anything like it in terms of the detail of local history.[39]

A good VCH remains the starting point for anyone interested in local history. As Christopher Elrington, one of the long serving general editors, has written, the VCH is a 'scholarly comprehensive encyclopaedia of English local history in all periods, a repository of essential information, and the starting point for further research'.[40]

The sources revolution has had a significant impact on local history. It has meant that the local historian has more material, in the sense of sources not previously available, such as probate inventories and the census enumerators' books, and in turn more knowledge about them through books, guides and, increasingly, the internet. This increases our ability to use the sources, and to develop the questions we ask. Genealogy and heraldry, the stock in trade of the county historian, have slowly given way to detailed research and writing about the community, encouraged by a recognition that local history is useful for answering questions which cannot easily be tackled at the national level.

Of course, it works both ways, since methodological developments in demographic studies, or in the use of sources such as oral testimony and photographs, enable the local historian to understand and appreciate their community in greater detail. Serious questions were raised in the past about antiquarianism, the collection of data for the sake of collection, and these accusations still regularly reappear when local history is discussed. As we will show in chapter XI, the rigour which the modern local historian can exercise in relation to genuine historical questions, partly as a consequence of the sources revolution, enables us to raise and answer searching questions at the local level. These may impact nationally, and are genuinely interesting historical questions in themselves.

The old debate about the relationship between local and national history seems scarcely relevant any more: local history may contribute to our understanding of the history of the nation, but its practitioners are asked, and are answering, important questions about individual localities and places, their evolution and development, and these questions are relevant independent of the contribution to an understanding of the national history. Nor is this simply a question of a professional methodology being developed and 'handed down': increasingly local history stands alone, with practitioners developing a methodology as a result of close study of the documents, both locally and in TNA, and an appreciation of landscapes, building structures, architectural features and so on, which enable us to understand and interpret the evolution of communities.

Notes

1 Printed guides for local historians include *Guide to the Contents of the Public Record* Office (3 vols, 1963–68), and Philip Riden, *Record Sources for Local History* (1987). Also useful for linking TNA material and local sources is Paul Carter and Kate Thompson, *Sources for Local Historians* (2005). Further help can be found in listings prepared by TNA, perhaps most notably as a result of the E179 project: M. Jurkowski, C.L. Smith and D. Crook, *Lay Taxes in England and Wales, 1188–1688* (Public Record Office Handbook 31, 1998).

2 *Scrutiny of the Public Record Office* (1991); S. Colwell, *The Family Records Centre* (2nd edn, 2002).

3 TNA provides numbered leaflets on different documents, available in hard copy at Kew or electronically on the web site: www.nationalarchives.gov.uk. Slightly bizarrely, Domestic Records Information 24, 'English Local History: a Note for Beginners', comments that TNA 'contains a wealth of material for the study of English local history from the Norman Conquest onwards', but says little about what this material is.

4 H.A. Clemenson, *English Country Houses and Landed Estates* (1982).

5 F.M.L. Thompson, 'Hrothgar John Habakkuk, 1915–2002', *Proceedings of the British Academy*, 124 (2004), 97–8.

6 Royal Commission on Historical Manuscripts, *Record Repositories in Great Britain: A Geographical Directory* (9th edn, 1992); B. Serjeant, 'Forty years on – an archival reminiscence', *LH*, 22/2 (1992), 74–5.

7 J. Foster and J. Sheppard, *British Archives: A Guide to Archive Resources in the United Kingdom* (4th edn, 2002). The best modern means of accessing information is through www.nationalarchives.gov.uk/nra, and for computerised lists of deposits (ongoing), www.a2a.org.uk.

8 K. Holland (ed.), *Mender of Disorders. Court and Community in the Archdeaconry of Nottingham, 1560–1756* (2004). Ex inf Dr. Dorothy Johnston.

9 M. Barley, *The Chiefest Grain* (1993).

10 It would be invidious to produce a long list of resources available on the internet, partly because so many sites come and go, but one I have found particularly useful is the Leicester trade directories project: http://www.historicaldirectories.org (June 2006)

11 R.B. Pugh, 'The Victoria History: its origin and progress', in R.B. Pugh (ed.), *General Introduction* (1970), 25.

12 D. Winterbotham and A. Crosby, *The Local Studies Library: A Handbook for Local Historians* (1998).

13 A. Armstrong, *Stability and Change in an English County Town: A Social Study of York, 1801–51* (1974); A. Armstrong, 'The interpretation of the census enumerators' books for Victorian towns', in H.J. Dyos (ed.), *The Study of Urban History* (1968); W.A. Armstrong, 'The use of information about occupation', in E.A. Wrigley (ed.), *Nineteenth-Century Society* (1972); M. Anderson, *Family Structure in Nineteenth-Century Lancashire* (1971).

14 With numerous Hearth Tax returns from the 1660s and 1670s now in print, there is little point in providing a listing. Publication of the returns began in the 1950s: see W.F. Webster (ed.), *Nottinghamshire Hearth Tax 1664: 1674* (Thoroton Society Record Series, 37 (1988), vii.

15 D. Hey, *Journeys in Family History* (2004).

16 E. J. Evans, *Tithes: Maps, Apportionments and the 1836 Act: A Guide for Local Historians* (1997); R.J.P. Kain and H.C. Prince, *The Tithe Surveys of England and Wales* (1985); R.J.P. Kain and H.C. Prince, *Tithe Surveys for Historians* (2000); Roger J.P. Kain and Richard R. Oliver, *The Tithe Maps of England and Wales: A Cartographic Analysis and County-by-County Catalogue* (1995).

17 R.J.P. Kain, *An Atlas and Index of the Tithe Files of Mid-Nineteenth Century England and Wales* (1986); J. Beckett, 'Tithe commutation in Nottinghamshire in the 1830s and 1840s', *Transactions of the Thoroton Society*, 96 (1992), 146–65; J. Beckett and J. Heath (eds), *Derbyshire Tithe Files 1836–50* (Derbyshire Record Society, 22, 1995); J. Beckett, 'The Lincolnshire tithe files', *Lincolnshire Past and Present*, 18 (1994–95), 11–12.

18 J. Beckett and T. Foulds, 'Landholding and society in Laxton in 1841', *Transactions of the Thoroton Society*, 90 (1986), 108–21; A. Henstock, 'House repopulation from the census returns of 1841 and 1851', *Local Population Studies*, 10 (1973), 37–52.

19 J.L. and Barbara Hammond, *The Village Labourer* (1912).

20 W.E. Tate, *A Domesday of English Enclosure Acts and Awards* (ed.) M.E. Turner (1978); W.E. Tate, *The English Village Community and the Enclosure Movements* (1967). J. Chapman, *Guide to Parliamentary Enclosures in Wales* (1992) is the equivalent guide for Wales.

21 M. Turner, *English Parliamentary Enclosure: Its Historical Geography and Economic History* (1980).

22 M.W. Beresford, 'Habitation versus improvement: the debate on enclosure by agreement', in F.J. Fisher (ed.), *Essays in Tudor and Stuart Economic History* (1961), 40–69.

23 M.W. Beresford, 'The decree rolls of chancery as a source for economic history, 1547–c.1700', *Economic History Review*, 32 (1979), 1–9.

24 VCH *Leicestershire*, 2 (1954), 254–9; A.R.H. Baker and R. Butlin, *Studies of Field Systems in the British Isles* (1973).

25 M. Turner and T. Wray, 'A survey of sources for parliamentary enclosure: the House of Commons' Journal and commissioners' working papers', *Archives*, 19 (1991), 257–88; J. Beckett, M. Turner and B. Cowell, 'Farming through enclosure', *Rural History*, 9 (1998), 141–55.

26 S. Hollowell, *Enclosure Records for Historians* (2000).

27 For an example, see D. Eastwood, 'Communities, protest and police in early nineteenth-century Oxfordshire: the enclosure of Otmoor reconsidered', *Agricultural History Review*, 44 (1996), 35–46.

28 P. Barnes, 'The adaptation of open field farming in an east Nottinghamshire parish, Orston, 1641–1793', *Transactions of the Thoroton Society*, 101 (1997), 125–32.

29 B. Short, *Land and Society in Edwardian Britain* (1997); B. Short, *The Geography of England and Wales in 1910: An Evaluation of Lloyd George's 'Domesday' of landownership* (Historical Geography Research Series, 22, 1989); B. Short and M. Reed, 'An Edwardian land survey: the Finance (1909–10) Act 1910 records', *Journal of the Society of Archivists*, 8 (1986), 95–103.

30 J.V. Beckett, *A History of Laxton: England's Last Open-Field Village* (1989), 270–2; Short, *Land and Society*, chapter 7.

31 TNA IR 58/63712–18. Because the books are not always compiled systematically, I found two streets in the parish (about 100 houses) scattered through all of the volumes.

32 Gillian Tindall, reviewing the book in the *Times Literary Supplement* (11 June 2004); *Sunday Times* (2 May 2004). In similar mode, Gillian Tindall has herself written *The House by the Thames and the People who Lived There* (2006).

33 N. Barratt, *Tracing the History of Your House* (2001), 2; P. Riden, *Local History* (1998), 59–69; N.W. Alcock, *Documenting the History of Houses* (2004).

34 B. Breckon et al., *Tracing the History of Houses* (2nd edn, 2000).

35 C.R. Elrington, *Handbook for Editors and Authors* (1970), 25.

36 C.R. Elrington, *The Victoria History of the Counties of England* (1990), 1–3.
37 *ECH* 354, 364–6; www.englandpast.net (June 2006).
38 C.P. Lewis, *Particular Places: An Introduction to English Local History* (1989), 64.
39 *ECH*, 23–5; *Times Literary Supplement*, 19 September 1986.
40 C.R. Elrington, 'The Victoria County History', *LH*, 22/3 (1992), 128, 136.

XI *Local history today*

In 1977 the Standing Conference for Local History established an independent committee to assess the pattern of interest, activity and study of local history in England and Wales. The committee, headed by the Oxford historian Lord Blake, met fourteen times between 1977 and 1979, received 701 items of written evidence, solicited comments from twenty-eight organisations and three individuals, and still found it could not really decide what local history actually was:

> There is no one accepted definition of local history. It has been suggested to us that the price of local history's 'coming of age' should be the formulation of a nationally acceptable definition . . . . We sympathise with the feeling expressed at the close of a session under that heading at the Eleventh Annual Meeting of the Standing Conference for Local History in 1959, when the response was that "We do not know and do not care what we mean by local history, but we are all determined to get on with it!" The rigidity of works afforded by a definition acts as a brake on flexibility of approach, while the scope of the work undertaken becomes limited within what has become a stated framework.[1]

Since the idea behind setting up the committee was to set an agenda, the absence of a clear definition was disappointing, but the Blake Committee, faced with the problem which has recurred many times in this book of deciding what is local, hesitated: 'local is surely a matter of scale, and our understanding of scale is dependent in large measure on experience and knowledge. Each person thinks of local in his own terms: a street, a town, a village, a series of hamlets, a mining area.' The nearest the committee would venture to a definition was to suggest that 'local history is the study of man's past in relation to his locality, locality being determined by an individual's interests and experiences'.[2] In this chapter we try to assess what local history now represents, in the light of developments since the 1960s.

Defining local history

What the Blake committee found, is that while local history might seem parochial – largely as a result of the pejorative meaning attached to 'local' – it squirms, wriggles, and escapes our grasp as soon as we try to find a suitable definition. No one would seriously doubt that local history is a generic term for studying communities at a level below that of the nation, but because local has all too often implied parochial and antiquarian, professional historians often prefer to talk of regional history. This is not because regions are straightforward units for the purposes of historical study: indeed, as we saw in chapter VIII, there has been an ongoing debate about what regions mean in a historic context. Rather, the term is used in contrast to local, as parochial and antiquarian, to imply that since history is contextualised and comparative, 'region' offers a clearer idea of what is being studied. Whether we prefer 'local' or 'regional' the intention is to draw a distinction between on the one hand local, parochial and antiquarian, and on the other regional, comparative and, perhaps subconsciously, real or proper history.

These distinctions are important. Since local history was sidelined in the nineteenth century, the accusation of local, parochial and antiquarian has conveyed a negative image from which it has proved difficult to escape. The fact that the local history torch was carried by the societies, and that often their proceedings and transactions really were local, parochial, and antiquarian, ensured a hostile 'academic' reception for the Department of English Local History when it was founded at Leicester in 1948, but it also stimulated a debate about the nature of the subject, which remains ongoing. Hoskins, and more so Finberg, found themselves performing a juggling act, accepting the stress on place – hence 'local' – while escaping from a tradition which placed equal emphasis on monumental brasses, local inns, church glass, heraldry and 'remarkable occurrences', into a comparative context which required an appreciation of patterns of development across long periods of time. In such circumstances, it was critical to develop a methodology, and the debates of the past fifty years have largely been focused in this direction. Reduced to essentials, it has been a debate about how 'community' is interpreted by the local historian.

It is an ongoing debate because there is not, and never will be, a right or wrong way of 'doing' local history. It is not like an accumulative subject such as the natural sciences or foreign languages where, without the basics, progress is not possible. More or less anyone can access and use documents by visiting an archive office or logging on to an internet site. They can walk fields, with or without a metal detector, visit National Trust and English Heritage properties, and go to the ubiquitous visitors' centres at places of historic interest. Once bitten, they soon get the bug, joining societies, subscribing to maga-zines, and generally taking an interest in their past, whether it is their family, their street, or their community, however defined.

In 1979 Lord Blake's committee located 875 organisations con-cerned primarily or exclusively with the promotion of local history, with a membership of over 130,000. This partly reflected a post-war development. Most counties now have a more popular magazine to place alongside the traditional county journal, offering an outlet for modest pieces of research. Almost every local society has a newslet-ter, and generally they follow the old county societies with a pattern of winter lectures and summer excursions. By no means all of this new generation of societies is research based. Many can more accurately be described as listening societies, devoted bands of people who gather in partially-heated church halls to hear speakers on a variety of subjects, some more local than others.

Since Blake, of course, has come the great boom in family history. The Federation of Family History Societies claims to 'represent, advise and support over 210 family history societies and other genealogical organisations world-wide, with a combined membership of over 300,000'. These newly established societies have helped to produce a fundamental shift of interests towards understanding com-munities. By contrast the Historical Association, founded in 1906 as a body which could speak for professional historians (in both sec-ondary and higher education) had about 8,000 members in 1994. It no longer gives a membership total on its website, although it does claim more than sixty branches. It still seeks to fly a flag for local history. Significantly more important for the community is the British Association for Local History (BALH), which grew out of the discus-sions which followed the Blake Report, and which publishes the *Local Historian*.[3]

There is not much doubt about our collective interest in local history, whether it is measured through visitors to historic sites and properties, or audiences for television series. Of course, much of this interest is passive. Participants may buy a guide book, and pick up free literature, perhaps even join the National Trust, but they are really looking to be casually entertained. What we need to do is to channel the work and outputs of those who are *active* in local history, in what-ever way, to make sure nothing is lost or wasted. We have to tap into the effort which Kate Tiller has described as the democratisation of local history. This is a world which no longer relies on the gentry, the clergy, and relatively under-employed lawyers who once populated the county societies. People of different social classes and ages, in towns, cities and country, are now active participants. They bring direct knowledge and often personal experience of the place they are study-ing, and often skills needed for study. They know the soils, field names, family connections, hedgerow species, and the plan of the church-yard. What we have to develop is a shared agenda of academic and lay practitioners, in which the professionals recognise the contri-bution of the enthusiastic amateurs, and the amateurs have at least some understanding of the seemingly arcane disputes about what is local and what is regional which often threaten to pass them by. As David Hey has written of the discussions conducted in the Centre for English Local History at Leicester, 'the great majority of local histo-rians remain untouched by these academic debates, for they are ama-teurs who are concerned with the places where they live or work, or with particular topics, but who have little interest in abstract justifi-cations of the subject'.[4]

Understanding past communities

How do we achieve a discourse? First, we have to understand the dif-ferent agendas that drive practitioners, and second we have to capture and facilitate the enthusiasm of all participants towards achieving the greater goal of understanding our past communities.

Everyone has a starting point when it comes to local history, which might range from a doctoral thesis to a passing interest in the family tree. The output of doctoral theses in which a local example is used to examine a national issue shows both the importance of local study for university historians, and also the way in which it is all too easily viewed just as a means to an end by graduate students. Finberg's 'national history localised', suggests that it is possible for a ready-made theory to be dropped on to a local case study, with the locality serving primarily to provide convenient empirical evidence. At the other end of this particular scale, the family tree compiler may have little interest in the quality and reliability of the documents, or in any consideration apart from where and when great Uncle Albert married. In this sense, both doctoral student and family historian are using local history for their own purposes, without much thought about context, themes and issues. John Marshall has noted gloomily of this approach that local history has suffered too much from 'the inciden-tal usefulness of the subject to many historians'.[5]

Once we have understood that practitioners come to local history with an agenda, we have to capture and facilitate the enthusiasm of all participants towards achieving the greater goal of understanding our past communities. To do this we have to marry an appreciation of the conceptual problems associated with studying local and regional history to the practical work of being local historians. This brings us back to training. The traditional teaching of university extra-mural and WEA classes in local history was designed to inform, and to encourage participation. Tawney's WEA classes were intellectually rigorous. After the Second World War this tradition remained strong, with a significant published output from adult education classes. In more recent years, something of this approach was lost as adult education became associated more strongly with leisure-learning than participatory or examinable work, although in a turning of the wheel this kind of class is now being squeezed out of university extra-mural departments by the requirement that courses should be accredited.[6]

Training

The idea of training, as a means of developing good local history, was taken up with some gusto in the Blake Report. Critical in this transformation has been the development of taught MA courses in local and regional history, providing a context for researching and writing local history, and training a generation of people who themselves often go forward to teach and research the subject. Hoskins, in his second spell at Leicester, set up the one-year MA in English Local History with a carefully chosen range of subjects including, for a time, approaches to the study of vernacular buildings. The course still runs, having been periodically reshaped since 1966, but the real breakthrough in training did not come from Leicester. The scholarly straitjacket worked against the Leicester approach: they sought full-time, fee paying postgraduates who would ideally go on to postgraduate research degrees.

The Blake Committee noted that 'strong representations have been made to us that the institution of an advanced course leading to a nationally approved qualification in local history would serve more assuredly than any other action to win wider acceptance of the subject in the minds of academics'. Leaving aside the issue of why academics should be the judges of these matters, the committee went on to recommend the development of MA degrees, diplomas, and other qualifications taught through Adult Education departments. The recommendations included: 'promote [the] idea that all courses in local history should include training in a knowledge and understanding of sources, a systematic method of investigation; the use of documentary material, in the original if possible, or otherwise in reproduced form; and group, as well as individual field or practical work of a research nature': also 'Develop MA degrees in local history', and 'extend scope for work leading to award of Certificates or Diplomas'.[7]

These recommendations offered a useful bridge between the academic study of the subject represented by Leicester, and the enthusiastic amateur who wanted to know and understand more of the subject in a structured way. As Marshall has noted 'never have so many historically untrained people come into contact with so many documents'. This was not a desire to stop them doing so, but a preference for channelling their enthusiasm, a recognition of the need for training to ensure they escaped from what he called 'primitive antiquarianism', the collection of data lacking the 'coherent, immediate, imaginative and above all *telling* context'.[8] He knew that since the Blake report, MA degrees and other qualifications have been introduced at universities up and down the country. The MA in Local and Regional History at the University of Nottingham, which I co-founded in 1983, has now graduated more than 130 students, of whom about one in ten have gone on to research degrees. Many of the students access the course through a Certificate in Local History taught in Adult (now Continuing) Education. It is one among many local history MA courses taught in Higher Education institutions across the country.[9] Where the main obstacle to following such courses may be constraints of time or finance, the would-be local historian can now follow a 'remote' course via the internet. The best known of such qualifications is the Oxford University's Department of Continuing Education's 'Local History via the Internet'.

Training provided a link between the true amateur ploughing a lonely furrow, and seldom lifting his or her eyes from the land in front of them to view the distant horizon, and the professional historian. Many amateurs now have 'accredited' training; indeed, there are hundreds, if not thousands of people passing through our institutions of higher education annually who have the basic techniques and skills of researching, understanding and writing local history.[10] The result is a body of trained local historians, many of whom have gone on to tutor others. Just as importantly, many of them bring their own skills to local history, whether in photography, architecture, medicine, computer technology, and many others. I can personally testify from the great number of MA and certificate dissertations I have read over the years, to the vital importance of this cross-disciplinary integration to the understanding of our past, whether it takes the form of a geo-morphologist's approach to flooding in nineteenth-century Derby, or a physicist's understanding of the use and working of scratch dials on medieval churches.[11] Among the publications of local history societies, I was particularly impressed by the work of a retired Southwell farmer, who used his experience of more than forty years working the land, to suggest how and how successfully that same land may have been farmed at the time of Domesday Book.[12]

Guidebooks

For the local historian who cannot or does not want the comfort of learning together with others, a stream of books has been published in relatively cheap formats. We have seen in chapter VI that books and guides were available in the 1930s and probably earlier on how to write a parish history. W.E. Tate's *The Parish Chest*, published for the first time in 1946,[13] offered local historians a guide to the available records, both ecclesiastical and civil, generated in the local community. By contrast, Lionel Munby has described R.B. Pugh's *How to Write a Parish History* (1954) as 'an alarming turn-off for the non-academically educated'. Pugh, general editor of the VCH, wrote in rather pompous tones that 'the local historian must know Latin . . . [and] may also need to read Old French and Middle English documents . . . A law dictionary is also essential'.[14] F.G. Emmison, the long-serving principal archivist at Essex Record Office, produced *Archives and Local History* (1966) in more modest tones. Francis Celoria's *Teach Yourself Local History* (1958), was popular with adult education tutors because it assumed no existing knowledge, while Hoskins was another early contributor. His *Local History in England*, was first published in 1959. A third edition, slightly updated by David Hey, appeared as late as 1984, but by then it was inevitable that a book written largely in the 1950s had dated – there are, for example, hardly any references to the census enumerators' books. Hoskins's style, and his capacity to evoke a lost past, mean this will long be the starting point for many would-be local historians, and it is an enjoyable read even for people who will never go on to research or write any local history.

Hoskins was followed by W.B. Stephens, whose *Sources for English Local History*, first published in 1973, was subsequently reprinted on a number of occasions because it is recognised as an invaluable guide to the sources. Stephens distinguished between local history and 'the antiquarian aspects of local studies', which he defined as heraldry, brass rubbing, genealogy, campanology 'and the like'. He was drawing, in other words, a distinction between antiquarian study and local history, but he also saw local history as distinct from other disciplines including archaeology, geology, palaeography and place-name studies.[15] In doing so he defined local history as the territory of *historians*. For Stephens the study of local history was a scholarly discipline and careful study of his book would enable the amateur to research and write good local history.

Stephens's book was joined in the 1980s by a whole series of guides which we could loosely term either as 'how to find and use archives',[16] or how to do local history. Philip Riden's *Local History: A Handbook for Beginners* (1983, 1998) came in this latter category. It was designed as 'a simple introduction to the study of local history in England and Wales' aimed at 'part-time amateur enthusiasts with no previous experience of historical research who are keen to discover something of the past around them'.[17] Written by an experienced adult education tutor who has also worked for the VCH it is, in practice, a guide to basic sources for local historians together with hints as to where to find them and what to do with them. Most recently Paul Carter and Kate Thompson's *Sources for Local Historians* (2005) deploys the skills of a TNA records specialist and a long-serving county archivist to show how local historians can research and write about a range of subject areas from the land to religion, housing and family life.

Group research

So far, I have discussed training in the context of the individual, but an alternative approach has been through group work, in which amateur and professional have often come together to study the local past, usually facilitated through university extra-mural or WEA classes. This type of work has its origins in the way some county histories were compiled, but it took on particular meaning in the post-war years with the expansion of university extramural classes and WEA evening classes. Many of these classes were designed to enable local people to find out about their locality, to undertake research and to publish local histories. A survey conducted in 1994 revealed that 287 published books and papers could be linked to group projects in local history over the period from the early 1950s to 1992.[18]

Almost invariably this kind of group work involved a professional tutor working with and training enthusiasts willing to spend time and energy on historical research. In recent times adult education and WEA classes have been less significant, partly as a result of changing directions in Continuing Education, but group work has been encouraged by the deployment of lottery funding. Initially this was through Millennium awards such as the Nottinghamshire Living History

Archive,[19] but more recently research has been encouraged through the Local Heritage Initiative scheme. Perhaps the most successful of these group projects in recent years, certainly in terms of funding, has been the £3.4 million HLF grant to the VCH for a five-year project entitled 'England's Past for Everyone'. This involves team leaders in a number of counties organising the research work of volunteers, and then writing a series of studies to be published electronically and in paperback.[20]

A further form of group work is where the participants cannot come together regularly, which is one of the major problems encountered by tutors of group projects. This provides an opportunity for individuals to work on particular topics, following a common theme, with 'tutorial' advice available and occasionally meetings to discuss findings and share difficulties. The Southwell and Nottingham Diocesan Church History Website project set up in 1998 as a joint initiative between the diocese, which is more or less co-terminous with the county of Nottinghamshire, and the University of Nottingham, is one such project. It was designed to compile a history of every church and church site in the diocese to a formula set down in a briefing paper circulated to all researchers. Not everyone will be able to follow such prescription, but twice-yearly group meetings help to keep the researchers in touch with the project and aware of wider developments. The project is aimed for completion in 2010, by which time it should provide a comprehensive guide to all the churches in the diocese.[21]

The hope behind these initiatives is that we can escape from the image of the local historian myopically studying the documents without any sense of understanding as to what they are doing, or without any real purpose behind their work – Marshall's vision of historically untrained people rampaging through the documents. We can identify several different types of local historian. First, there is the fact grinder, the local historian who, within the true antiquarian tradition, piles up fact after fact and allows the particular set of facts to 'speak for themselves' with little or nothing by way of interpretation. Second, is the thoughtful local historian who provides a careful account of the place, but without indicating that it might have, or ever had, any relationship with any other place or indeed might have a history which relates in any way to broader issues. Third, there is the local historian who writes with an understanding of context.

There is value in each of these approaches, but the obvious danger is that without a context what comes to be published is likely to be of dubious quality, especially as it is likely to lack the essential quality control of being read and criticised by others. It is the image of the fact grinder, however rough and ready, which has fostered accusations that the subject is inadequately formulated, and that the lack of direction is shown by the published output of local historians. The output, in other words, reflects the input, and the input tends to be defined in terms of methodology – the 'how'. It does not matter that it is local history, because the thinking behind it is no different from any other history. What is crucial is the interpretation and context.

Good local history

Consequently it is the third approach, the local historian who writes with an understanding of context, which is widely recognised as good local history. As David Dymond, for many years local history tutor at Cambridge, has written in an excellent practical guide, aimed at both research students and amateur local historians, 'the ultimate aim in writing is to design an unbroken chain of systematic argument, which not only describes what happened in the past but almost simultaneously tries to explain why it happened'.[22] This is what we might call a question-led approach to local history rather than a place-led approach. In the hands of professional historians it might even provide celebrity status for a relatively obscure community, as happened with the demographic studies based on Colyton, Devon (chapter VIII). It is possible that local people knew nothing of this wider work taking place with their village at its epicentre.[23]

The alternative is to work the other way around, to ensure that the local historian can usefully handle population data within the context of something like Malthus' population theory, or church history within the context of the Dissolution of the Monasteries, or the Gothic revival, to assess their significance when mediated through the experience and circumstances of a particular place. Kate Tiller accepted that there was plenty of scope for understanding and appreciating documents, but that local historians were less well equipped when it came to understanding issues. Her response was to try to set some benchmarks for local research. What exactly did parliamentary enclosure mean for local communities? Was the new post-1834 Poor Law actually imposed, and was outdoor relief denied to the able bodied? Tiller set out to introduce local historians to the comparative topics where they can make a difference, and to encourage them to keep their eyes above the parapet.

In one sense this is Hoskins's view of local history nationalised, but Tiller expressed it in terms of local historians looking up from their interesting but rather parochial research to test more widely held historical ideas from local evidence. 'Local history', she has written, 'should understand itself, and be understood by other historians, as part of the same intellectual enterprise as general history, and as bringing unique value to that general history'.[24] Although conceived in a modern context, her suggestions echo those made by Sir Henry Lambert in 1934 when he talked about relating locality to broader issues such as the Dissolution of the Monasteries and the Civil War. At the time this was an innovative approach, and it reminds us that the methodological debates surrounding local history were not invented after the Second World War.[25] Of course, the danger is that this can occur only if the amateur enthusiast follows the rules laid down by the professional historian. That will not always be possible, and it may not even be wanted.

Local history needs to be issue driven, and should not just be source driven. A local historian might become interested in studying the past because they 'find' a collection of documents, whether these are house deeds or newspapers or something similar, but studying only the one source is never going to produce good quality local history. As the range of sources has widened, the need to link the material together has also grown. All historians recognise that the wealthier the evidence, the stronger the case being made. Training is partly designed to raise awareness. Thus the local historian interested in the social structure of the Durham coalfield in the nineteenth century would be significantly disadvantaged by not knowing or understanding the nature of evidence given to the 1842 Royal Commission on the Employment of Children. This is because of the light it sheds on the communities of the Durham coalfield, which can usefully be combined with evidence from local newspapers and literary sources.[26]

Historians have always appreciated the significance of record linkage, but the sophistication of techniques has increased in recent decades, driven by the power of modern computer software. Locating the sources is now much easier with web-based indexes and, increasingly, usage is facilitated by digitisation. But it is with the analysis of data that historians have benefited most. Probate inventories, discovered by Hoskins in the 1940s, survived in vast numbers, but were simply too numerous to use other than as individual examples or in the study of small communities. Today, fed into a modern database or spreadsheet, they can be used much more inventively to study agricultural change in the early modern period, as well as household goods and possessions – particularly in relation to post-1660 consumerism. Material from census enumerators' books can be compared through time in order to establish patterns of change in the community.[27] Modern and contemporary maps can be overlaid using Geographical Information System techniques to establish change through time, and to collate evidence relating to individual places.[28]

Perhaps the most interesting development of all, however, is the linking together of different documents and types of document to reconstruct whole communities, and tease out from the sources something of the lives of ordinary people.[29] What seemed impossibly difficult when this type of work began, using university mainframe computers in the 1970s, and was still a formidable challenge when computer 'memory' was still limited in the 1980s, was worth undertaking because of the light it shed on how individual communities worked. My own research on the Nottinghamshire village of Laxton was significantly aided by reconstructing the village in 1841 from tithe and census data. Even for a village of 600 or so people, this created a huge number of individual records, which could be linked together to reconstruct households, landownership and occupancy, farming tenancies and labour, as well as to locate some unexpected problems relating to who owned or farmed which land in the village. In turn this had important implications for our understanding of 'peasant proprietorship'.[30]

Even a few years ago the technical challenges were formidable, but today a Microsoft Excel spreadsheet running on a desktop PC will do much the same thing just as efficiently, enabling us to link together data from the census, parish records, school log books etc. as well as tithe and related evidence as we saw in chapter X. Physical and documentary sources can also be brought together through record linkage techniques including working from field boundaries on modern large-scale Ordnance Survey maps and present-day field-names through successive earlier maps, terriers, deeds, leases and so forth to produce field-name maps and then apply questions about settlement, land-use and ownership, field systems or archaeological features.[31]

Issues, geographies and time periods

How can we pull all these points together? First, of necessity there is a limit to what any local historian or group of local historians working together can achieve, and few of them, even with an MA or a Certificate behind them, will tackle some of the more contentious regional issues. They will, Hoskins-like, accept the borders as given. What does it matter whether local historians should be studying *pays*, or other forms of distinctive countrysides, identifiable topography, economically functional market areas and hinterlands, communities of social and cultural identity, and so forth, when their real interest is in a single community with identifiable boundaries, and (often) identifiable sources to fit within those boundaries? In any case the size of the unit is critical. One reason why urban history is now so clearly an academic discipline in its own right is not just the comparative method favoured by its practitioners, but the fact that it is impractical for a single scholar working alone to write the history of an English city or large town over a long time span without help. The recent studies of Glasgow, Norwich, Nottingham, and Sheffield, were all the outcome of collaboration, and a study of Liverpool currently in progress has adopted the same approach.

Second, local history does not need to be constrained by boundaries. Since it is issue driven, the place may be the house, the family, the street, the community, the village, the parish, the town, or the region, but it does not *have* to be any one of these. It is the constraints of time and resources which have generally persuaded local historians to favour the study of villages or other small communities. In this sense, the link with the rural community which we looked at in earlier chapters, has a practical as well as an ideological formulation.

Third, local history does not need to be limited by time period. Professional historians talk about their 'period', in other words they divide themselves into medievalists, early modernists, modernists, twentieth-century specialists, and so on. Local history does not need to recognise such boundaries, but it does tend, even so, to be subject to other constraints. Few local historians have felt happy working in the twentieth century, despite the fact that it is, in many respects, the best documented of all because we have people, pictures and other sources that do not exist for earlier periods. There are of course genuine problems of confidentiality in writing twentieth-century local history, particularly in the case of people who are still alive, but given the extraordinary wealth of material it is remarkable how few local history studies give adequate attention to the post-1914 period. Photographic evidence and oral testimony provide us with new types of source, and more recently film and video add a personal dimension to local history which simply cannot be recaptured for earlier generations. Reconstructing the history of the community, even if not of individual families, is relatively straightforward.

Despite this, many local historians are loathe to travel much further forward in time than the First World War, reflecting perhaps the tyranny of the census enumerators' books. Since they first became available in the 1950s, the CEBs have become the stock-in-trade for local and family historians alike in examining the Victorian community. They are full of useful information, and with modern technology – encouraged by TNA – are now so easily available that they have come to dominate our way of thinking. Thus, there is almost an acceptance that for periods where no enumerators' books are available, there is no local history, hence the current cut-off point of 1901.[32]

In practice, our understanding of the local community can be greatly aided by starting with the present and working backwards into the past. This is how family history works, but it is also relevant to the way we understand and study a community. Often it begins by recording the present, perhaps for an anniversary exhibition, and then using the sources to work backwards. By moving in this way, the individual, or even the group, can stop when they have had enough, or when they reach a point at which they feel unable to go on.[33]

Fourth, local history needs to be disseminated. Collecting data is a pointless exercise unless something is done with it. Hoskins, perhaps optimistically, wrote that 'I assume that the local historian who has spent some years studying every detail about the past history of his chosen place, or some special aspect of it which more particularly appeals to him, will wish to see the results of his labours in print'.[34] As a professional historian with a string of books and articles to his name, Hoskins can be forgiven for making such an assumption, but in truth many local historians either fear publishing, or are simply not interested. There are plenty of guides,[35] but even MA students have often proved reluctant to revise their work for publication either in book or article form. In fact, just as the local historian is not confined by place or period, so they are not subject to the tyranny of the published books and research papers which drive professional historians. Even *The Local Historian* can appear formidable, hence the founding in 1984 of *Local History Magazine* 'to encourage local historians to communicate with each other and with the widest possible public, so that the relevance of local history to all sections of the community can generally be appreciated'. *Current Archaeology*, founded in 1967, plays a not dissimilar role in popularising archaeology.[36]

The county societies keep alight the flame of quality local history writing and archaeological reporting. That does not necessarily require them to be edited by academics, but it does need an understanding of historical issues, usually with the help of specialist commentators, to recognise the strengths of particular contributions.

Published local history in other forms is more problematic. There are only a few specific local history publishers, partly because of the adverse economics usually involved in producing books, and these publishers may want local historians to write to a formula that helps them to sell books. One consequence is that much local history has been produced via a sort of domestic industry, perhaps employing nothing more than a desk-top package on a home PC, and a local printer who will run off copies to be paid for and sold by the author. In this world there are no quality controls, and perhaps very little assessment of basic accuracy. It is a world often reminiscent of our antiquarian past. Yet, as we all know, local history books, cheaply produced and fully illustrated, are always likely to sell on the pre-Christmas market. Authors can, alternatively, recoup their outlay by pre-publication subscription, which once again takes us back to the county historians.

The written word is still the traditional form of finished output, perhaps typified most clearly in the 'big red books' published by the VCH, selling at about £95, and feeling remarkably like many of the earlier county histories when we pick them off the shelf. However, although books are a very satisfying way of producing work, they are not alone. Local history can be presented in exhibitions and displays, it can be burned on to CD-Roms – perhaps adding oral and other forms of output to the tradition of text and pictures – and, above all, it can be presented on websites. It may be of varying quality, given that websites have no quality control, but the internet provides plenty of scope in terms of the ratio of text to pictures and, even more significantly, websites can be built up through time. Perhaps we shall never reach the stage where books are outlawed, but for local historians the possibilities opened up by electronic publication are seemingly endless. Yet many local historians have been, and remain, so unsure of themselves that they refuse to expose their work to public appraisal through any form of publication.

No one has a copyright on local history, and this is what makes it such a hybrid. Just because anyone can pick it up and run with it, the possibilities for confusion, let alone straightforward error, are increased. It leads to professional/academic snobbery, which reflects a division within the community between academic scholarship in one corner, and the continuing (and flourishing) amateur tradition in the other. Ultimately, what we do, and how we do it, is a matter of taste, and there are no hard and fast rules about the compilation and production of local history. As Jill Wishart, Chair of the Cumbria Local History Federation, has written, 'How far does the modern local historian differ from an antiquarian?' Even by asking the question she recognised that 'today's local historians may involve themselves in social, economic and landscape change, as well as recording and collecting any relevant historical information', with the usefulness of such work depending 'on the willingness on our part to leave a credible record, together with some observations relating the locality to the regional or national scene'.[37]

The development of qualifications was designed to address the potential for haphazard and unfocused work, and at the same time to prevent a drift whereby academic history becomes separated from local history outside universities. It can and never will be more than partially successful, because so many local historians never go near a university or have any intention of following a course. What we have is a subject which has strongly developed academic strands (particularly through Leicester, the VCH, the regional centres, the regional journals and other groups), but with a much wider constituency ranging from seriously interested people with qualifications, and a determination to publish issue-driven and focused studies, to a community for whom local history bears the hallmarks of heritage and may even be viewed primarily as a form of modern entertainment. Yet it is all local history – and rightly so.

Notes

1 *Report of the Committee to Review Local History* (1979) [Blake Report], 2; P. Riden, 'The Blake Report: a personal reaction', *LH*, 14/1 (1980), 18–23.

2 Blake Report, 2–3.

3 www.ffhs.org.uk (May 2006); www.history.org.uk (May 2006); www.balh.co.uk (May 2006).

4 D. Hey, *The Oxford Companion to Local and Family History* (1996), 283–4.

5 J.D. Marshall, *The Tyranny of the Discrete: A Discussion of the Problems of Local History in England* (1997), 22.

6 L. Munby, D.H. Owen, and J. Scannell (eds), *Local History Since 1945: England, Wales and Ireland* (2005), 15–17.

7 Blake Report, 12, 13, 54.

8 Marshall, *Tyranny of the Discrete*, 72.

9 J. Beckett, 'Teaching regional history: some possibilities and pitfalls', *Bulletin of Local History: East Midlands Region*, 20 (1985), 1–7.

10 M. Noble and J. Crowther, 'Adult education and the development of regional and local history: east Yorkshire and north Lincolnshire', in P. Swan and D. Foster (eds), *Essays in Regional and Local History* (1992), 163–8.

11 Graham Conway, 'The "Great Flood" of Derby, 1 April 1842' (University of Nottingham MA thesis, 1991); Alan Thompson, 'The use of scratch dials by the rural church and laity as evidenced from their occurrences on

churches in the East Midlands' (University of Nottingham MA thesis, 1995).

12 R.E. Hardstaff, *Norman Southwell: Food, Fuel and Farming 1086 AD* (2003).

13 W.E. Tate, *The Parish Chest: A Study of the Records of Parochial Administration in England* (1946, 1969)

14 Munby et al., *Local History*, 13–14; R.B. Pugh, *How to Write a Parish History* (6th edn, 1954), 12–14.

15 W.B. Stephens, *Sources for English Local History* (1973), 1–2.

16 D. Dymond, *Researching and Writing History: A Practical Guide for Local Historians* (1999, updating his 1981 book); A. Macfarlane, *A Guide to English Historical Records* (1983); J. West, *Town Records* (1983, 1992); S. Porter, *Sources for Local Historians* (1990); J. West, *Village Records* (rev. edn 1997); D. Iredale, *Enjoying Archives: What They Are, Where to Find Them, How to Use Them* (1989); L. Munby (ed.), *Short Guides to Records* (1994 revision) and, ed. K.M. Thompson, Vol. 2 (1997).

17 P. Riden, *Local History for Beginners* (1998), 1.

18 Munby, et al., *Local History*, 15–17; J. Unwin, 'Local history group research projects in adult continuing education', *LH*, 24/1 (1994), 28–35; B. Jennings, 'Authors by the score – adult education classes and the writing of local history', *LH*, 22/2 (1992), 58–67.

19 S. Meredeen, *Nottinghamshire History Comes Alive!* (2002). For an example of a community project researched by volunteers and funded by the lottery, see S. Hollowell, *A Century of Change: Cogenhoe 1901–2000* (Cogenhoe and Whiston Heritage Society, 2003), and the related *Voices of Cogenhoe* (CD Rom by Cogenhoe and Whiston Heritage Society, 2003).

20 www.englandpast.net (May 2006).

21 http://southwellchurches.nottingham.ac.uk (May 2006).

22 Dymond, *Researching and Writing History*, 31.

23 K. Shurer, 'The future for local history: boom or recession?', in Richardson, 181. The same point is made by Marshall, *Tyranny of the Discrete*, chapter 2.

24 K. Tiller, *English Local History: The State of the Art* (1998), 6, 19; idem, *English Local History: An Introduction* ([1992]; 2nd edn. 2002), 181, 195.

25 Sir Henry Lambert, *The Value of Local History* (1934).

26 Tiller, *English Local History: An Introduction*, 187–8.

27 M. Overton, 'The diffusion of agricultural innovations in early modern England: turnips and clover in Norfolk and Suffolk, 1580–1740', *Transactions of the Institute of British Geographers*, 10 (1984); L. Weatherill, *Consumer Behaviour and Material Culture in Britain, 1660–1760* (1988); J. Beckett and C. Smith, 'Urban renaissance and consumer revolution in Nottingham, 1688–1750', *Urban History*, 27 (2000), 31–50; J.V. Beckett, *A History of Laxton: England's Last Open Field Village* (1989).

28 D. Gregory, *A Place in History: A Guide to Using GIS in Historical Research* (2003); www.visionofbritain.org.uk (May 2006). Many of the

latest methods of using computers with historical data are presented in the journal *History and Computing* founded in 1988.

29 P. Hudson, 'A new history from below: computers and the maturing of local and regional history', in Richardson, 173–7.

30 J.V. Beckett and D.K. Smith, 'The land tax returns as a source for studying the English economy in the eighteenth century', *Bulletin of the Institute of Historical Research*, 56 (1981), 54–61; J.V. Beckett and T. Foulds, 'Reconstructing an English village using FAMULUS 77: Laxton, Nottinghamshire', in P. Denley and D. Hopkin (eds), *History and Computing* (1987), 45–9; J.V. Beckett and T. Foulds, 'Beyond the micro: Laxton, the computer and social change through time', *LH*, 16/8 (1985), 451–6; idem, 'Landholding and society in Laxton in 1841', *Transactions of the Thoroton Society*, 90 (1986), 108–21.

31 Tiller, *English Local History: The State of the Art*, 5.

32 E. Lord, *Investigating the Twentieth Century: Sources for Local Historians* (1999).

33 V. Norrington, *Recording the Present* (1989); G. Moshenska, 'The Sedgeford village survey: digging for local history in the back garden', *LH*, 35/3 (2005), 159–67; J.V. Beckett, 'Reconstructing the English village', *The Harborough Historian*, 8 (1989), 14–17; idem, *Laxton*, chapter X; D. Hey, *Journeys in Family History* (2004).

34 W.G. Hoskins, *Local History in England* (3rd edn, 1984), 263.

35 Ibid., 263–74; Riden, *Local History for Beginners*, 160–76; Dymond, *Researching and Writing History*; B. Trubshaw, *How to Write and Publish Local and Family History Successfully* (2005).

36 Munby et al., *Local History*, 21.

37 Jill Wishart, 'Local historians and antiquarians', *Local History News*, 74 (Spring, 2005), 28.

XII *Conclusion*

Local history is one of the major leisure interests in this country today. Every week thousands of people attend lectures, read documents in archive offices and books in local studies libraries, study artefacts in museums and heritage centres, and watch television programmes and read magazines, which in one way or another tap into this huge national interest. Local history ties together all sorts of disciplines, including academic subjects such as history and geography, and adult education and WEA classes. It brings together librarians, archivists, museum curators, and heritage centre managers. The practitioners of local history come in all shapes and sizes from family historians simply trying to track down their ancestors, to university professors writing detailed studies of particular places. Within this community of interests there is an inevitable tendency towards fragmentation, both in respect of the different skills, interests and subject matters, and also in relation to the sometimes acrimonious debate about methodology. Admittedly this has tended to be confined to universities, where it remains largely isolated in much the same way as few churchgoers know much about the Biblical criticism practised in university theology departments.

Without much doubt, interest in the many aspects of local history at a non-academic level has burgeoned. Those authors influenced by the work of professional historians try to widen the context in which they work, or to treat special themes or periods. Others are content to produce old photographs of trams, people, street scenes, picture post-cards, and items with nostalgia value. Videos and visual displays for heritage centres serve a similar function. Sometimes it is excellent, sometimes it is worthy or commendable, and sometimes poor. Yet, at root, we are all doing the same thing, even if in different ways and with different ends in view. Good local history does not have to be written, but it does need to be communicated, through whichever medium is most appropriate. The problem is that because it is not an accumulative subject, anyone can have a go, and local historians in universities inevitably have to defend themselves against accusations of dumbing down when some – but by no means all – amateur enthusiasts produce work which fails the quality test of being issue driven. The danger of one group judging the other, of a return to the days of professional historians claiming the scholarly high ground, is considerable, hence the scholarly disdain for family history. Spending hours tracking down baptisms and burials of long departed relatives, building up family trees (an enthusiasm all too reminiscent of the seventeenth-century gentry), and swapping notes through email and internet sites, seems somehow rather trivial in comparison with the greater task given to the professional historian of understanding and interpreting how past societies have operated.

One of the key themes of this book has been the stress on local history as being unbounded. No one has a right to define local history in an exclusive way. What we have to do is assess the output, because collectively that may well build towards a major body of evidence which will be of great value to our understanding of the past. Professional historians, had they existed in the sixteenth and seventeenth centuries, might well have objected to the modus operandi of the county historians, and raised questions about their objectivity and methodology, but today those great studies are used as source materials for quarrying detail of local communities. Who can say how family trees, often so disparaged by 'real' historians, might one day provide a vast database which will help us to link together our society in new ways? Already work is under way which shows how migration pattern trends can be established when we bring together the evidence from large samples of family trees.[1] All local history is potentially of value, even if we have to sift for accuracy and relevance.

Local history began in England almost by accident. It was rooted in the search for a national past following the Reformation, and where the early practitioners such as Camden and Saxton thought in national terms, it was soon clear that the study of the county was more manageable for the gentlemen authors prepared to take on this work. In theory, someone was needed to pull everything together, but in practice that did not happen. Instead, authors began to study counties, and to assemble information relating to their past, whether documentary or artefactual. The county histories grew in scale and in physical size, but eventually almost every English county had a great mine of information about its past. Some, indeed, had two or more such compilations. Other authors turned to studying towns and occasionally parishes, and the threefold structure of English local history had been born. The books became larger, the content increased, and the work of disentangling public and private records to yield up their secrets continued down to the nineteenth century. By then, local history was changing. The great county histories were too expensive, took too long to compile, and no longer seemed the appropriate

means of presenting local history to an audience increasingly com-
posed of the urban middle-classes who looked to join the newly
forming archaeological and antiquarian societies of Victorian
England. While Baines, in his study of Lancashire, managed to appeal
to both the older and the newer audience, the future did not lie with
the old-style history. Parish histories could be summarised in trade
directories, and updated as information became available, and the
urban book-buying public wanted shorter, more manageable texts
without the long and sometimes turgid pedigrees of established
county families. Yet there was still a yearning for county histories,
which would incorporate parish studies, hence the last flowering of
this type of local history with the foundation in 1899 of the Victoria
County History.

Quite where all this was leading was unclear, but what is not in
doubt is that the old style of compilation, drawing on documents,
coins, place-names and other evidence was gradually being superseded as subjects like archaeology began to establish their own, separate identity. Once history was established as a separate discipline
within the universities, with its emphasis on the state and the nation,
and on interpretation rather than narrative, what was left of local
history was easily dismissed as antiquarian, a term which moved from
respect in the eighteenth century to scarcely disguised contempt by the
twentieth. Antiquaries, now known as antiquarians, were collectors,
whether of heraldic insignia, or coins, or documents, or whatever, as
long as it was about the past, but historians used documents maintained by others (notably the keepers of TNA) to interpret the past.
Local history was sidelined in these circumstances. While the county
societies, the printing societies, and the archaeological societies, even
the architectural societies thrown up by the Gothic revival, flourished,
professional historians looked askance at the county societies, and
dismissed their work as amateur and, by implication, valueless. This
scholarly contempt may have been missed by the societies, which continued to produce their annual transactions full of articles about heraldry, church bells and bell frames, family pedigrees, and other local
material, but it severely hampered the development of local history
within the universities. It was sidelined into adult education and
Workers Educational Association classes, and treated by professional
historians as a mine in which to hew for the occasional Ph.D thesis,
rather than having any serious significance of its own. The fact that it
might open up insights which would impact on history more generally was not even considered. Only in the newly developing, but still
relatively low key discipline of economic history was local history

welcomed, because of the way local studies shed light on the process of industrialisation.

This slightly schizophrenic existence lasted until the years after the Second World War, when a combination of academic acceptance in the form of the Department of English Local History at Leicester, the opening up of a new generation of local archive offices, and the revival of the VCH, provided a significant boost to the idea that the study of local communities was a worthwhile exercise in itself. Finberg's definition may have been a little too narrow for some tastes, but the idea it expressed – that each community was worthy of study in its own right – began a long debate about the methodology of local history, a debate which was critical to the establishment of local history in university courses. The debate has ranged through discussion of local communities, *pays*, regions (of various sorts), and the ways in which economic and social history, as well as political and other types of history, impact on the study of local history. At times the debate has seemed esoteric and rather divorced from the continuing work of the county societies, but it was both necessary and important for the development of local history in the wake of the Blake Report if it was to have academic viability in relation to university taught certificates, diplomas and Masters degrees. And, once local historians could gain qualifications, the subject began to take on a life of its own in terms of training, study, and an understanding of how our local societies have worked in the past. Since many of the new students, invariably mature (and sometimes very mature – a student joining our MA course at the age of eighty said he wanted an alternative to attending funerals!) – brought skills developed in other walks of life to their study of local history, the two-way interaction ensured that important new insights were brought into our understanding of past communities. When we add into this mix the huge new interest arising out of the development of family history, increased life expectancy for people beyond their working life, the accessibility of the sources – and of new sources – and the range of courses, television programmes, internet sites, and other information outlets, the growth of interest in the subject post-1960 or so is not so remarkable, but it is still hugely impressive.

Where issues remain is in the quality of this work, and in what it all adds up to. University courses demand scholarly dissertations written from the sources and addressing properly formulated historical questions, whereas many amateur local historians are happy to plough their own particular furrow without any necessary contact with the wider world beyond. There is, naturally, the danger that an amateur pursuing his own course of action will simply give the whole subject a bad name, if only because he or she works away without a question, an issue, or even a purpose. Anyone who has worked in local history for a period of time meets such people, best described as collectors, or modern antiquaries. Often their work is of value, or could be if channelled in the right direction, as with people who spend hours photographing old chapels, or mills, or other threatened buildings. The information is useful, but what happens to it when they lose interest or even die? Perhaps wrongly, I tend not to be judgemental, taking the view that everyone should have the right to do the research that interests them, as long as it does not damage documents or artefacts, and that it is up to people who have an academic interest or concern to liaise with them, and perhaps to interrogate their research if it can be of wider use in understanding and interpreting our communities.

The key issue is to avoid ending up with several local history communities, not always talking to each other. Once local history became tied into debates about methodology, it easily became divorced from the amateur audience, while offering a range of new ideas and thinking developed by academics. Most notable among these was the study of parish records for family reconstitution, which in one sense is simply a more academic approach to building a family tree; but there are others, and this can produce tension between the academic and the non-academic – sometimes expressed in relation to what are perceived to be the priorities pursued by archivists.

This is pointless. There are large numbers of amateurs, especially if we count family historians, and many do excellent work on family reconstitution and other types of study, and the danger of one group judging the other is both considerable and unnecessary. What we have to achieve is good local history without necessary boundary constraints, or time restrictions. Crucially, it needs to be disseminated in one form or another, not simply to be accumulated, but the form can vary from the written word to websites, CD-Roms, exhibitions and heritage displays. No one, ultimately, has a patent on local history, and our aim should be to make sure that what is researched and produced contributes to our overall understanding of the past, not just the collection of information about that past.

This book has been an attempt to show how local history is history, not simply data collection or even antiquarianism. It is about studying, analysing, and discussing the past, so that we can present that past in a fair manner without fear of misrepresentation. What we are faced with in researching and writing local history today are some interesting, and in some senses contradictory problems. First, the source materials are more available and more numerous than ever before, and twentieth-century sources are the best ever, if the least researched by local historians. We have the resources of the archive office, and of the library structure. We have the technology for video and audio research, and, increasingly for online searching as a result of digitisation.

Second, we have desk-top publishing and internet sites which make the presentation of local history much easier than in the past.

Third, we have the analytical tools to discuss the past in an informed manner, and to tackle issues which were once thought to be beyond us. Against this we have old habits and the antiquarian – realist – tradition, as well as a sense that many local historians lack either the skills, or the desire or both to produce the level of analysis that many professional historians would like to see from them. This was certainly Hoskins's view in the 1950s but given the experience of many so-called amateurs, particularly those who have been trained, this seems less relevant today. For the same reason I would also question John Marshall's judgement that 'the state of popular local history gives real cause for worry, in that practitioners are all too inclined to risk embracing antiquarianism – or, to use current publicity jargon, Heritage – in order to survive through the insurance of an adequate inflow of student numbers'. This seems to me to overlook, for example, architects attending heritage conservation courses, and people with non-relevant degrees studying Certificate and Diploma courses to enable them to work more effectively in local history.[2]

Local history today can hardly be defined in a simple, straightforward manner. Perhaps no history can, but there is a particular difficulty with local history because it is place-specific rather than subject-specific. It is neither rural nor urban, despite the growth of urban history, medieval or modern, economic or political, and therein lies the problem, because 'local' still has overtones in our society of parochial: thus local history has neither the grand sweep of the nineteenth century narrative historians, nor the detailed focus of academics used to writing about the state and the nation from the perspective of political history, foreign policy, international relations, and similar perspectives. In university history departments it is passed by in favour of the student demand for Holocaust studies and the fascist dictatorships of twentieth-century Europe. It still inhabits a world of voluntary societies and some surviving adult education classes where it can be safely sidelined by professional historians, who can rest assured that their study of contexts, issues and concepts, published by academic presses after a rigorous process of peer review, represent real scholarship.[3]

It is hardly surprising that the danger remains of the amateur local historian and the professional academic historian viewing each other across a chasm filled with misunderstanding. The amateur has been and still is associated with the myopic case study, and every time a poor quality desk-top publication appears on our shelves the image is reinforced. The need for methodological integrity, which is often provided by certificates, diplomas and MA courses, helps to narrow the gap between the professional and the amateur, but just by running such courses those people who teach them are viewed as the professionals as opposed to the 'amateur' students.

To end on a negative note as if the chasm is unbridgeable would be wrong. The Blake report noted in 1979 that the establishment of English Local History at Leicester had given local history 'a limited academic standing . . . . The study of local history at a high level of scholarship and research is fundamental, for it allows for the properly conducted exploration of techniques and sets standards.'[4] Leaving aside the occasional tendency at Leicester to lofty pomposity – notably the often quoted desire, still on their website, not to be mistaken for the Department of Leicestershire Local History – the department has provided a focus for discussing the methodology of the subject, and some of the alternative meanings and interpretations of local history. These debates have been pursued elsewhere to the long-term benefit of local historians generally. Since there are now hundreds of trained university local historians in the wider community we can, surely, expect a greater understanding of what the subject is, and how it can be developed in terms of methodology and output in future years, as well as how it can take place in the community. Interest in localities certainly does not seem likely to diminish, so it is really up to professional local historians, if they wish to see standards of output maintained, to act as facilitators or guides in ensuring that local history has at least the same respect accorded to it today as the great county historians did in their time.

Does it really matter? Local historians will continue to research and write about their communities, to follow their interests and instincts, to learn from, or even ignore, the scholarly community, and, in the end, to contribute in some way to the great body of knowledge built up since the sixteenth century which is, and will continue to be, English local history.

Notes

1 C. Pooley and J. Turnbull, *Migration and Mobility in Britain Since the Eighteenth Century* (1998).

2 W.G. Hoskins, *Local History in England* (3rd edn, 1984), 30; J.D. Marshall, *The Tyranny of the Discrete: A Discussion of the Problems of Local History in England* (1997), 108.

3 J. Kenyon, in *The History Men* (1983) made no mention of local history or any of its practitioners, and J. Cannon, in *The Blackwell Dictionary of Historians* (1988), had an entry on local history, but no recent scholar merited a brief biography despite the fact that Hoskins had been awarded a CBE in 1971 'for services to local history'.

4 *Report of the Committee to Review Local History* (1979), 5. For the journal *East Midland Historian*, published annually by the School of Education at the University of Nottingham, we consciously ask for less rigorous reviews of some amateur publications than of those written by individuals with university affiliations. This seems fair, but there is always a danger of it being seen as patronising.

Bibliography

Primary Sources

Nottinghamshire Archives Office
 DD/TS/6/4/4, papers of William Stretton (1800–24)
 PR 4082–6, papers of Rev. Christopher Collinson, 1898–1916
 Probate inventory, Charles Deering 1748
 DD 121/1, Village histories
Bromley House Library, Angel Row, Nottingham
 Manuscript history of Nottingham, by Charles Deering
The National Archives
 IR 58/63712–18

Printed Sources

Atkyns, R., *The Ancient and Present State of Gloucestershire* (1712)

Baker, G., *The History and Antiquities of the County of Northampton* (1836–41)

Beckett, J. and Heath, J. (eds), *Derbyshire Tithe Files 1836–50* (Derbyshire Record Society, 22, 1995)

Blackner, John, *History of Nottingham* (1815)

Borlase, William, *Antiquities, Historical and Monumental, of the County of Cornwall* (1769)

Brand, John, *The History and Antiquities of the Town and County of the Town of Newcastle upon Tyne* (2 vols, 1789)

Bray, William, *Sketch of a Tour into Derbyshire and Yorkshire* (2nd edn, 1783)

Bridges, J., *The History and Antiquities of Northamptonshire* (1791)

Britton J. and Brayley E.W. (eds), *Topographical, Historical and Descriptive Delineations of Cumberland* (1803)

Camden, William, *Britannia: Or a Chorographicall Description of the Most Flourishing Kingdoms, England, Scotland, and Ireland, and the Islands Adjoyning, Out of the Depth of Antiquitie* (1637)

Chamberlayne, Edward, *Angliae Notitia or The Present State of England* (18th edn, 1694)

Chynoweth, J. et al. (eds), *The Survey of Cornwall by Richard Carew* (Devon and Cornwall Record Society, 47, 2004)

Cooke, G.A. *Topographical and Statistical Description of the County of Nottingham* (c.1810)

Cooper, C.H., *Annals of Cambridge* (3 vols, 1842)

Corringham, R.W, 'Agriculture in Nottinghamshire', *Journal of the Royal Agricultural Society of England*, 6 (1845)

Cotton, Charles, *The Wonders of the Peak* (2nd edn, 1744)

Curtis, J.A., *Topographical History of Nottinghamshire* (1843–44)

Cussans, John Edwin, *History of Hertfordshire* (3 vols, 1879–81)

Deering, C., *Nottinghamia Vetus Et Nova: Or, an Historical Account of the Ancient and Present State of the Town of Nottingham* (1751)

Defoe, Daniel, *A Tour Through the Whole Island of Great Britain* (1726)

Dickinson, William, *Antiquities Historical, Architectural, Chorographical and Itinerary in Nottinghamshire and the Adjacent Counties* (1801)

Drake, Francis, *Eboracum: Of the History and Antiquities of the City of York from its Original to the Present Times, Together With the History of the Cathedral Church and the Lives of the Archbishops of the See* (1736)

Dugdale, Sir William, *The Antiquities of Warwickshire* (2nd edn, in 2 volumes, revised, augmented and continued down to this present time by William Thomas D.D., sometime rector of Exhall in the same county, 1730)

Enfield, William, *An Essay Towards the History of Liverpool* (1773)

Ford, J.R. (ed.), *John Lucas's History of Warton Parish, Compiled 1710–40* (1931)

Foster, C.W. and Longley, T. (eds), *The Lincolnshire Domesday and the Lindsay survey* (Lincolnshire Record Society, 19, 1924)

Fowles, J. and Legg R. (eds), *Monumenta Britannica* (1982 reprint)

Gilpin, William, *Observations Relative Chiefly to Picturesque Beauty, Made in 1772, on Several Parts of England* (1786)

Glover, S., *Glover's Derby: The History and Directory of the Borough of Derby Intended as a Guide to Strangers Visiting the Town* (1843)

Gough, R., *Myddle*, ed. D. Hey (1981)

Harvey, J.N. (ed.), *The Itineraries of William of Worcester* (1969)

Hasted, Edward, *The History and Topographical Survey of the County of Kent Containing the Antient and Present State of it Civil and Ecclesiastical; Collected from Public Records, and Other the Best Authorities, both Manuscript and Printed*, I (1778)

Hitchins, Fortescue, *A History of Cornwall* (2 vols, 1824)

Hoare, Richard Colt, *The Modern History of South Wiltshire* (5 vols, 1822–44)

Horsfield, T.W., *History, Antiquities and Topography of Sussex* (1835)

Hutchins, John, *The History and Antiquities of the County of Dorset* (4 vols, 1861–70)

Hutchinson, William, *The History of the County of Cumberland* (1794)

Hutton, W., *The History of Derby from the Remote Ages of Antiquity to the Year MDCCXCI . . .* (1791)

Hutton, William, *A History of Birmingham* (2nd edn, 1783)

Laird, F.C., *The Beauties of England and Wales* (1812)

Lambarde, William, *A Perambulation of Kent* ([1576] new edn, 1970)

Lambarde, William, *Dictionarium Angliae Topographicum et Historicum* (1730)

Macky, John, *A Journey Through England* (1722)

Manning, Owen, *The History and Antiquities of the County of Surrey* (3 vols, 1814)

Marshall, William, *Rural Economy of Western England* (1796)

Morant, Philip, *The History and Antiquities of the County of Essex* (1763–68)

Morant, Philip, *The History and Antiquities of Colchester* (1789)

Mordaunt, J., *The Natural History of Northamptonshire* (1712)

Moritz, C.P., *Journeys of a German in England in 1782* (1965)

Morris, C. (ed.), *The Journeys of Celia Fiennes* (1947)

Nichols, John, *The History and Antiquities of Hinckley in the County of Leicester* (1782)

Nicolson, J, and Burn, R., *The History and Antiquities of the Counties of Westmorland and Cumberland* (1777)

Ogilby, John, *Britannia Depicta or Ogilby Improved* (1720; reprinted 1970)

Orange, James, *History and Antiquities of Nottingham* (2 vols, 1840)

Owen, D.M. (ed.), *The Minute Books of the Spalding Gentlemen's Society, 1712–55* (Lincoln Record Series, 73, 1981)

Phelps, W., *History and Antiquities of Somerset* (1839)

Piercy, J.S., *The History of Retford* (1828)

Pilkington, J., *A View of the Present State of Derbyshire with an Account of its Most Remarkable Antiquities* (1789)

Polwhele, R., *History of Devonshire* (3 vols, 1793–1806)

Polwhele, R., *History of Cornwall* (1816)

Report of the Committee to Review Local History (1979) [Blake Report]

Records of the Borough of Nottingham, 6 (1914)

Riden, P., and Glover, C. (eds), *William Woolley's History of Derbyshire* (Derbyshire Record Society, 1981)

Royal Commission on Historical Manuscripts, *Record Repositories in Great Britain: A Geographical Directory* (9th edn, 1992)

Sanders, Robert, *Complete English Traveller* (1772)

Speed, John, *The Counties of Britain: A Tudor Atlas* (1988)

Surtees, Robert, *The History and Antiquities of the County Palatine of Durham* (1816)

Throsby, John (ed.), *The Antiquities of Nottinghamshire by Robert Thoroton* (3 vols, 1790–96)

Tomlin Smith, Lucy (ed.), *The Itinerary in Wales of John Leland in or About the Years 1536–39* (1906)

Tomlin Smith, Lucy (ed.), *The Itinerary of John Leland* (5 vols, 1964 edn)

Webster, W.F. (ed.), *Nottinghamshire Hearth Tax 1664: 1674* (Thoroton: Society Record Series, 37 (1988)

Whitaker, John, *The History of Manchester in Four Books* (2 vols, 2nd edn, 1773)

Winchester, A.J.L. and Wane, M. (eds.), *Thomas Denton: Perambulation of Cumberland 1687–88* (Surtees Society, 2003)

Secondary Sources

Ackroyd, Peter, *London: The Biography* (2000)

Alcock, N.W., *Documenting the History of Houses* (2004)

Alsop, J.D., 'Lambarde, William (1536–1601)', *Oxford Dictionary of National Biography* (2004)

Anderson, M., *Family Structure in Nineteenth-Century Lancashire* (1971)

Andrews, J.H., 'Defoe and the sources of his tour', *Geographical Review*, 126 (1968)

Anon, 'Proceedings', *Transactions of the Lancashire and Cheshire Antiquarian* Society, 2 (1884)

Armstrong, A., 'The interpretation of the census enumerators' books for Victorian towns', in H.J. Dyos (ed.), *The Study of Urban History* (1968)

Armstrong, A., *Stability and Change in an English County Town: A social study of York, 1801–51* (1974)

Armstrong, W.A., 'The use of information about occupation', in E.A. Wrigley (ed.), *Nineteenth-Century Society* (1972)

Baker, A.R.H. and Butlin, R., *Studies of Field Systems in the British Isles* (1973)

Barker, T.C., 'The beginnings of the Economic History Society', *Economic History Review*, 30 (1977)

Barley, M., *The Chiefest Grain* (1993)

Barley M.W. and Train, K.S.S., 'Robert Thoroton', in J. Simmons (ed.), *English County Historians* (1978)

Barnes, P., 'The adaptation of open field farming in an east Nottinghamshire parish, Orston, 1641–1793', *Transactions of the Thoroton Society*, 101 (1997)

Barr, C.B.L., 'Drake, Francis (1696–1771)'. *Oxford Dictionary of National Biography* (2004)

Barratt, N., *Tracing the History of Your House* (2001)

Barron, H.M., *Your Parish History: How to Discover and Write it* (1930)

Bastian, F.H. 'Defoe's tour and the historian', *History Today*, 17 (1967)

Beckett, J., 'Teaching regional history: some possibilities and pitfalls', *Bulletin of Local History: East Midlands Region*, 20 (1985)

Beckett, J.V., *The East Midlands from AD1000* (1988)

Beckett, J.V., *A History of Laxton: England's Last Open Field Village* (1989)

Beckett, J.V., 'The Church of England and the working class in nineteenth-century Nottingham: the building of St. Stephen's Church, Hyson Green', *Transactions of the Thoroton Society*, 92 (1988), 59–73

Beckett, J.V., 'Reconstructing the English village', *The Harborough Historian*, 8 (1989)

Beckett, J.V., 'Lincolnshire and the East Midlands: a historian's perspective', *Lincolnshire History and Archaeology*, 27 (1992)

Beckett, J., 'Tithe commutation in Nottinghamshire in the 1830s and 1840s', *Transactions of the Thoroton Society*, 96 (1992)

Beckett, J., 'The Lincolnshire tithe files', *Lincolnshire Past and Present*, 18 (1994–95)

Beckett, J., 'Our green and pleasant land', *Journal of British Studies*, 38 (1999)

Beckett, J., 'The guardian of the nation's heritage: Sir Neil Cossons, OBE', *East Midland Historian*, 10 (2000)

Beckett, John, 'Derbyshire and the establishment of the diocese of Southwell in 1884', in Riden, P. (ed.), *Essays in Derbyshire History* (2006)

Beckett, J. (ed.), *A Centenary History of Nottingham* (1997)

Beckett, J. (ed.), *The Thoroton Society: A Commemoration of its First 100 Years* (1997)

Beckett, J. (ed.), *Nottinghamshire Past* (2003)

Beckett, J.V. and Foulds, T., 'Beyond the micro: Laxton, the computer and social change through time', *LH*, 16/8 (1985)

Beckett, J. and Foulds, T., 'Landholding and society in Laxton in 1841', *Transactions of the Thoroton Society*, 90 (1986)

Beckett J.V. and Foulds, T., 'Reconstructing an English village using FAMULUS 77: Laxton, Nottinghamshire', in Denley P. and Hopkin D. (eds.), *History and Computing* (1987)

Beckett, J. and Heath, J., 'When was the Industrial Revolution in the East Midlands?', *Midland History*, 13 (1988)

Beckett, J. and Smith, C., 'Dr Charles Deering: Nottingham's first historian', *Nottinghamshire Historian*, 63 (1999)

Beckett, J and Smith, C., 'Urban renaissance and consumer revolution in Nottingham, 1688–1750', *Urban History*, 27 (2000)

Beckett, J.V. and Smith, D.K., 'The land tax returns as a source for studying the English economy in the eighteenth century', *Bulletin of the Institute of Historical Research*, 56 (1981)

Beckett, J., Turner, M. and Cowell, B., 'Farming through enclosure', *Rural History*, 9, 2 (1998)

Beresford, M.W., 'Deserted villages of Warwickshire', *Transactions of the Birmingham and Midlands Archaeology Society* (1950)

Beresford, M., *The Lost Villages of England* (1954, reissued 1998)

Beresford, M.W., 'Habitation versus improvement: the debate on enclosure by agreement', in Fisher, F.J. (ed.), *Essays in Tudor and Stuart Economic History* (1961)

Beresford, M.W., *New Towns of the Middle Ages* (1967)

Beresford, M.W., 'The decree rolls of chancery as a source for economic history, 1547–c.1700', *Economic History Review*, 32 (1979)

Beresford, M. and Hurst, J.G. (eds), *Deserted Medieval Villages* ([1972], reissued 1989)

Beresford, M.W. and Hurst, J.G., *Wharram: A Study of Settlement on the Yorkshire Wolds* (1990)

Beresford, M.W. and St. Joseph, J.K., *Medieval England: An Aerial Survey* (1979)

Berg, M. and Hudson, P., 'Rehabilitating the Industrial Revolution', *Economic History Review*, 45 (1992)

Bettey, J.H., *Wessex from AD1000* (1986)

Bevan, A., *Tracing Your Ancestors in the National Archives* (7th edn, 2006)

Biggs, B.J., 'J.S. Piercy, Retford historian', *Transactions of the Thoroton Society*, 79 (1985)

Binfield, C., et al. (eds), *The History of the City of Sheffield 1843–1993, Vol. I: Politics, Vol. II: Society, Vol. III: Images* (1993)

Borsay, Peter, *The English Urban Renaissance: Culture and Society in the Provincial Town, 1660–1770* (1989)

Boyd Haycock, David, *William Stukeley: Science, Religion and Archaeology in Eighteenth-Century England* (2002)

Brace, C., 'Looking back: the Cotswolds and English national identity, c.1890–1950', *Journal of Historical Geography*, 25 (1999)

Brandon, P. and Short, B., *The South East from AD1000* (1990)

Brayshay, M. (ed.), *Topographical Writers in South-West England* (1996)

Breckon, B. et al., *Tracing the History of Houses* (2nd edn, 2000)

Broadway, J., 'William Dugdale and the significance of county history in Early Stuart England' (*Dugdale Society Occasional Paper*, 39, 1999)

Broadway, Jan, *'No historie so meet': Gentry Culture and the Development of Local History in Elizabethan and Early Stuart England* (2006)

Brooke, C.J., *Safe Sanctuaries: Security and Defence in Anglo-Scottish Border Churches, 1290–1690* (2000)

Brundage, A., *The People's Historian: J.R. Green and the Writing of History in Victorian England* (1994)

Buchanan, R.A., *Industrial Archaeology in Britain* (1972)

Burgoyne, S., *A Scholar and a Gentleman: Edward Hasted, the Historian of Kent* (2001)

Burke, P., *The French Historical Revolution: The Annales School, 1929–89* (1990)

Burke, P., *New Perspectives on Historical Writing* (1991)

Burrow, J.W., 'Victorian historians and the Royal Historical Society', *Transactions of the Royal Historical Society*, 5th series, 39 (1989)

Burrow, J.W., ' "The Village Community" and the uses of history in late nineteenth-century England', in N. McKendrick (ed.), *Historical Perspectives: Studies in English Thought and Society* (1974)

Burrow, J.W., *A Liberal Descent – Victorian Historians and the English Past* (1981)

Butlin, R.A., 'Regions in England and Wales c.1900–14', in Dodgshon, R. and Butlin, R.A. (eds), *Historical Geography of England and Wales* (2nd edn, 1990)

Cameron, K., *English Place Names* (new edn, 1996)

Camp, A.J., 'Society of Genealogists', *LH*, 22/2 (1992)

Cannadine, D., *Lords and Landlords: The Aristocracy and the Towns, 1774–1967* (1980)

Cannon, J., *The Blackwell Dictionary of Historians* (1988)

Cantwell, J.D., *The Public Record Office 1838–1958* (1991)

Carter, P. and Thompson, K., *Sources for Local Historians* (2005)

Caunce, S., *Oral History and the Local Historian* (1994)

Celoria, F., *Teach Yourself Local History* (1958)

Chambers, J.D., 'The open fields of Laxton', *Transactions of the Thoroton Society*, 32 (1928)

Chambers, J.D., *Modern Nottingham in the Making* (1945)

Chambers, J.D., *A Century of Nottingham's History, 1851–1951* (1952)

Chambers, J.D., 'The Vale of Trent, 1670–1800: a regional study of economic change' (*Economic History Review*, Supplement 3, 1957)

Chambers, J.D., 'Population change in a provincial town: Nottingham, 1700–1800', in Pressnell, L.S. (ed.), *Studies in the Industrial Revolution* (1960)

Chambers, J.D., *Nottinghamshire in the Eighteenth Century* (2nd edn, 1966)

Chapman, J., *Guide to Parliamentary Enclosures in Wales* (1992)

Christian, P., *The Genealogist's Internet* (2002)

Church, R., *Economic and Social Change in a Midland Town: Victorian Nottingham, 1815–1900* (1966)

Clark, J., 'Sovereignty: the British experience', *Times Literary Supplement*, 29 November 1991

Clark, P., 'Visions of the urban community: antiquarianism and the English city before 1800', in Fraser, D. and Sutcliffe, A. (eds), *The Pursuit of Urban History* (1983)

Clark, P., *British Clubs and Societies, 1580–1800: the Origins of an Associational World* (2000)

Clark, P. (ed.), *The Cambridge Urban History of Britain, II, 1540–1840* (2000)

Clemenson, H.A., *English Country Houses and Landed Estates* (1982)

Collini, S., *Public Moralists: Political Thought and Intellectual Life in Britain 1850–1930* (1991)

Colls, R., *The Pitmen of the Northern Coalfield: Work, Culture, and Protest, 1790–1850* (1987)

Colls, R., *Identity of England* (2002)

Colwell, S., *The Family Records Centre* (2002)

Cossons, A., 'The villagers remember', *Transactions of the Thoroton Society*, LXVI (1962)

Cossons, A., *Coaching Days: The Turnpike Roads of Nottinghamshire* (1994 edn)

Cossons, A., *The Turnpike Roads of Leicestershire and Rutland* (2003)

Cox, J.C., *How to Write the History of a Parish: An Outline Guide to Topographical Records, Manuscripts and Books* (5th edn, 1909)

Crosby, A., '*The Amateur Historian* and *The Local Historian*: some thoughts after fifty years', *LH*, 32/3 (2002)

Crosby, A.G., '*A Society with No Equal': The Chetham Society, 1843–1993* (1993)

Currie, C.R.J., 'The history of the VCH series', in C. Sturman (ed.), *Some Historians of Lincolnshire* (1992)

Currie, C.R.J., and Lewis, C.P. (eds), *English County Histories: A Guide* (1994)

Cust, R., 'Catholicism, antiquarianism and gentry honour: the writings of Sir Thomas Shirley', *Midland History*, 23 (1998)

Daniels, S., *Fields of Vision: Landscape Imagery and National Identity in England and the United States* (1992)

Darby, H.C., 'Some early ideas on the agricultural regions of England', *Agricultural History Review*, 2 (1954)

Daunton, M. (ed.), *The Cambridge Urban History of Britain, III, 1840–1950* (2000)

Deane P. and Cole, W.A., *British Economic Growth, 1688–1959* (2nd edn, 1967)

Devine, T.M. and Jackson, G., *Glasgow I, Beginnings to 1830* (1995)

Dyer, C., 'Maurice Beresford and local history', *LH*, 36/2 (2006)

Dymond, D., *Researching and Writing History: A Practical Guide for Local Historians* (1981, 1999)

Dymond, D., *Writing Local History* (1996)

Dyos, H.J. and Wolff, M. (eds), *The Victorian City: Images and Realities* (1973)

Dyos, H.J., *Victorian Suburb: A Study of the Growth of Camberwell* (1961)

Eastwood, D., 'Communities, protest and police in early nineteenth-century Oxfordshire: the enclosure of Otmoor reconsidered', *Agricultural History Review*, 44 (1996)

Elrington, C.R., *Handbook for Editors and Authors* (1970)

Elrington, C., *The Victoria History of the Counties of England* (1990)

Elrington, C., 'The Victoria County History', *LH*, 22/3 (1992)

Emery, F.V., 'English regional studies from Aubrey to Defoe', *Geographical Journal*, 124 (1958)

Evans, E.J., *Tithes: Maps, Apportionments and the 1836 Act: A Guide for Local Historians* (1997)

Evans, G.E., *The Horse in the Furrow* (1960)

Evans, G.E., *The Pattern Under the Plough* (1966)

Evans, G.E., *The Farm and the Village* (1969)

Evans, G.E., *Spoken History* (1987)

Evans, J., *A History of the Society of Antiquaries* (1956)

Evans, N. (ed.), 'National identity in the British Isles' (Coleg Harlech: *Occasional Papers in Welsh Studies*, 3, 1989)

Everitt, A., *The Community of Kent and the Great Rebellion, 1640–60* (1966)

Everitt, A., 'The making of the agrarian landscape of Kent', *Archaeologica Cantiana*, 92 (1976)

Everitt, A., 'River and wold: reflections on the historical origin of regions and pays', *Journal of Historical Geography*, 3 (1977)

Everitt, A., 'Country, county and town: patterns of regional evolution in England', *Transactions of the Royal Historical Society*, 29 (1979)

Everitt, A., 'Place names and pays', *Nomina*, 3 (1979)

Everitt, A., *Landscape and Community in England* (1985)

Everitt, A., 'Edward Hasted', in Simmons, *English County Historians*

Fawcett, C.B., *Provinces of England* ([1919], reprinted 1960)

Finberg, H.P.R., *Approaches to History* (1962)

Finnegan, R. (ed.), *Studying Family and Community History: 19th and 20th Centuries* (4 vols, 1994)

Fletcher, A., *A County Community in Peace and War: Sussex 1600–60* (1975)

Foster, J. and Sheppard, J., *British Archives: A Guide Archive Resources in the United Kingdom* (4th edn, 2002)

Fox, H.S.A., 'The people of the wolds in English settlement history', in Aston, M., Austin, D. and Dyer, C. (eds), *The Rural Settlements of Medieval England* (1989)

Fraser, W.H. and Maver, I., *Glasgow II: 1830–1912* (1996)

French, C., 'Taking up "the challenge of micro-history": social conditions in Kingston upon Thames in the late nineteenth and early twentieth centuries', *LH*, 36/1 (2006)

Furedi, F., *Mythical Past, Elusive Future: History and Society in an Anxious Age* (1992)

Garside, P.L. and Hebberet, M. (eds), *British Regionalism, 1900–2000* (1989)

Gelling, M., *Signposts to the Past: Place-Names and the History of England* (1978)

Gelling, M., *Place Names in the Landscape* (2000)

Gilbert, E.W., 'The idea of a region', *Geography*, 45 (1960)

Goodacre, J., *The Transformation of a Peasant Economy: Townspeople and Villagers in the Lutterworth area, 1500–1700* (1994)

Gover, J.E.B., Mawer, Allen and Stenton, F.M., eds., *The Place Names of Nottinghamshire* (1940)

Grace, F., *The Late Victorian Town* (1992)

Greenslade, M.W., 'The Potteries: a question of regional identity', in Phillips, A.D.M. (ed.), *The Potteries* (1993)

Gregory, D., 'The production of regions in England's Industrial Revolution', *Journal of Historical Geography*, 14 (1988)

Gregory, D., *A Place in History: A Guide to Using GIS in Historical Research* (2003)

Guide to the Contents of the Public Record Office (3 vols, 1963–68)

Hackett Fischer, D., *Albion's Seed: Four British Folkway in America* (1989)

Halliday, F.E. (ed.), *Richard Carew of Antony: the Survey of Cornwall* (1953)

Hammond, J.L. and B., *The Village Labourer* (1912)

Hanks, P., et al. (eds), *The Oxford Names Companion* (2002)

Hardstaff, R.E., *Norman Southwell: Food, Fuel and Farming 1086 AD* (Southwell and District Local History Society, 2003)

Harmsen, Theodor, *Antiquarianism in the Augustan Age: Thomas Hearne, 1678–1735* (2000)

Harvey, P.D.A., *Maps in Tudor England* (1993)

Hayns, D., 'County local history organisations in England and Wales: a report on the recent BALH survey', *LH*, 22/2 (1992)

Henstock, A., 'House repopulation from the census returns of 1841 and 1851', *Local Population Studies*, 10 (1973)

Henstock, A. and Train, K., 'Robert Thoroton: Nottinghamshire Antiquary, 1623–78', *Transactions of the Thoroton Society*, 81 (1977)

Hewison, R., *The Heritage Industry: Britain in a Climate of Decline* (1987)

Hey, D., *An English Rural Community: Myddle under the Tudors and Stuarts* (1974)

Hey, D., *Yorkshire from AD1000* (1986)

Hey, D., *Family History and Local History in England* (1987)

Hey, D., *The Fiery Blades of Hallamshire: Sheffield and Its Neighbourhood, 1660–1740* (1991)

Hey, D., *The Oxford Companion to Local and Family History* (1996)

Hey, D., *Family Names and Family History* (2000)

Hey, D., *Journeys in Family History* (2004)

Hey, D. (ed.), *The Oxford Guide to Family History* (1993)

Higgs, E., *Making Sense of the Census Revisited: Census Records for England and Wales 1801–1901* (2005)

Hill, F., 'From Canon Foster to the Lincolnshire Archives Office', *Lincolnshire History and Archaeology*, 13 (1978)

Hill, J.W.F., *Georgian Lincoln* (1966)

Hill, J.W.F., *Medieval Lincoln* (1948)

Hill, J.W.F., *Tudor Lincoln* (1956)

Hill, J.W.F., *Victorian Lincoln* (1974)

Hindle, P., *Maps for Historians* (1998)

Historical Manuscripts Commission, *Papers of British Antiquaries and Historians* (Guides to Sources for British History, 12, 2003)

Hitch, D., 'Cambridgeshire emigrants to Australia, 1842–75: a family and community perspective', *Family and Community History*, 5/2 (2002)

Holland, K. (ed.), *Mender of Disorders. Court and Community in the Archdeaconry of Nottingham, 1560–1756* (2004)

Hollowell, S., *Enclosure Records for Historians* (2000)

Hollowell, S., *A Century of Change: Cogenhoe 1901–2000* (Cogenhoe and Whiston Heritage Society, 2003)

Hollowell, S., *Voices of Cogenhoe* (CD Rom 2003)

Holmes, C., *Seventeenth-century Lincolnshire* (1980)

Hoskins, W.G., 'The deserted villages of Leicestershire', *Transactions of the Leicestershire Archaeological Society*, XXII (1944–45)

Hoskins, W.G., 'Regional Farming in England', *Agricultural History Review*, 2 (1954)

Hoskins, W.G., *The Making of the English Landscape* (1955)

Hoskins, W.G., *Essays in Leicestershire History* (1956)

Hoskins, W.G., *The Midland Peasant: The Economic and Social History of a Leicestershire Village* (1957)

Hoskins, W.G., *Local History in England* ([1959], 3rd edn, 1984)

Hoskins, W.G., *Fieldwork in Local History* (1967)

Hoskins, W.G., *The Age of Plunder: King Henry's England, 1500–47* (1976)

Hoskins, W.G., 'English local history: the past and the future', in Richardson, 137

Howarth, H.H., 'Old and new methods of writing history, being the opening address of the historical section at the Dorchester Meeting', *Archaeological Journal*, 55 (1898), 122–44

Howarth, K., *Oral History: A handbook* (1999)

Howkins, A., *Poor Labouring Men: Rural Radicalism in Norfolk,1870–1923* (1985)

Hudson, P., *Regions and Industries: A Perspective on the Industrial Revolution in Britain* (1989)

Hudson, P., *The Industrial Revolution* (1992)

Hudson, P., 'Industrialisation in Britain: the challenge of micro-history'. *Family and Community History*, 2/1 (1999)

Hudson, P., 'Regional and local history: globalisation, postmodernism and the future', *JORALS*, 20 (1999)

Hudson, P., 'A new history from below: computers and the maturing of local and regional history', in Richardson, 173–7

Hutton, R., 'The religion of William Stukeley', *Antiquaries Journal*, 85 (2005)

Hunter, M. (ed.), *Preserving the Past: The Rise of Heritage in Modern Britain* (1996)

Hunter, M., *John Aubrey and the Realm of Learning* (1975)

Iredale, D., *Enjoying Archives: What They Are, Where to Find Them, How to Use Them* (1989)

Jackson, J.W., 'Genesis and progress of the Lancashire and Cheshire Antiquarian Society', *Transactions of the Lancashire and Cheshire Antiquarian Society*, 49 (1933)

Jennings, B., 'Authors by the score – adult education classes and the writing of local history', *LH*, 22/2 (1992)

Jobey, George, 'The Society of Antiquaries of Newcastle upon Tyne', *Archaeologia Aeliana*, 5th series, 18 (1990)

Johnson, R., 'Cultural traditions in the Potteries', in Phillips, A.D.M. (ed.), *The Potteries* (1993)

Johnston, R., Hauer, J., and Hoekveld, G. (eds), *Regional Geography: Current Developments and Future Prospects* (1990)

Jurkowski, M., Smith, C.L. and Crook, D., *Lay Taxes in England and Wales, 1188–1688* (Public Record Office Handbook 31, 1998)

Kain, R.J.P., *An Atlas and Index of the Tithe Files of Mid-Nineteenth-Century England and Wales* (1986)

Kain, R.J.P. and Oliver, R.R., *The Tithe Maps of England and Wales: A Cartographic Analysis and County-by-County Catalogue* (1995)

Kain, R.J.P. and Prince, H.C., *The Tithe Surveys of England and Wales* (1985)

Kain, R.J.P. and Prince, H.C., *Tithe Surveys for Historians* (2000)

Kammen, C., *On Doing Local History* (2nd edn, 2003)

Kearney, H., *The British Isles: A History of Four Nations* (1989)

Kellett, J.R., *The Impact of Railways on Victorian Cities* (1969)

Kenyon, J., *The History Men* (1983)

Kidd, A.J., 'Between antiquary and academic: local history in the nineteenth century', *LH*, 26/1 (1996); Richardson, 97–9

Lambert, H., *The Value of Local History* (1934)

Langton, J., *Geographical Change and Industrial Revolution: Coalmining in south-west Lancashire 1590–1799* (1979)

Langton, J., 'The Industrial Revolution and the regional geography of England', *Transactions of the Institute of British Geographers*, new series, 9 (1984)

Langton, J., 'The production of regions in England's Industrial Revolution: a response', *Journal of Historical Geography*, 14 (1988)

Langton, J., 'The continuity of regional culture: Lancashire Catholicism from the late sixteenth to the early nineteenth century', in Royle, E., ed., *Issues of Regional Identity* (1998)

Laslett, P., *The World We have Lost* (1965, 3rd edn, 1983)

Laslett, P. (ed.), *Family Life and Illicit Love in Earlier Generations* (1977)

Laslett, P. (ed.), *Household and Family in Past Time* (1972)

Le Roy Ladurie, E., *The Peasants of Languedoc* (1966; English translation, 1974)

Leach, T.R., 'Edward Trollope and the Lincoln Diocesan Architectural Society', in C. Sturman (ed.), *Some Historians of Lincolnshire* (1992)

Lees, L.H., 'The challenge of political change: urban history in the 1990s', *Urban History*, 21 (1994)

Levine, P., *The Amateur and the Professional: Antiquarians, Historians and Archaeologists in Victorian England, 1838–86* (1986)

Levy, F.J., 'The founding of the Camden Society', *Victorian Studies*, 7 (1964)

Lewis, C.P., *Particular Places: An Introduction to English Local History* (1989)

Liddell, J.R., 'Leland's lists of manuscripts in Lincolnshire monasteries', *English Historical Review*, 54 (1939)

Lobel, M., *The Borough of Bury St Edmund's: A Study of the Government and Development of a Monastic Town* (1935)

Lord, E., 'The boundaries of local history: a discussion paper', *JORALS*, 11 (1991)

Lord, E., *Investigating the Twentieth Century: Sources for Local Historians* (1999)

Lummis, T., *Listening to History: The Authenticity of Oral Evidence* (1987)

Macfarlane, A., 'The study of communities', *Social History*, 5 (1977)

Macfarlane, A., *A Guide to English Historical Records* (1983)

Maine, H., *Village Communities in the East and West* (7th edn, 1895)

Maitland, F.W., *Domesday Book and Beyond, Township and Borough* (1897)

Mandler, P., *The Fall and Rise of the Stately Home* (1997)

Marcombe, D., *Sounding Boards: Oral Testimony and the Local Historian* (1995)

Marshall, J.D., 'Local and regional history – or both? A dialogue', *LH*, 13/1 (1978)

Marshall, J.D., 'Why study regions? (1)', *Journal of Regional and Local Studies*, 5/1 (1985)

Marshall, J.D., 'Why study regions? (2): some historical considerations', *Journal of Regional and Local Studies*, 6/1 (1986)

Marshall, J.D., 'Communities, societies, regions and local history, perceptions of locality in High and Low Furness', *LH*, 26 (1996)

Marshall, J.D., *The Tyranny of the Discrete: A Discussion of the Problems of Local History in England* (1997)

Marshall, J.D. and Walton, J.K., *The Lake Counties from 1830 to the mid-Twentieth Century* (1981)

Martin G.H. and Spufford, P. (eds), *The Records of the Nation: The Public Record Office, 1838–1988; The British Record Society, 1888–1988* (1990)

Mathias, P., *The First Industrial Nation, 1700–1914* (1969)

Matlass, D., 'One man's England: W.G. Hoskins and the English culture of landscape', *Rural History*, 4 (1993), 187–207

Matthew, H.C.G., *Leslie Stephen and the New Dictionary of National Biography* (1995)

McCord, N., 'The regional identity of north-east England in the nineteenth and early twentieth centuries', in Royle, E. (ed.), *Issues of Regional Identity* (1998)

McIntosh, M.K., *Autonomy and Community: The Royal Manor of Havering, 1250–1500* (1986)

McIntosh, M.K., *A Community Transformed* (1991)

McKisack, May, *Medieval History in the Tudor Age* (1971)

Mendyk, S., 'Blome, Richard (c.1635–1705)', *Oxford Dictionary of National Biography* (2004)

Mendyk, S., 'Sir William Dugdale and the antiquities of Warwickshire (1656)', *West Midlands Studies*, 17 (1984)

Mendyk, S., *'Speculum Britanniae': Regional Study, Antiquarianism and Science in Britain to 1700* (1989)

Meredeen, S., *Nottinghamshire History Comes Alive!* (2002)

Mingay, G.E., 'The contribution of a regional historian: J.D. Chambers, 1898–1970', *Studies in Burke and His Times*, 13 (1971)

Moir, E., *The Discovery of Britain: The English Tourists, 1540–1840* (1964)

Morgan, V., 'The cartographic image of "the country" in early modern England', *Transactions of the Royal Historical Society* 5th series, 29 (1979)

Morrill, J., *Cheshire, 1630–60: County Government and Society During the English Revolution* (1974)

Morris, R.J., 'Clubs, societies and associations', in Thompson, F.M.L. (ed.), *The Cambridge Social History of Britain, 1750–1950*, 3 (1990)

Morrish, P.S., 'History, Celticism and propaganda in the formation of the diocese of Truro', *Southern History*, 5 (1983)

Mortimer, N. (ed.), *Stukeley Illustrated: William Stukeley's Rediscovery of Britain's Ancient Sites* (2003)

Moshenska, G., 'The Sedgeford village survey: digging for local history in the back garden', *LH*, 35/3 (2005)

Mott F.T. and Carter, T. (eds), *The Transactions of the Leicester Literary and Philosophical Society from June 1835 to June 1879* (1884)

Muir, R., *Reading the Landscape* (1981)

Muir, R., *The New Reading the Landscape: Fieldwork and Landscape History* (2000)

Mullins, E.L.C., *A Guide to the Historical and Archaeological Publications of Societies in England and Wales, 1901–33* (1968)

Mumford, L., *Technics and Civilisation* (1934)

Munby, L. (ed.), *Short Guides to Records* (1994)

Munby, L., Owen, D.H., Scannell, J. (eds), *Local History Since 1945: England, Wales and Ireland* (2005)

Nasse, E., *On the Agricultural Community of the Middle Ages, and Inclosures of the Sixteenth Century in England* (1872)

Noble, M. and Crowther, J., 'Adult education and the development of regional and local history: east Yorkshire and north Lincolnshire', in Swan, P. and Foster, D. (eds), *Essays in Regional and Local History* (1992)

Norrington, V., *Recording the Present* (1989)

Norton, J. E., *Guide to National and Provincial Directories, Excluding London, Before 1856* (1950)

Nurse, B., 'The 1610 edition of Camden's *Britannia*', *The Antiquaries Journal*, 73 (1993), 158–60

Obelkevich, J., *Religion and Rural Society: South Lindsey 1825–75* (1976)

Olney, R.J., *Rural Society and County Government in Nineteenth-Century Lincolnshire* (1979)

Orwin, C.S. and Orwin, C.S., *The History of Laxton* (1935)

Orwin, C.S. and Orwin, C.S., *The Open Fields* (1938)

Overton, M., 'The diffusion of agricultural innovations in early modern England: turnips and clover in Norfolk and Suffolk, 1580–1740', *Transactions of the Institute of British Geographers*, 10 (1984)

Owen, D., 'Sir Francis Hill', preface to *Medieval Lincoln* (1990 reprint)

Owen, D., 'William Oswald Massingberd', in C. Sturman (ed.), *Some Historians of Lincolnshire* (1992)

Palliser, D. (ed.), *The Cambridge Urban History of Britain, I, 600–1540* (2000)

Palmer, M. and Neaverson, P., *Industry in the Landscape, 1700–1900* (1994)

Palmer, M. and Neaverson, P., *Industrial Archaeology: Principles and Practice* (1998)

Palmer, M. (ed.), *The Onset of Industrialisation* (1977)

Parry, G., *The Trophies of Time: English Antiquarians of the Seventeenth Century* (1995)

Payton, P., *Cornwall* (1966)

Phythian-Adams, C., *Local History and Folklore: A New Framework* (1975)

Phythian-Adams, C., 'Re-thinking English local history' (*University of Leicester, Occasional Paper*, fourth series, 1, 1987)

Phythian-Adams, C., 'Local history and national history: the quest for the peoples of England', *Rural History*, 2 (1991)

Phythian-Adams, C., 'Hoskins's England: a local historian of genius and the realisation of his theme', *Transactions of the Leicestershire Archaeological and Historical Society*, 66 (1992), 143–59

Phythian-Adams, C., *Land of the Cumbrians: a Study in British Provincial Origins, A.D. 400–1120* (1996)

Phythian-Adams, C. (ed.), *Societies, Cultures and Kinship, 1580–1850: Cultural Provinces and English Local History* (1993)

Piggott, S., *Ruins in a Landscape: Essays in Antiquarianism* (1976),

Piggott, S., *Ancient Britons and Antiquarian Imagination* (1989)

Piggott, S., 'William Camden and the Britannia', in Richardson, 12–29

Pollard, S., *Peaceful Conquest: The Industrialisation of Europe, 1760–1970* (1981)

Pollard, S., *Marginal Europe: The Contribution of Marginal Lands Since the Middle* Ages (1997)

Pooley, C. and Turnbull, J., *Migration and Mobility in Britain Since the Eighteenth Century* (1998)

Porter, S., *Exploring Urban History: Sources for Local Historians* (1990)

Powell, A., *John Aubrey and His Friends* (1948)

Powell, W.R. 'Antiquaries in conflict: Philip Morant verses Richard Gough', *Essex Archaeology and History* 20 (1989)

Power, M.J., 'John Stow and his London', in Richardson, 30–51

Prince, H.C., 'The changing rural landscape, 1750–1850', in Mingay, G.E. (ed.), *The Agrarian History of England and Wales, vol. VI (1750–1850)* (1989).

Pugh, R.B., *How to Write a Parish History* (6th edn, 1954)

Pugh, R.B., 'The Victoria History: its origin and progress', in Pugh, R.B. (ed.), *General Introduction* (1970)

Rackham, O., *Trees and Woodland in the British Landscape: The Complete History of Britain's Trees, Woods & Hedgerows* (2001)

Ralph, E., 'The Society 1876–1976', in McGrath, P. and Cannon, J. (eds), *Essays in Bristol and Gloucestershire History* (1976)

Ravenhill, W., *Christopher Saxton's 16th Century Maps: The Counties of England and Wales* (1992)

Rawcliffe, C. and Wilson, R. (eds), *Medieval Norwich* (2004)

Rawcliffe, C. and Wilson, R. (eds.), *Norwich since 1550* (2004)

Rawding, C., *The Lincolnshire Wolds in the Nineteenth Century* (2001)

Readman, P., 'Landscape preservation, "advertising disfigurement", and English national identity, c.1890–1914', *Rural History*, 12 (2001)

Readman, P., 'The place of the past in English culture, c.1890–1914', *Past and Present*, 186 (2005)

Reay, B., *Microhistories: Demography, Society and Culture in Rural England, 1800–1930* (1996)

Redmonds, G., *Surnames and Genealogy: A New Approach* (2002)

Redmonds, G., *Christian Names in Local and Family History* (2004)

Richardson, R.C. (ed.), *The Changing Face of English Local History* (2000)

Richardson, R.C., 'Camden and the re-discovery of England', *Transactions of the Leicestershire Archaeological and Historical Society*, 78 (2004)

Richardson, R.C., 'Writing urban history in the eighteenth century: Milner's Winchester', Richardson, 83–93

Riden, Philip. 'John Hieron, William Woolley, Samuel Sanders and the history of Derbyshire', *Derbyshire Miscellany*, 7 (1974–76)

Riden, P., 'The Blake Report: a personal reaction', *LH*, 14/1 (1980)

Riden, P., *Record Sources for Local History* (1987)

Riden, P., *Local History for Beginners* (1998)

Rix, M., 'Industrial Archaeology', *Amateur Historian*, 2, 8 (1955)

Robbins, K., 'Local history and the study of national history', *The Historian*, 27 (1990)

Robbins, K., *Great Britain: Identities, Institutions and the Idea of Britishness* (1998)

Roberts, B.K., *The Making of the English Village* (1987)

Roberts, B.K., 'Rural settlement and regional contrasts: questions of continuity and colonisation', *Rural History*, 1 (1990)

Roberts, Elizabeth and Westall, O.M., 'J.D. Marshall: the making of the identity of a regional historian', in Royle, E. (ed.), *Issues of Regional Identity* (1998)

Roberts, S.K. (ed.), *A Ministry of Enthusiasm* (2003)

Robinson, G.W.S., 'The geographical region: form and function', *Scottish Geographical Magazine*, 69 (1953)

Rodger, R., 'Urban history: prospect and retrospect', *Urban History*, 19 (1992)

Rogers, C.D., *The Family Tree Detective: Tracing your Ancestors in England and Wales* (new edn, 2006)

Rollason, D., *The Local Origins of Modern Society: Gloucestershire 1500–1800* (1992)

Rowlands, M.B., *Masters and Men in the Small Metalware Trades of the West Midlands* (1975)

Rowlands, M.B., *The West Midlands from AD1000* (1987)

Royle, E. (ed.), *Issues of Regional Identity* (1998)

Samuel, R., 'Local history and oral history', *History Workshop*, I (1976)

Samuel, R., 'Urban history and local history', *History Workshop Journal*, 8 (1979)

Samuel, R., *Theatres of Memory* (1994)

Scrutiny of the Public Record Office (1991)

Seebohm, F., *The English Village Community, Examined in its Relations to the Manorial and Tribal Systems and to the Common or Open Field System of Husbandry* (4th edn, 1905)

Seed, J., 'From "middling sort" to middle-class in late eighteenth and early nineteenth-century England', in Bush, M.L. (ed.), *Social Order and Social Classes in Europe Since 1500* (1992)

Serjeant, B., 'Forty years on – an archival reminiscence', *LH*, 22/2 (1992)

Shakespeare, William, *Richard II* (1597)

Sharpe, K., *Sir Robert Cotton, 1586–1631* (1979)

Sharpe, P., 'The total reconstitution method: a tool for class specific study', *Local Population Studies*, 44 (1990)

Sharpe, P., 'Literally spinsters: a new interpretation of local economy and demography in Colyton in the seventeenth and eighteenth centuries', *Economic History Review*, 44 (1991)

Shaw G. and Tipper, A., *British Directories: A Bibliography and Guide to Directories Published in England and Wales (1850–1950) and Scotland (1773–1950)* (1989)

Sheeran, G. and Y., 'Discourses in local history', *Rethinking History*, 2 (1998)

Sheeran, G. and Y., 'Reconstructing Local History', *LH*, 29/4 (1999)

Short, B., The geography of England and Wales in 1910: an evaluation of Lloyd George's 'Domesday' of landownership (*Historical Geography Research Series*, 22, 1989)

Short, B., *Land and Society in Edwardian Britain* (1997)

Short, B and Reed, M., 'An Edwardian land survey: the Finance (1909–10) Act 1910 records', *Journal of the Society of Archivists*, 8 (1986)

Shurer, K., 'The future for local history: boom or recession?', in Richardson, 179–93

Simmons, J., *Local, National and Imperial History* (Inaugural Lecture, University of Leicester, 1948, published 1950)

Simmons, J. (ed.), *English County Historians* (1978)

Skipp, V., *Crisis and Development: An Ecological Case Study of the Forest of Arden, 1570–1674* (1978)

Skipp, V., 'Local history: a new definition', *LH*, 14/6 and 7 (1981)

Snell, K.D.M., 'Gravestones, belonging and local attachment in England, 1700–2000', *Past & Present*, 179 (2003)

Speight, S., 'An officer and an antiquary: Major Hayman Rooke and the beginnings of archaeology in eighteenth-century Nottinghamshire', in Beckett, J. (ed.), *Nottinghamshire Past* (2003)

Spufford, M., *Contrasting Communities: English Villagers in the Sixteenth and Seventeenth Centuries* (1974)

Spufford, Margaret, 'Poverty portrayed: Gregory King and Eccleshall in Staffordshire in the 1690s', *Staffordshire Studies*, 7 (1995)

Stenton, F.M., ed., *Documents Illustrative of the Social and Economic History of the Danelaw: From Various Collections* (1960)

Stephens, W.B., *Sources for English Local History* (1973)

Stobart, J., 'Regions, localities and industrialisation: evidence from the East Midlands, circa 1780–1840', *Environment and Planning A*, 33 (2001)

Stobart, J., *The First Industrial Region: North-west England, c.1700–60* (2004)

Stocker, D., 'Blomefield, Francis (1705–52)', *Oxford Dictionary of National Biography* (Oxford, 2004)

Stocker, David, 'Francis Blomefield as a historian of Norfolk', *Norfolk Archaeology*, 44 (2003)

Stokes, W., 'Regional finance and the definition of a financial region' in Royle, E. (ed.), *Issues of Regional Identity* (1998)

Stone, L. and Stone, J.C.F., *An Open Elite? England 1540–1880* (1984)

Stoyle, M., *West Briton: Cornish Identities and the Early Modern British State* (2002)

Sturman, C. (ed.), *Some Historians of Lincolnshire* (1992)

Sweet, R., 'The production of urban histories in eighteenth-century England', *Urban History*, 23 (1996)

Sweet, R., *The Writing of Urban Histories in Eighteenth-Century England* (1997)

Sweet, R. *Antiquaries: The Discovery of the Past in Eighteenth-Century Britain* (2004)

Tate, W.E., *Parliamentary land enclosures in the county of Nottingham during the 18th and 19th centuries (1743–1868)* (Thoroton Society Record Series, 5, 1935)

Tate, W.E., *The Parish Chest: A Study of the Records of Parochial Administration in England* (1946, 1969)

Tate, W.E., *The English Village Community and the Enclosure Movements* (1967)

Tate, W.E., *A Domesday of English Enclosure Acts and Awards* (ed. M. Turner, 1978)

Tawney, R.H., *The Agrarian Problem in the Sixteenth Century* (1912)

Taylor, C., 'People and places: local history and landscape history', *LH*, 32/4 (2002)

Thirsk, Joan, *Fenland Farming in the Sixteenth Century* (1953)

Thirsk, Joan, 'Industries in the countryside', in Fisher, F.J. (ed.), *Essays in the Economic and Social History of Tudor and Stuart England* (1961)

Thirsk, J., *England's Agricultural Regions and Agrarian History* (1987)

Thirsk, J., 'William George Hoskins 1908–92', *Proceedings of the British Academy*, 87 (1994)

Thirsk, J., 'From farming to food: forty years in Lincolnshire history', *Lincolnshire History and Archaeology*, 32 (1997)

Thirsk, J., 'The British Agricultural History Society and *The Agrarian History of England and Wales*: new projects in the 1950s', *Agricultural History Review*, 50 (2002)

Thirsk, J., 'Hasted as Historian', in Richardson, 69–82

Thirsk, J. (ed.), *The Agrarian History of England and Wales* (vol. 4, 1500–1640) (1967)

Thirsk, J. (ed.), *The Agrarian History of England and Wales* (vol. 5, 1640–1750) (2 vols, 1984–85)

Thirsk, J. (ed.), *Rural England: An Illustrated History of the Landscape* (2000)

Thomas, K., *Changing Conceptions of National Biography: the Oxford DNB in Historical Perspective* (2005)

Thompson, A.H., *The Surtees Society, 1834–1934* (Durham, Surtees Society, 150, 1939)

Thompson, E.P., *The Making of the English Working Class* (1968 edn)

Thompson, F.M.L., *Hampstead: Building a Borough, 1650–1964* (1974)

Thompson, F.M.L., 'Hrothgar John Habakkuk, 1915–2002', *Proceedings of the British Academy*, 124 (2004)

Thompson, P., *The Voice of the Past: Oral History* (2nd edn, 1988)

Thornton, G., *A History of Clare, Suffolk* (1928)

Tiller, K., *English Local History: An Introduction* (Stroud, [1992]; 2nd edn 2002)

Tiller, K., 'The VCH: past, present and future', *Historian*, 42 (1994)

Tiller, K., *English Local History: The State of the Art* (University of Cambridge, Board of Continuing Education, 1998)

Tindall, G., *The House by the Thames and the People who Lived There* (2006)

Tomlinson, V.I., 'The Lancashire and Cheshire Antiquarian Society, 1883–1983', *Transactions of the Lancashire and Cheshire Antiquarian Society*, 83 (1985)

Tosh, J., *The Pursuit of History* (3rd edn, 2000)

Trinder, B., *The Making of the Industrial Landscape* ([1982], 1987)

Trubshaw, B., *How to Write and Publish Local and Family History Successfully* (2005)

Tupling, G.H., *The Economic History of Rossendale* (Chetham Society, 86, 1927)

Turnbull, G., 'Canals, coal and regional growth during the Industrial Revolution', *Economic History Review*, 40 (1987)

Turner, M., *English Parliamentary Enclosure: Its Historical Geography and Economic History* (1980)

Turner, M. and Wray, T., 'A survey of sources for parliamentary enclosure: the *House of Commons' Journal* and commissioners' working papers', *Archives*, 19 (1991)

Tyacke, S. and Huddy, J., *Christopher Saxton and Tudor Map-Making* (1980)

Underdown, D., *Fire From Heaven: Life in an English Town in the Seventeenth Century* (1994)

Unwin, J., 'Local history group research projects in adult continuing education', *LH*, 24/1 (1994)

Urdank, A., *Religion and Society in a Cotswold Vale: Nailsworth, Gloucestershire, 1780–1865* (1990)

VCH Hampshire, 1 (1900)

VCH Lancashire, 3 (1907)

VCH Leicestershire, 2 (1954)

VCH Staffordshire, 8 (1963)

Venn, P., 'Exceptional Eakring: Nottinghamshire's other open field parish', *Transactions of the Thoroton Society*, 94 (1990)

Vinogradoff, P., *Villainage in England* (1892)

Vinogradoff, P, *The Growth of the Manor* (2nd edn, 1911)

Wadsworth, A.P., 'The history of the Rochdale woollen trade', *Transactions of the Rochdale Literary and Scientific Society*, 15 (1923–25)

Wadsworth, A.P., 'The early factory system in the Rochdale district'. *Transactions of the Rochdale Literary and Scientific Society*, 19 (1935–37)

Wadsworth, A.P., 'The history of coal mining in Rochdale district', *Transactions of the Rochdale Literary and Scientific Society*, 23 (1947–49)

Wadsworth, A.P. and de L. Mann, J., *The Cotton Trade and Industrial Lancashire, 1600–1780* (1931)

Wagner, A., *English Genealogy* (1960)

Wagner, A., *Pedigree and Progress* (1975)

Wake, J., *How to Compile a History and Present-Day Record of Village Life* (1925)

Walker, H.H., 'Centenary lecture: the story of the Devonshire Association, 1862–1962', *Transactions of the Devonshire Association*, 99 (1962)

Warnicke, R.M., *William Lambarde* (1973)

Weatherill, L., *Consumer Behaviour and Material Culture in Britain, 1660–1760* (1988)

West, J., *Town Records* (1983, 1992)

West, J., *Village Records* (new edn 1997)

Williams, P., 'The Crown and the counties', in Haigh, C. (ed.), *The Reign of Elizabeth I* (1984)

Winstanley, M., 'Researching a county history: Edwin Butterworth, Edward Baines and the *History of Lancashire* (1836)', *Northern History*, 32 (1996)

Winterbotham, D. and Crosby, A., *The Local Studies Library: A Handbook for Local Historians* (1998)

Wishart, J., 'Local historians and antiquarians', *Local History News*, 74 (Spring, 2005)

Wood, A.C., 'Doctor Charles Deering', *Transactions of the Thoroton Society*, 45 (1941)

Wood, A.C., 'Local history', *Transactions of the Thoroton Society*, 49 (1945)

Wood, A.C., 'Fifty years of the Transactions', *Transactions of the Thoroton Society*, 50 (1946)

Wood, A.C., *A History of Nottinghamshire* (1947)

Wood, A.C., 'The history of trade and transport on the River Trent', *Transactions of the Thoroton Society*, 54 (1950)

Woodward, L., 'The rise of the professional historian in England', in Bourne, K. and Watt, D.C. (eds), *Studies in International History* (1967)

Worth, R.N., 'William of Worcester: Devon's earliest topographer', *Transactions of the Devonshire Association*, 18 (1886)

Wrightson, K., and Levine, D., *Poverty and Piety in an English Village: Terling, 1525–1700* (1979)

Wrightson, K., and Levine, D., *The Making of an Industrial Society: Whickham, 1560–1765* (1991)

Wrigley, E.A., 'Family limitation in pre-industrial England', *Economic History Review*, 19 (1966)

Wrigley, E.A., 'The changing occupational structure of Colyton over two centuries', *Local Population Studies*, 18 (1977)

Wrigley, E.A. and Schofield, R.S., *The Population History of England, 1541–1871: A Reconstruction* (1981)

Theses

Conway, G., 'The "Great flood" of Derby, 1 April 1842' (University of Nottingham MA thesis, 1991)

Eakle, A.H., 'Antiquaries and the writing of English local history, 1750–1800 (Genealogy, Heraldry, 18th Century Art, Folklore)' (University of Utah, Ph.D thesis, 1985)

Honeybone, M., 'The Spalding Gentlemen's Society: the communication of science in the East Midands of England, 1710–60' (Open University, Ph.D thesis, 2001)

Thompson, A., 'The use of scratch dials by the rural church and laity as evidenced from their occurrences on churches in the East Midlands' (University of Nottingham MA thesis, 1995)

Websites

http://www.britarch.ac.uk/baa.
http://freebmd.rootsweb.com
www.archon.org.uk www.A2A.gov.uk
www.pro.gov.uk
www.englandpast.net
www.visionofbritain.org.uk
www.ffhs.org.uk
www.englandspast.net
http://southwellchurches.nottingham.ac.uk
http://www.nottshistory.org.uk.
www.nationalarchives.gov.uk
http://www.historicaldirectories.org
www.history.org.uk
www.balh.co.uk

Index

n. after a page reference indicates the number of a note on that page.